CHURCH-STATE RELATIONS

CHURCH-STATE RELATIONS

Tensions and Transitions

Edited by

THOMAS ROBBINS

and

ROLAND ROBERTSON

Transaction Books
New Brunswick (U.S.A.) and Oxford (U.K.)

Library of Congress Catalog Number: 86-14215
ISBN: 0-88738-108-1 (cloth); 0-88738-651-2 (paper)
Printed in the United States of America

Library of Congress Cataloging in Publication Data

Church-state relations

   Includes index.
   1. Church and state.   I. Robbins, Thomas, 1943-
II. Robertson, Roland.
BV630.2.C59   1986   322′.1   86-14215
ISBN 0-88738-108-1
ISBN 0-88738-651-2 (pbk.)

Contents

To Tom's "loving cat, Burmela."
And to Roland's sons: Mark, Tom, and Joel

Acknowledgments

We would like to thank Irving Louis Horowitz for his encouragement and Pushpa Desai of Maya Word Processing of Mt. Pleasant, Michigan. Jo Stagno Caiazzo, of the Department of Sociology, University of Pittsburgh, has been of enormous help in preparing the final manuscript, and we are both very grateful to her.

Introduction

One of the difficulties in preparing a reader on church-state relations in comparative perspective is that the very concepts of *church* and *state* imply a somewhat parochial Anglo-American cultural standpoint. Although the value of religious pluralism is (by most modern interpretations) ingrained in the American constitutional foundation, the familiar notion of *church-state relations* is derived partly from the British *establishmentarian* context. In other words, we tend to assume a single relationship between two clearly distinct, unitary and solidly but separately institutionalized entities. In the implicit model built into the American conceptualization of the religiopolitical nexus there is one state and one church, whose jurisdictional boundaries must be carefully delineated. We safeguard separation, as well as pluralism, in large part, because we assume the church to be groping toward hegemonic establishment. Similarly, we insist that *the state* should respect individual rights, because we assume the state to be inherently disposed toward aggrandizement at the expense of personal liberty.

The very idea of a church-state hiatus is therefore somewhat culture-bound. It is difficult to apply, for example, to the Soviet Union, where a monolithic unity and an institutional interpenetration of political–administrative and religioideological orders is clearly assumed and enforced. To a lesser degree, the idea of contemporary tensions between church and state is problematic in those West European societies where, notwithstanding a long tradition of separately institutionalized governmental and ecclesiastical entities, the identification of the dominant religion with the *ancien regime* has meant the apparent decline of religion subsequent to the passing of the latter, which has ultimately reduced the saliency of church-state issues. Finally, the conceptual framework of church-state relations will appear alien within and with respect to many Third World and Middle Eastern societies which exhibit a lesser degree of political integration compared to European or American models, as well as a smaller tendency for religion to be clearly institutionalized in a hierarchical–ecclesiastical (or any comprehensive national) structure.

The United States is if not unique, at least extreme in its formal articulation of normative concerns about church-state separation in its constitution. The state is solemnly enjoined not to establish religion and to respect

1

the latter's sacred free exercise. These insistent demands, now backed by powerful lobbies and movements, may indicate that Americans are really fixated on the negative model of established religion. Similarly, Americans' strident demand that government respect the rights of individuals reflects a basic conception of the state as inherently disposed toward aggrandizement at the expense of individual liberty. The explicit formality of American constitutional norms with regard to religion creates a clear "church-and-state" theme, as well as legalistic subthemes, such as free exercise—religious liberty issues and separation-incorporation issues, and so on. This neat formalism and resulting analytical framework cannot be easily applied cross-culturally, although it has considerable heuristic value for the analysis of American trends and attitudes.

Almost half of the essays in this volume, primarily part two, deal with the "American case." Articles in the first section explore key concepts and themes involving the religiopolitical nexus in the contemporary world, and the implications which arise for the contemporary study of religion; while our final section deals with church-state relations in a number of European and other countries, excluding the United States. No one state or society, however, is explored with the depth and breadth of the seven papers of part two dealing with the United States.

Part I
GENERAL CONSIDERATIONS

1

General Considerations in the Study of Contemporary Church-State Relationships

Roland Robertson

It can hardly be said that the putatively relevant academic disciplines were ready for the encounters involving agencies of the state or of secular political actors, on the one side, and religious organizations or movements, on the other, that we have witnessed in many parts of the world in recent years. Those specializing in the empirically focused study of religion had concerned themselves with religion in its more peripheral manifestations—with quite a few sociologists maintaining that what is most characteristic of religion in the modern world is, indeed, its peripheral status— while those studying the "harsh" realities of modern life, particularly those of politics and economics, were seemingly disdainful of the idea that religion had much to do, except in a few isolated cases, with the comprehension of the central issues of modern life.

Widespread acceptance of one or another version of the secularization thesis formed the immediate backdrop to this state of unreadiness. The social sciences had for long promoted the idea that religion is more or less irrelevant—and increasingly so—to the governmental, political, economic and other major domains of modern life. In no small measure such a perception has been a desideratum of scientific study of human societies, and when religion has reared its head it has thus often been regarded as an ephemeral, atavistic annoyance on the analytical terrain. Not unironically the prevalence of the secularization thesis has, on the other hand, constituted a major target of some modern religious or politicoreligious movements. Be that as it may, the study of religion has, for the most part, been regarded for the past fifty years or so as "wallpaper in the halls of academe" (a characterization which is adopted from Beckford's more detailed discussion of the preoccupations of some influential sociologists of religion in the following chapter). Specialists in the study of religion have themselves often reflected that attitude, sometimes by maintaining that the "wallpaper" is in fact the most interesting thing about social systems, by which I specifically mean that the claim that religion has primarily to do with meaning, identity and the like has frequently been made on the basis of the idea that these aspects of human life are ultimately the most important—that they are transcendent and do not need to be systematically related to the supposedly more mundane themes of politics, government, violence, revolution, economic crisis, and so on.

The academic disciplines have, in effect, followed the course broadly indicated by those classical sociologists in their characterization, to use Max Weber's phrase, of the "parcelling-out" of modern life. The perception that modern life in general is characterized by its being functionally differentiated into increasingly autonomous and distinct spheres has been consolidated by a parallel differentiation of academic life itself. This had led, inter alia, to sociologists of religion being greatly preoccupied—as if that were the point of the subdiscipline—with producing general theories of religion per se (including its decline or demise). What thus has been greatly neglected until quite recently is the *interpenetration* of religious and other spheres.

Few, if any, of the great intellectuals whose work has been resoundingly influential in the study of religion, were concerned with religion per se. That was not Kant's pivotal concern, nor was it Rousseau's. Hegel did not study only religion nor did de Tocqueville, Troeltsch, Freud, Max Weber, Durkheim or Parsons. Each of these, in their different ways, had an agenda for the analysis of general or specific aspects of the modern world per se and attended to religion as a crucial part—but, nonetheless, only a part—of their respective foci of concern. The circumstances which have produced a professional sociology of religion concerned so much with religion per se cannot, indeed should not, receive attention here. Nor can, nor should there be analysis of the crystallization of political science and political sociology—neither of which have displayed much interest in religion until very recently. In other words, examining the courses of professionalization and the modes of self-identification of academic disciplines is not directly relevant to the concerns of this book. Nonetheless, insofar as academic disciplines refract significant aspects of the societies in which they emerge, congeal and become subject to mutation or demise, it *is* relevant to consider more generally how we have overlooked—or at least been taken by surprise by the sudden reemergence of—apparently consequential connections between church and state, religion and politics, religion and government, religion and international relations, and so on.

For the most part, those who have advocated the secularization thesis have not seriously explored the question as to the terms in which modern societies function. Many have at one and the same time strongly insisted

on the historical significance of religion as providing the symbolic foundations of societies or in legitimating the political realm and the operation of
the state, on the one hand, and denied such significance in the modern
world, on the other—without paying much, if any, attention to the bases of
modern regimes. More broadly, there has been a tendency to insist on the
centrality of religion to the operation of human societies in broad anthropological perspective but a lack of interest in how societies which used
to "need" religion now persist. The latter problem has largely been left by
students of religion to other specialists.

Meanwhile, after a long period of neglect of what Bagehot, in his influential work on the British constitution, called the dignified parts of government (symbolism, ritual, and so on) and, more generally, the theme of
legitimacy (in other than highly restricted form), political scientists and
political sociologists have, in recent years, become increasingly preoccupied with such matters—but particularly the themes of legitimacy and
legitimation. However, blossoming of interest in the modern state and the
question of its legitimacy and forms of legitimation has not resulted as
such in a revitalization of concern with religion; although the situation has
significantly changed since 1979, the year of the Iranian and Nicaraguan
revolutions and the Polish protorevolution.

That church-state relations have become more visible and often problematic in recent years does not, of course, constitute in itself evidence
against the thesis that the modern state largely stands without need of
religious legitimation. One certainly has, for example, to entertain the
possibility that the recent proliferation of religion-based challenges to the
authority of the modern state are merely ephemeral reactions to the onward march of secularization. Moreover, even if—as some significant figures in social science have claimed—the modern state is particularly
vulnerable to legitimation crises or even if many states lack legitimacy that
does not in itself mean that religion (or the church) becomes again auto-
matically relevant to the functioning of state apparati. Moreover (as
Thomas Robbins makes clear in his introduction to part two), quite a few
of the more publicized of church-state encounters in recent years have
arisen from the attempt on the part of state agencies to expand their reg-
ulative control, rather than from attempts by religious organizations to
assert a monitoring role vis à vis the state (or the domain of secular-
political activity) or from a diffuse upsurge in religiosity.

Nevertheless, with such caveats firmly in mind, it would seem that in the
modern world religious factors are coming to play more rather than less
significant roles in affairs of state. Since church-state and/or religious-
political issues have emerged in nearly every corner of the modern world in
recent years—in societies which have relatively little in common in terms

of histories and sociocultural attributes—the question immediately arises as to whether there is something about the world as a whole, the modern world system, which gives rise to them. I deal with the central aspects of that theme in the third essay in this section, in particular reference to the idea that the "tightening" of the entire world into a single sociocultural system places strong constraints upon individual societies to identify and legitimate themselves in relation to the global circumstance and, more diffusely, humanity. Emphasis is also given to the ways in which heightened consciousness about the raison d'être and fate of the world and the human species is a pivotal factor in the rise of religious and religiopolitical (as well as secular-political) movements oriented to the global-human circumstance per se. At this point, however, an even more general introductory theme should be mentioned.

Particular sensitivity to church-state problems, tensions, conflicts, and the like is, virtually by definition, likely to occur most from within societies which erect—in varying degrees—walls of separation (to invoke Jefferson's famous phrase) between church and state and that stress the necessity for constitutional and legal safeguards against the impingement of religion on the societal political system and vice versa. It is also likely to be found in societies—such as those of Eastern Europe—in which the state has been greatly secularized, regardless of the degree to which there is a tradition in such societies of safeguarding the religious realm from state encroachment or protecting the religious rights of individuals. Additionally, in societies of both of those types the idea that societies—including the ostensibly secularized state systems thereof—are not beholden to or reliant upon transcendent forms of religious or quasi-religious symbolism is likely to be evident.

Sahlins (1976:220) has pinpointed a crucial aspect of this theme. What Marx said about primitive societies not being able to exist unless they disguised to themselves "the real basis of that existence, as in the form of religious illusions" may be more true of modern societies in that the latter conspire "to conceal the symbolic ordering of the system," not least in the form of "those academic theories of praxis by which we conceive ourselves and the rest of the world."[1] Geertz (1980:121-22), in speaking of the etymological history of "that master noun of modern political discourse, *state*," notes that

> Each of the leading notions of what the state 'is' that has developed in the West since the sixteenth century—monopolist of violence within a territory, executive committee of the ruling class, delegated agent of the popular will, pragmatic device for conciliating interests—has [led to] those dimensions of authority not easily reducible to a command-and-obedience conception of

political life [being] left in an indefinite world of excrescences, mysteries, fictions, and decorations.

To be sure, neither Sahlins nor Geertz are speaking directly to the theme of church-and-state. Nonetheless their striking formulations point to matters which have a considerable bearing on that theme. Sahlins indicates that modern life is actually founded much, much more on symbolism, including religious symbolism, than is normally recognized in either quotidian or academic contexts. Geertz (1980:123) cogently maintains, to again use his own words, that in the mainstreams of Western life "the semiotic aspects of the state . . . remain so much mummery." And while his main concern is with Bageot's dignified parts of government—myth, political symbology, ceremony, and so on—his comments surely indicate that the segregation of the exercise of power and authority from general, cultural symbolism is a form of modern false consciousness (to reverse, in tandem with Sahlins, the usual Marxist perspective). Put simply, affairs of state cannot be regarded simply as a sphere for the autonomous operation of what Weber called material interests, any more than the *church* can be appropriately conceived of as being almost exclusively the domain of ideal interests (the latter idea being effectively destroyed by Beckford in the following chapter). Even more important there is the question of how the two are connected.

For, to adopt Sahlins (1985) again, we have to be interested in *the structure of the conjuncture*. In the present context that means paying attention to the ways in which church and state are coordinated. We cannot take the American term *separation* literally, for if church and state were to be truly—as opposed to constitutionally—separated, there would be no society at all. This theme has been evident in writing, particularly on the part of Americans, on the theme of *civil religion*. Indeed, in some formulations civil religion is conceptualized precisely to refer to the ways in which a rationale is provided for their being held apart and the ways in which they should interact.[2] (The more typical formulation, which does not necessarily exclude the latter, is centered upon the idea of civil religion as a set of symbols concerning sacred themes, ceremonials, places and events in a nation's history.) The formulation of civil religion as rationale for the autonomy-within-interdependence of religion and state-centered politics has usually been applied to Western societies, most notably the United States, in which Christianity has been the dominant religious tradition. For Christianity is, of course, distinctive in the degree to which it raises ongoing dilemmas about the relationship between active involvement in worldly affairs and the salvation of souls.[3] As will be seen more fully in the introduction to part three, other religious traditions have displayed much less ambivalence in this regard, although in societies in which there is a problematic plurality of religious cultures, civil–religious themes are very likely to emerge, regardless of the particular faiths involved—centered on the problem of coexistence of such faiths relative to national loyalty and societal identity (Markoff and Regan 1981).[4]

A pressure to connect religious and state domains in the modern world, regardless of the degree to which there is formal, constitutional separation, arises from the fact that increasingly we face the problem of the plurality of cultures and faiths at the global level. And that circumstance is almost certainly also a source for our now becoming more conscious of the "deeper" aspects of modern life. By the same token, consciousness of roots, tradition, heritage, and so on, increases the likelihood that societies will draw upon religiocultural resources in defining their identities and that movements within and across societies will invoke religious symbols. Thus we have become increasingly conscious in recent years of the religious aspects of revolutionary situations, revolutionary and revitalization movements and of revolutions themselves (Lewy 1974).

The modern idea of revolution, as it developed during and in the aftermath of the French Revolution at the end of the eighteenth century, acquired a strongly secular cast (in spite of the quasi-religious activities of the French Revolutionaries themselves). In fact it is not too much to say that until very recently the revolutionary myth has to a considerable extent been predicated upon and has heralded a more-or-less totally secularized world (Robertson 1985). Thus we are now only beginning to realize the extent to which nineteenth century revolutionary activity in fact involved a distinctly religious dimension (Billington 1980). On the other hand, recent events in Asia, the Middle East, Eastern Europe and Latin America compel us to reexamine the relationship between religion and revolution—and, in turn, the connection between that conjunction and the modern state.

The circumstances under which revolutionary movements are likely to invoke and deploy religious ideas and symbols is directly addressed by Leland Robinson in his contribution to this section. Thus in the papers which follow we have, first, an analysis of the ways in which sociologists of religion have tended to ignore power, largely by concentrating on the meaning- and identity-conferring aspects of religion. Beckford's persuasive analysis has obvious implications for the discussion of church-state relationships and encounters. Next I endeavor to frame discussion of contemporary church-state encounters, including conflicts, by consideration of the world system. Third, Robinson identifies six major variables which increase or decrease the likelihood of revolutionary movements using religion as a tool.

Notes

1. I have taken the liberty of expanding Sahlins' comment to refer to all industrial or post-industrial societies. He himself speaks only of "capitalist" societies.
2. A good example is Hammond (1980).
3. The most important recent work on this theme, with special reference to the intensification of theological and political-philosophical discussion of church-state encounters in early Christendom, has been done by Dumont (1982).
4. For further discussion of the societal circumstances which encourage "civil religion talk" see Robertson (1978:148-85).

Bibliography

Billington, James H. 1980. *Fire in the Minds of Men: Origins of the Revolutionary Faith.* New York: Basic Books.

Dumont, Louis. "A Modified View of Our Origins: The Christian Beginnings of Modern Individualism." *Religion* 12 (1982):1-27.

Geertz, Clifford. 1980. *Negara: The Theatre State in Nineteenth-Century Bali.* Princeton: Princeton University Press.

Hammond, Phillip E. 1980. "The Conditions of Civil Religion: A Comparison of the United States and Mexico." Pp. 40-85 in Robert N. Bellah and Phillip E. Hammond, eds., *Varieties of Civil Religion.* San Francisco: Harper and Row.

Lewy, Guenther. 1974. *Religion and Revolution.* New York: Oxford University Press.

Markoff, John and Daniel Regan. "The Rise and Fall of Civil Religion." *Sociological Analysis* 42 (Winter 1981):333-52.

Robertson, Roland. 1978. *Meaning and Change: Explorations in the Cultural Sociology of Modern Societies.* New York: New York University Press.

———. 1985. "The Development and Modern Implications of the Classical Sociological Perspective on Religion and Revolution." Pp. 236-65 in *Religion, Rebellion, Revolution,* Bruce Lincoln, ed. New York: Macmillan.

Sahlins, Marshall. 1976. *Culture and Practical Reason.* Chicago: Chicago University Press.

———. 1985. *Islands of History.* Chicago: Chicago University Press.

2

The Restoration of *Power* to the Sociology of Religion*

James A. Beckford

Introduction

In the past few years the notion of *power* in the sociology of religion has shown signs of emerging from an eclipse which had begun to take place in the 1960s. More precisely, a variety of notions of power is becoming apparent both in the everyday practice of religion in the Western world and in sociologists' interpretations of that practice. The first part of this chapter will chart the eclipse of *power*; the second will scan the signs of its emergence from obscurity; and the conclusions will discuss the broad implications of this trajectory for the sociology of religion.

David Martin (1966) was entirely justified in claiming in the mid-1960s that the sociology of religion faced downhill on an inclined plane. He said that sociologists of religion were doubly defensive: to be a sociologist was bad enough, but to study a declining phenomenon was even worse. The subject matter was said to be disappearing fast, and if some of it still seemed to persist, it is taken to be "either a residue or a false front for another more genuine reality. . . . Of all the different enclaves of contemporary specialization the sociology of religion most resembles the republic of Venice just before Napoleon snuffed it out for ever" (Martin 1966:354-55).

The metaphor of the inclined plane could be extended to suggest that it was cross-cut by numerous little streams of sectarian and cultic vitality which often caught the imagination of observers. Here was canalized religiosity bubbling along in apparent defiance of the general lay of the land.

---

*An earlier version of this chapter was delivered as the Paul Hanley Furfey lecture to the Annual Meeting of the Association for the Sociology of Religion, Providence, R.I., October 1982 and published in *Sociological Analysis* 44 (1983):11-32. I am grateful for permission to reprint the article in modified form.

But even these streams were treated as exceptions which proved the rule—or as eventual tributaries to the major water-course of secularization. Water does not flow uphill, however holy it might be. All in all, the significance of religion for many sociologists in the 1960s was that it was declining. The trend was toward progressive secularization, rationalization, bureaucratization, alienation, massification, and depersonalization.

There were three main responses from sociologists of religion. The first was to concentrate on the supposedly declining functional capacity of religion to solve people's problems of meaning or identity. The second was to measure religion in all its empirical detail, so that, again to quote David Martin, "We now know the Standard Deviation of the time spent on shaving by Members of the Society of Jesus" (Martin 1966:359). The third response concentrated on the deviant and exotic fringe of religious phenomena, whose curiosity value could hardly be denied, but whose relevance to what most sociologists considered to be the major developments of the time was weak indeed.

An examintion of the most favored textbook presentations of the sociology of religion in the 1950s and 1960s shows that the treatment of the topic of "power" was, at best, cursory and, at worst, nonexistent. More often than not, it was actually precluded by explicit concern with religion's supposedly functional capacity to overcome so-called powerlessness. Yet, this had not always been the case. A more robust approach had characterized the work of earlier writers such as Max Weber, H. Paul Douglass, Reinhold and Richard Niebuhr. Furthermore, their keen awareness of the intimate associations between power and religion was reflected in such classics as Liston Pope's *Millhands and Preachers* and in J. Milton Yinger's *Religion in the Struggle for Power*.

The orientation toward the functional capacity of religion to solve problems of meaning or identity was dominant throughout the late 1960s and 1970s, and the eclipse of the notion of power was largely a consequence of this orientation. I shall document this thesis by reference to the seminal works of Peter Berger, Thomas Luckmann and Hans Mol. In their different ways they each constitute religion as primarily a matter of knowledge susceptible to understanding in the same way as other cognitive products in particular, language. If the sociology of knowledge was to serve as a new paradigm for the sociology of religion, then the recommended analytical strategy was to focus on language as the key to religious phenomena. Indeed, the religious enterprise was constituted as a search for knowledge about the taken-for-granted basis of the world's orderliness. Religious practice was seen as a matter of regenerating the self-evident knowledge of the ultimate order of things through social interaction. Religious meaning was thereby equated with the social perception of various kinds or order; and theodicies were said to protect the sense of order by virtue of "the redeeming assurance of meaning itself" (Berger 1969:58).

Peter Berger

The limited use that Berger makes of the concept of power tells us a lot about his deep assumptions about man and religion. The concept is virtually confined to statements about "the surrender of self to the ordering power of society" (Berger 1969:54). "Concrete relations with individual others" are taken to be the source of "the masochistic attitude" in religion, through which "the self-denying submission to the power of the collective nomos can be liberating" (Berger 1969:56-57). "Above all, society manifests itself by its coercive power" (Berger 1969:11). "The institutions of sexuality and power first appear as thoroughly alienated entities, hovering over everyday social life as manifestations from an 'other' reality" (Berger 1969:92).

It is highly significant that the experience and perception of power in human relationships is not selected by Berger as one of the signals of transcendence. The reason for this surprising omission may be that he subsumes *power* under his concept of *order* which, in turn, is subsumed under the concept of *meaning.* There is clearly a strong connection (if not identity) between *order* and *meaning* in Berger's work, for which he has been criticized (Radcliffe 1980). His sense of *power* is also heavily influenced by this close connection. It seems to refer ultimately to the background "noise" of the social system—a pervasive sense of something constraining and "out there." Consequently, Berger pays little or no attention to power in human relationships or in the relationships between groups, social categories and collectivities. His usage is very largely abstract and disembodied. Power is never treated as a phenomenon experienced by human beings directly: it merely underwrites the human condition in society.

Thomas Luckmann

The relegation of the concept of power to an abstract status or a background position in Berger's work on religion is taken one step further by Thomas Luckmann, whose *The Invisible Religion,* in particular, helped to shape the dominant concerns of much sociology of religion in the 1960s and 1970s. This book is a systematic treatise on the changing ways in which human beings are said to transcend their biological nature and thereby to generate world views in a process deemed to be religious:

> The historical priority of a world-view provides the empirical basis for the "successful" transcendence of biological nature by human organisms, de-

taching the latter from their immediate life context and integrating them, as persons, into the context of a tradition of meaning. We may conclude, therefore, that the world-view, as an "objective" and historical social reality, performs an essentially religious function and define it as an elementary social form of religion. This social form is universal in human society [Luckmann 1967:53].

What is meant by *religious function* seems to be the provision of continuous sense in human life, which is derived from "the coherence of meaning in the world view" (Luckmann 1967:70). Religion is therefore said to be "present in nonspecific form in all societies and all normal (socialized) individuals" (Luckman 1967:78).

Luckmann insisted that specific contents or themes of religion vary with social-cultural circumstances. In the modern Western world the process of institutional differentiation created a "private sphere" in which individual consciousness was liberated from the dominant social structures, thereby giving rise to what Luckmann terms "the somewhat illusory sense of autonomy which characterized the typical person in modern society" (Luckmann 1967:97). As a result, the "thematic unity of the traditional sacred cosmos breaks apart. . . . Once religion is defined as a 'private affair' the individual may choose from the assortment of 'ultimate' meaning as he sees fit—guided only by the preferences that are determined by his social biography" (Luckmann 1967:98-99).

As a consequence of Luckmann's focus on religion as transcendence through world views, the notion of power is excluded from the agenda. It seems to have no part to play in a theoretical scheme emphasizing the normality of transcendence-through-socialization, no matter whether in traditional or modern forms. In Luckmann's scheme, religion is constituted as a social process in which meaning is conveyed from generation to generation by means of themes and symbols reflecting the texture of everyday social interactions.

One is entitled to ask whether Luckmann's scheme can cope with events and experiences which threaten to overload the capacity of sacred meaning systems to make sense of existence. Is there nothing in life which cannot be handled by religion? Certainly, Luckmann's claim has a hollow ring to it: ". . . death does not appear even as a subordinate topic in the sacred cosmos of a modern industrial society. Nor are growing old and old age endowed with 'sacred' significance" (Luckmann 1967:14). There is certainly a sharp contrast with Berger's view that

> Every human society is in the last resort, men banded together in the face of death. The power of religion depends, in the last resort, upon the credibility of the banners it puts in the hands of men as they stand before death, or more accurately, as they walk, inevitably, toward it [Berger 1969:52].

It is one thing to describe the mechanics of the way in which men may transcend their biological nature by means of sacred world views; but it is quite another to imply that the categories of transcendence can always cope with the flux of experience. Meaning systems are certainly objectivated, but it is an empirical question whether men actually succeed in making sense of their lives in terms of them. This may be an instance of the oversocialized conception of religious man—to adopt Dennis Wrong's celebrated expression. Or, to change the authority to Clifford Geertz, it may be a case where the human capacity to hold beliefs has given way to the inhuman state of being held by beliefs. In order to restore the balance, we need more studies of the failure of religion to achieve the functions so readily attributed to it by sociologists. Paradoxically, this would tell us more about the power of religion by exposing its empirical limitations.

I am entirely in agreement with Timothy Radcliffe's criticism of those who equate religious meaning with a sense of unitary order:

> Man is only driven to question the meaning of anything and everything because he finds himself at the intersection of many orders, employing many languages, playing many roles. It is the plurality of *nomoi* that provokes the question of meaning [Radcliffe 1980:158].

Nobody seriously doubts the plurality of today's world views (although the use of the word *plurality* masks conflict and contradiction, and may even suggest that a single world view had previously held sway), and Luckmann is surely right to insist that modern man has a choice to make among them. But it would be wrong to suggest that everybody actually makes such a choice to the exclusion of other world views or that the chosen world view always succeeds in making sense of life.

The experiences of conflict, tension and contradiction are no less meaningful simply because they frustrate the neat categories afforded by discrete world views. The creative bricolage, experimentation, alternation, revision, and special pleading which partly characterize our everyday reasoning are a significant element in religious thought and feeling. But theoretical schemes which tie meaningfulness too closely to perceived order have little place for such quintessentially human action.

In short, the orientation toward the sociological study of religion through meaning systems and language has been helpful in illuminating complex social, cultural, and mental processes through which religious values, ideas, thoughts and feelings are transmitted. But it has also brought with it the negative implication that, since meaning systems and world views are expressed in terms which reflect particular social structures and roles, the meaning of religion was somehow contained in those terms.

There is the distinct danger in this of mistaking the operative terms of meaning for the essential limits of meaning.

To put this central point differently, the emphasis on the social construction of world views (unintentionally perhaps) turned the purely formal processes of socialization into the sacred content of religion. Social form was equated with sacred content. (Reinhold Niebuhr would probably have castigated this approach for mistaking "the image of God in man for God himself" [Niebuhr 1940:206]). One might even go so far as to say that social form obliterated sacred content, albeit ironically in the name of freeing the sociology of religion from a fixation with formal religious organizations. It might, in fact, be salutary to be reminded of the wide gulf separating the emergent orthodoxy of the sociology of religion in the 1960s from earlier positions such as that held by Reinhold Niebuhr:

> All superficial questions about the meaning of life, all simple religions which imagine that faith in any god is better than no faith at all, fail to recognize that the ultimate question is not whether life has a meaning (which it must have or no one could live), but whether or not the meaning is tragic [Niebuhr 1940:213].

Perhaps *meaning* ousted *tragedy* as well as *power* from the dominant sociological perspectives on religion?

Hans Mol

Proof of the seminal value of the orientation of the sociology of religion toward meaning systems and language can be found in many examples of sociological analysis produced in the 1970s. I shall take as an illustration the work of Hans Mol who has probably achieved the greatest systematization of thinking along the general lines laid down by Berger and Luckmann in the 1960s. But I also want to stress that his work is obviously independent and unique in very many respects.

Mol's main interest has been the processes whereby personal identity is sacralized in the modern world. By this, he means that in the life process of individuals and collectivities there is a continuing dialectic between the forces of evolutionary adaptation and integration. This is because human beings have a need for identity in the sense of finding "a stable niche in this whole complex of physiological, psychological and sociological patterns of interaction. . . . Order means survival; chaos means extinction" (Mol 1976:8). The function of religion, then, is to give "special underpinning to particular conceptions of order within a culture, thus making the security of the individual less precarious. . . . Identity, order and view of reality are all intertwined" (Mol 1976:9).

The process of sacralizing identity on the personal and social levels is said to be carried out by the four mechanisms of objectification, commitment, ritual and myth. The effect of the mechanisms is to stabilize the system by incorporating change in the way that an oyster accommodates an intruding grain of sand by coating it with mother-of-pearl. Thus, the forces of disorder are reintegrated into the system in a delicate dialectical process with cybernetic safeguards. This is the ground for Mol's optimistic view that

> The future therefore seems to be with those religious commitments to order and identity that intricately and sensitively reestablish the social authority necessary for the safeguarding of pivotal social values (such as responsibility, charity, reliability, etc.) and yet involve sufficient individualism and personal motivation to keep the motor of human existence humming with a minimum of friction [Mol 1976:266].

This is not the place to comment on the functionalist teleology of Mol's basic position, for the more pressing task is to draw out the underlying assumption that meaning and identity are necessarily on the side of integration and order in the dynamic or social change. Even when religious ideas are treated as the motive force of change, it is assumed that their ultimate function is to introduce order and stability as the prerequisite for successful identity-maintenance. In this way, the apparently disruptive and disturbing phenomena of conversion and charisma are reduced to "means by which religions continue to integrate" (Mol 1976:54) through the continual creation of stable identity.

Among the more obvious implications of Mol's position is the notion that identity depends upon stability and order and is therefore weakened to the extent that doubt, conflict, and change are regularly experienced. This seems to limit severely the possibilities of both personal identity and the religious life. But perhaps more important for present purposes is the implication that any experience which threatened or managed to overflow the categories of order (and therefore meaningfulness) would, ipso facto, also undermine identity in Mol's sense of the term. It would follow that sacralization had failed, and I find this inherently implausible.

By contrast, and by way of showing that the notion of identity does not have to be associated with rigid postulates about the anthropological need for order, Robertson and Holzner (1980) have articulated the process of variable identity-formation with variable conceptions of social structure. They show, for example, that identity-formation in underprivileged groups may involve conceptions of legitimate social order which are totally at odds with those of more powerful and privileged groups. The choice of conception is clearly not haphazard; nor is it mechanical and universal. Order is as much negotiated as it is perceived as coercive. Consequently, struggles commonly occur for the power to define the nature of the prevailing order. Identity-formation is not therefore a simple matter of finding a niche or location offering to make sense of prevailing order. It is the object of frequently intense struggle, competition and tension between actors and collectivities. Identity may be attributed and rejected as well as sought and found.

It seems perverse to consider the products of all such processes as the source of religion. And if the response is that sacralization of identity occurs only when the individual or collectivity is successfully integrated into the systems of order and meaning, one wonders whether the analysis has overlooked something vital. I have in mind the ancient traditions, found in all major religions, of spiritual skepticism, struggle, pessimism, fatalism, etc.—in short, the sense of grappling with something internal or external to the person which refuses to be bound by the available systems of meaning.

To sum up, the orientation of the sociology of religion toward the processes whereby religion is socially constructed as order, meaning and identity carries with it the danger that other aspects of the religious phenomenon may be precluded from consideration. The overall effect is a kind of reductionism which may empty religion of significance just as effectively as earlier and more positivistic approaches have done. An interpretivist or *verstehende* approach which operates with a notion of meaning tied to the allegedly anthropological or societal prerequisites for particular kinds of order or identity runs the risk of reducing religion to a state of blandness or neatness unrecognizable to many of its practitioners.

It would be entirely wrong, however, to give the impression that no attention was paid in the late 1960s and early 1970s to issues transcending the identity-and-meaning-conferring capacities of religion. Of course, there were clear signs of conflict and tension within religious groups, and sociologists were not slow to pick up on them. I am thinking of such seminal studies as Hadden's *Gathering Storm in the Churches,* Hammond's *Campus Clergyman,* and Berton's *The Comfortable Pew.* But sensitive as these books and others were to struggles within churches, the issues were only implicitly presented as struggles for power. They were mainly concerned with problems of organizational structure, innovative doctrines, ecumenical relations, and the so-called New Breed of activist clergyman. The dominant questions were therefore about the churches' problematic capacity to adapt their policies to changing circumstances and thereby to protect the material prosperity and moral influence that they had enjoyed in the mid-1950s.

Most commentators refused to swallow the bromides of the end of ideology thesis; but at the same time they nevertheless seemed to share an assumption that religion was remote from power struggles. Stormy weather was certainly forecast in the area of civil rights; and the pew was becoming a noticeably less comfortable place from which to contemplate persistent social problems in the early 1970s. But the difficulties were primarily diagnosed as matters internal to religious groups, i.e., belief, doctrine, and organization.

The prospect of religious mobilization for direct political and legal action in the pursuit of more generalized power was still remote in the 1960s. And the challenge to the use of power in the name of religion was still weak in the United States, although contemporary events in other countries as diverse as India, Burma, Egypt, Israel, and Ireland might have suggested the need to take more seriously the relationship between religion and power. I find it strange, for example, that, aside from the egregious case of the Berrigans, the deep ideological fissures gouged at the time of the wars in South East Asia found such weak expression in organized religion. This was one of the "Sounds of Silence" which gave Rodney Stark pause for thought at the time (Stark 1970). Perhaps only now, as Walter Capps (1982) has recently pointed out, are American religious groups coming to terms with the questions about power precipitated by those wars.

Since my objective has so far been to argue that the notion of power remained in eclipse in the sociology of religion for about fifteen years, it has not been necessary to stipulate a precise meaning for it. Nor do I intend to do so now. But it is necessary for my purposes to recognize at this juncture that power has been conceptualized and defined in widely differing ways by sociologists of diverse theoretical persuasions (Lukes 1974 and Wrong 1980). And, while it would be impossible to review all the different meanings here, it will be helpful simply to point out that the meanings which have tended to prevail in the sociology of religion over the past fifteen years or so are significantly different from those which are now coming into use. Let me be more specific.

So long as religion was constituted mainly as world view or meaning system, *power* was conceptualized mainly as *functional capacity*. It was therefore used in such typical expressions as "the power of religion to provide meaning and identity" or "the power of radical ministers to overcome lay resistance to civil rights activism." But there are many other possible meanings of the term. And the general thesis of the second part of this chapter will be that different, and more widely differing, senses of the term *power* have been at work in more recent sociological analyses of religion. In fact, virtually the whole gamut of conceptualizations of power in general sociology can be found in recent studies of religious phenomena. My plan is to review in turn a small number of individual works and topics which illustrate the diversity of connections between religion and power. For the sake of a convenient mnemonic, I shall deal with them under the headings of religion and the experience of power as: confounding; convincing; contesting; controlling; cultivating; and curing.

Religion and the Power Which Confounds

Let me begin with a brief review of some of the ideas of a scholar who has revolutionized the study of the Christian religion in Late Antiquity—Peter Brown. His study of Augustine of Hippo is justly celebrated, but more recently he has demonstrated the importance to be attributed to what he calls *the holy man* in the Eastern part of the late Roman Empire. In his books *Society and the Holy in Late Antiquity* and *The Making of Late Antiquity* he emphasizes that between the fourth and sixth centuries A.D., a period bridging the classical age and the middle ages, the focus of power in religious matters was disputed between the formal institutions of the Church and the entirely informal practices of numerous individual holy men.

They were mainly ascetics who claimed to enjoy unmediated access to God and, consequently, wide-ranging powers. They claimed the power to curse effectively, to heal physical and mental ailments, and to resolve disputes between people living in societies which were being slowly disengaged from Roman dominion. His own words are crystal-clear and require no gloss:

> The predominance of the holy man, therefore marked out late Antiquity as a distinct phase of religious history. The classical period conjures up the image of a great Temple; the middle ages, of a Gothic cathedral. In between, it is the portraits that strike the imagination, the icons of the holy men, the austere features of the philosophers, the ranks of staring faces in frescoes and mosaics. For some centuries the locus of the supernatural was thought of as resting on individual men. The rise of the holy man coincides . . . with the erosion of classical institutions; his decline . . . coincides with the reassertion of a new sense of the majesty of the community [Brown 1981:151].

I want to emphasize three points. First, holy men were considered to be the repository or locus of supernatural power and were therefore in competition with the "vested hierarchy of church and state" (Brown 1981:140). Second, the locus of spiritual power was as precarious as the society in which holy men flourished was fluid. And third, the manifestation of spiritual power was inextricably bound up with associated notions of suffering, evil, or misfortune. These three observations, which really do not do justice at all to the full richness of Brown's interpretations of Late Antiquity in Byzantium, nevertheless underscore the importance of treating the notion of power in religion as variable, flexible, and contestable.

Power is not a fixed attribute or property of individuals, relationships or social systems. Whether it is defined as pure potential or as actual effectiveness, the distribution of power should be conceptualized as an emergent feature of changing circumstances. As such, of course, it may vary in scope, intensity, and durability. Its fortunes cannot be divorced from the vicissitudes of many other social phenomena. Indeed, Brown makes the important point that the actual embodiment of religious power may even be paradoxical, for in the Eastern Empire there were

> ... Men with "reputation for power"; yet this power was thought to have been drawn from outside any apparent niche in the power structure of society. It was gained in the desert . . . beyond human sight, and depended upon a freedom to speak to God, the exact extent of which lay beyond human power to gauge [Brown 1981:183-184].

This view is a very useful corrective to the unfortunate tendency to think of power solely in terms of its prevailing form and distribution.

One further observation on Brown's work will lead us on to a different way of examining the intimate connection between power and religion. He emphasizes on several occasions the need for would-be holy men to affirm and confirm their spiritual power by speaking authentically.

In his own words, authenticity "demands histrionic and theoretical performances as a guarantee" (Brown 1981:134). In societies in which the traditional formulae of religion have lost credibility and the extent of taken-for-granted agreement on the locus of the sacred is small, would-be holy men must continually re-create and maintain their authenticity by overt actions. In the case of the ascetic martyrs and holy heroes of, for example, Syria in the fifth century A.D. this meant a constant struggle to demonstrate that their access to God was direct *and* mysterious. It was a struggle against competitors for the allegiance and reverence of ordinary mortals who sought their patronage.

In the sense in which Peter Brown makes such profitable use of the term, power has little to do with coercion or control. It concerns, rather, religious experiences which are riveting and confounding in the sense of totally transcending normal comprehension. In fact, the elements of meaning and orderliness, of which so much was made in the functionalist sociologies, have little or nothing to do with this sense of the term *power*.

As a postscript to this section I must acknowledge that many insights similar to those made by Brown had previously been made in a more generally applicable way by Bryan Wilson. His *Magic and the Millennium* and *The Noble Savages* are both eloquent testimony to the power exerted in the name of religion mainly in preliterate or slowly developing societies (see also Burridge 1969 and Gilsenan 1973). In particular, he showed how rare, how precarious, and how paradoxical have been instances of genuine religious charisma in which faith in a person's supernatural powers has sustained effective relationships between him or her and a band of devoted followers. In the modern world especially, this endangered species of religious power is said to be confined to the periphery "almost always as a leisure-time activity, rather than as a dynamic force for innovation and transformation. Charisma is now merely for fun; its public is of fans rather than as followers" (Wilson 1975:125).

All that remains of the Noble Savage is the derived charisma of the revivalist preacher, the diffuse charisma of neo-Pentecostalism, and the leaderless charisma of mass entertainers. This is all true, but the cynical observation of Thomas Hobbes in *Leviathan* is equally valid: "Reputation of power is power; because it draweth with it the adherence of those that need protection."

Since Wilson was careful to describe charisma as only one social manifestation of religious power, it is possible to accept his account of its demise without also granting that the possibilities of religious power are thereby necessarily exhausted. Indeed, I regard his obituary for charisma as an invitation or challenge to identify the other sources of surviving religious power on which faith is founded (if at all) in the modern world.

Religion and the Power Which Convinces

I shall now argue that Richard Fenn's stimulating book, *Liturgies and Trials,* also reasserts the centrality of power to an understanding of religion in its social dimensions. The book's express concern is with the place of language in the struggle between the forces of secularization and religion. It ranges widely over many fields, but some of its main subject matter is taken from famous court cases in which the power of the state to impose its own secular criteria of technical justice has conflicted with the insistence of some people on a religious interpretation of their actions. The court records of cases concerning, first, the claimed right of Karen Ann Quinlan's father to suspend the extraordinary medical means of supporting her comatose life; second, the refusal of two employees of the Episcopalian Church to give evidence on the whereabouts of a Puerto Rican church member suspected of terrorism; and, third, the trial of the Catonsville Nine for burning the files of a local draft board, are examined for what they reveal about the power of the state, through the judiciary, to determine what can count as religious grounds for action.

Fenn's general thesis is that against the "overriding powers of the secular state, private commitments and sacred duties will not survive unless they are protected by liturgical words" (Fenn 1981:xxiv). The reason for this is that liturgy attempts to reestablish powerful connections between words and deeds, between people, and between situations in such a way that the intentions and sincerity of speakers are guaranteed. "The liturgy is as close as humans ordinarily come to reentering the closed linguistic garden of paradise" (Fenn 1981:xv). Liturgy is therefore regarded as powerful: it has the power to authenticate feelings, words, promises, and pronouncements. It functions as a last resort in attempts to resolve ambiguities in human speech on important matters. Thus, "oaths, sacraments, and signs are liturgical expressions of speech that have become unambiguous, serious and binding both on those who speak and on those who listen" (Fenn 1981:xi).

In the light of Fenn's specific interpretation of the power of religious language, the problem of secularization takes on a special significance. It refers to the process whereby secular institutions reduce "authoritative declarations to mere assertions of personal opinion in the court or in the classroom" (Fenn 1981: xxxiv). The authenticity previously guaranteed to a speaker by religious language is ruled literally out of court. The only admissible expressions of religion are confined to a very narrow range of statements of a largely nondoctrinal kind. For example, the content of Karen Ann Quinlan's father's Roman Catholic convictions was ruled inadmissible in court. All that mattered was the question of whether he was a suitable guardian of his own daughter. In this way, the paramount importance attributed to the rule of law in the United States diluted the significance of Joseph Quinlan's specifically religious beliefs and reduced them simply to the technical matter of his suitability as a guardian.

Religious terms allegedly lose their prophetic power when used in secular contexts. This is reminiscent of Yinger's dilemma of power argument (1946), but Fenn's focus on the linguistic aspect of the dilemma is both novel and insightful. His position is summarized as follows:

> The process of secularization therefore dissolves the powerful speech of the religious community, in which the same words are both sign and symbol, into the two distinct vocabularies and rules for speaking. One, in which words are taken literally, is a vocabulary of symbols that obey rules of relevance and reliability in secular courts and classrooms. The other is a liturgical language that creates . . . a community of common faith and hope [Fenn 1981:164-65].

Incidentally, there are many suggestive points of convergence between, on the one hand, Fenn's thesis on the corrosive effects of secular rationality on the power of religion to guarantee sincerity and, on the other hand, Alasdair MacIntyre's monumental survey of the self-defeating moral philosophies of the post-Enlightenment age, *After Virtue*. Like Fenn, MacIntyre is exercised by the allegedly illusory freedom enjoyed by members of societies in which virtually every aspect of life is treated as a matter of personal choice. And again, they share a similar concern with the near-impossibility of reaching agreement on fundamental values or virtues in societies dominated by the logic of rational efficiency. In their respective ways, they seem to reach similar conclusions about the baneful effects of a loss of vision of the serious ends of life. For MacIntyre this means the abandonment of virtues conceptualized teleologically. For Fenn, it means the progressive erosion of the social and intellectual conditions allowing people to harness the power of religion to say anything seriously and convincingly.

Nevertheless, Fenn's theory does not simply consign religious speaking to the anthropoligical museum, for it also suggests that the hegemony currently enjoyed by secular institutions and professional elites within them actually creates an unfulfilled demand for opportunities for people to speak sincerely, i.e., to declare, to pronounce, and to direct. Thus,

> A speech-act theory of secularization must therefore focus first of all on power: power defined as the ability to engage in such forceful acts as declarations and directions. . . . A theory of secularization utilizing these concepts would then be able to assess the relative power of religious institutions and the spokespersons in various non-ecclesiastical contexts [Fenn 1981:120].

Fenn's analysis of the Quinlan case and of the case of the Episcopal Church employees who refused to testify about a suspected terrorist on the grounds that it would be an infringement of their First Amendment rights turns on the issue of where the power lies to define religion in a secular society. One might wish to go further and to suggest that being religious nowadays entails a struggle to assert the power of religion over agencies whose effects are generally to exclude the relevance of religion to any but the most private and nonmaterial concerns.

It should be added here that the struggle to preserve the power of religious language does not merely oppose the religious to the nonreligious. It also involves tensions within religious groups between the advocates of literal and metaphoric uses of language. Indeed, Fenn's view is that the secularization of religious language begins within the religious community with the disposition to take religious pronouncements as mere metaphors or slippery symbols of "togetherness." The original power of prophetic speech is consequently dissipated, or, as Fenn renders the point more poetically, "out of the metaphor's Trojan-horse belly come the soldiers of deviant interpretation and rival claims to the holy city" (Fenn 1981:180). Thus, words which originally evoked commitment by speaking powerfully of common values and historical myths eventually degenerate into words which merely point to everyday objects.

This new and basically political approach to the sociology of religion represents a shift away from the kind of work which emphasized the largely subjective importance of religion as a set of precarious cognitions sustained by social interaction and conversation with significant others. The emphasis has been shifted toward a concern with the practical processes whereby religion is actually lived out at both the individual and collective levels in a struggle for power. The struggle is over the power to define situations, to effect the course of events, and, above all, to gain a hearing for religious testimony, declarations, and directions. I have been trying for some time to describe the cross-national ways in which this struggle is currently being acted out in the controversy surrounding cultism and anticultism (Beckford 1979, 1985).

This approach takes us into a realm of power defined by Steven Lukes (1974) as the capacity to set the agenda, i.e., to decide what will, and what will not, count as relevant topics for consideration or criteria for evaluation. By this, he means that the exercise of power is frequently invisible and involves far more than simply having one's orders obeyed in the face of resistance from others. It involves, notably, being in a position to determine how critical issues are to be presented and understood by others.

Religion and the Power Which Contests

A clear illustration of the shift toward a concern with the experience of religion as powerfully contesting the status quo can be seen in the ways in which the notion of Civil Religion has evolved in the last fifteen years or so. The career of the Civil Religion concept exemplifies a drift away from its organic, meaning-conferring functions as delineated by Robert Bellah in 1967 toward a concern with the struggles waged by numerous interest groups to acquire power for their particular (and often, exclusive) version of the concept. Studies by Michael Novak (1974) and by Roderick Hart (1977), for example, have opened our eyes to a kind of underground war being conducted by the advocates of various extremist interpretations of the sacred origins, mission and millennial future of the American nation. These intense ideological struggles center on the perceived threats to America's sacred mission. And their participants make no secret of their conviction that the exercise of the power to contest is the only way to block the advance of the many-headed monsters of anti-Christ and unAmericanism. These studies have destroyed the image of American Civil Religion as a peaceful and courtly preserve of elite groups and invisible opinion-makers. It is becoming clear that the power to impose particular versions of Civil Religion is the object of continuous and occasionally naked conflict, although it must be conceded that the level of fervor rarely reaches the pitch of the Reverend Dallas F. Billington's exhortation:

> I want you . . . to pray this prayer beside your bed every night: that God kill [Madlyn Murray O'Hair]. . . . Now we have no right to go out and take a gun and kill her, but we can sure pray for God to kill Her. . . . It is not wrong for you to pray God to destroy your enemy .. . . (quoted in Hart 1977:24).

The "Moonies" are probably the most visible and controversial of groups presently working hard to spread a sectarian version of American Civil Religion (See Robbins et al. 1976).

For me, the most poignant symbol of the current struggle to stake out America as sacred space was a violent confrontation that I witnessed in Berkeley between Eldridge Cleaver, speaking on a Unification Church-sponsored platform in October 1982 about "America's future and the world revolution," and sundry radical opponents claiming that he had sold his famous soul for a mess of Korean C.I.A. pottage. Both sides made a bid to speak for "the real American people," the Constitution and democracy. Yet, neither side was prepared to allow the other's legitimacy. And on their right flank the Moonies have formidable, if less visible competitors in such groups as the Christian Government Movement, the National Association for Christian Political Action, the Christian Anti-Communist Crusade, the Church League of America, and the American Coalition of Patriotic Societies. Far from signalling the end of ideology, then, it seems that American Civil Religion has become yet one more occasion or site for power contests nowadays extending well beyond the clash of pulpit orators. Moreover, virtually every country sports one or more Civil Religions, and similar struggles for power are to be observed in many of them.

Religion and the Power Which Controls

The study of Civil Religions shades off naturally into the more inclusive topic of religiously inspired movements for moral reform. But I shall not examine any particular study of the New Christian Right here. The reason for this is that so many studies of this phenomenon and of its most visible component, the Moral Majority, have appeared recently that it is unnecessary to belabor the obvious point that the relationship between religion and power is also crucial to this whole phenomenon.[1] I shall simply take the opportunity to add the observation that, while electoral politics has rightly been the primary focus of attention, the phenomenon also includes issues bearing on what I would call *moral power*. And this concept extends beyond the scope of purely electoral studies. By *moral power* I mean that, aside from influencing legislators and executives, this movement for the mobilization of large numbers of people in pursuit of the allegedly inerrant principles of biblical Christianity is also disseminating (or at least, reinforcing) specific and categorical notions of right and wrong in all spheres of everyday life. The increased pressure on politicians may be the most novel aspect, but the longer term impact may be more lasting in the moral life of the person-in-the-street responsive to the blandishments, exhortations, and excoriations of, for example, the aptly named "prime time preachers" or "televangelists."

This is all the more likely to happen, of course, to the extent that the clergy of local churches are exposed to pressure from a newly militant laity to conform with the guidelines issued by the more conservative electronic churches. There are already signs that the moral power inspired in part by the New Christian Right is making itself felt in local politics on such issues as law and order, school board syllabuses and zoning policies. But resistance from more liberal sources is also growing at both national and local levels. The result is a struggle for the moral power to control wide swatches of life.

If I have one regret about the studies of the New Christian Right, it is that they tend to isolate the phenomenon from other developments in religion and morality. In particular, I am surprised that so little attention has been paid to parallel campaigns being waged to control, for example, so-called cults. Admittedly, the scale of anticultism is meagre compared with Moral Majority, but it raises issues which touch upon some of the New Christian Right's central concerns: the family, education, and Americanism. Yet, at the same time, anticultism is also fed by currents of secular rationalism and liberal humanism. *They* are more exercised by perceived threats to the freedom of cultists' minds and the rationality of their thinking processes. There is therefore as much tension and disagreement with the New Christian Right as there is agreement. This is just one small example of the cross-cutting lines of interest which indicate that the current struggles for moral power are anything but simple or one-dimensional.[2] It is only when separate studies of the New Christian Right and of other phenomena, such as the Catholic campaigns for respect for life, are juxtaposed that the complexities, tensions, alliances, and conflicts in the struggle to control moral sentiment are thrown into relief.

Let me add that I do not believe that the struggle for what I have called *moral power* can be subsumed under Gusfield's notion of *symbolic politics* or *status politics*. For there is no evidence to show that the present-day moral indignation of so many Protestants and Catholics alike represents a displacement of material deprivations or status frustrations. The truth is that morality can be as real as bread-and-butter; and is no less the staff of life for some people.

Religion and the Power Which Cultivates

If we turn our attention to sociological studies of new religious movements in the last fifteen years or so, I think it is clear that the dominant perspective has been a mixture of functionalism and American phenomenology. That is to say, the most salient question has been of the kind "how have new religious movements fulfilled the function of supplying meaning and identity to their followers?" The philosophical presuppositions of such a perspective have rarely been examined (but see Beckford 1981), and alternative approaches have received little attention on the western side of the Atlantic. But I do not wish to spend time on the reasons for this now. Rather, I intend to sketch the outlines of a different interpretation which throws a distinctive notion of power into sharp relief. Again, I shall refrain from analyzing one particular piece of work but shall draw on my own studies and on those of my colleagues in various parts of the world.

The sociocultural conditions engendering a loosening or relaxation of the bonds linking young adults to particular statuses, careers, occupations, geographical locations, etc., have been well enough researched to need no further comment here. Let us simply acknowledge that people between the ages of, say, eighteen and thirty now constitute an unprecedentedly large section of most Western societies and have acquired a strategic and economic importance virtually unknown by their predecessors. At the same time as the aggregate strength of young adults has reached new levels, their sources of possible support, protection, patronage and legitimation from people outside their age category have diminished.

The price that has been paid for their emergent autonomy has included the weakening of social ties to kin, locality and workplace. For the vast majority of young adults this situation may amount to nothing less than an unalloyed benefit of increased freedom of opportunity and action. Some young adults have taken advantage of their relative freedom to experiment with novel forms of consciousness, experience, social relations, and ideology. In current jargon they enjoy more space for themselves. Indeed, some may even feel themselves under pressure to be experimental in outlook; and others may experience experimental failure. New religious movements no doubt offer something useful to young adults in both categories, as the literature amply testifies. But it would be a great mistake to believe that the recruits to new religious movements were exclusively unwilling or failed experimenters—just as it would be equally wrong to treat all new religious movements and analagous enterprises as if they were alike in most respects. For the fact is that there is enormous variety in the motivations to join new religious movements, just as the movements themselves display a wide diversity of aims, values and strategies.

In a nutshell, my interpretation of the new religious movements with which I am familiar is that they are seen by prospective and actual members alike as sources of various kinds of power. Their expectation, and the experience of many, is that membership empowers them to cultivate and to achieve a number of things more easily than through other means. The chance to cultivate various spiritual qualities, personal goals or social relationships is the attraction. This is a necessarily condensed statement of my general interpretation, but I want to emphasize a few salient points here. First, there are frequent discrepancies between members' expectations and the actual possibilities for cultivation made available to them. Second, members' beliefs frequently bear only a passing resemblance to the official doctrines of new religious movements. Third, it is possible for members with very diverse motives and intentions to derive equally satisfactory benefits from membership of the same movement. Fourth, some members are prepared to tolerate high levels of discrepancy between their beliefs, experiences and the movement's practices for the sake of exploring their potential for development in unforeseen and only dimly perceived directions.

Of course, once members have invested time, resources, personal reputation and even self-respect in the attempt to tap the power to cultivate all the things on offer from new religious movements, they are unlikely to abandon them lightly. The theory of cognitive dissonance and attribution theory would both confirm this general point. And one does not have to be a deprogrammer to realize how resistant some members can be to any and all efforts to induce them to abandon movements about which they may already have serious misgivings. If one's understanding of human action is based on a narrow cost-benefit model, the tenacity of many members of new religious movements can only signify pathology. But if one is sensitive to the importance of such human activities as willing, experimenting, striving for coherence (rather than consistency), and cultivating a sense of overall integrity, then both membership and apostasy can be understood in terms other than pathology. But most importantly, it must be appreciated that recruits to new religious movements perceive in them (rightly or wrongly, clearly or confused, and for a wide variety of motives) the opportunity to tap sources of power—power which will supposedly enable them to cultivate any number of personal ends and end-states.

Here I wish to introduce an idea which helps to explain the popularity of so many collective experiments in new religious practices and experiences.

Today's new religious movements may offer relatively safe sites for experimentation with types of consciousness and modes of social relationships which entail quite serious risks. Indeed, these risks have alarmed not only anticultists but also more sophisticated commentators such as Christopher Lasch (1980), Edwin Schur (1976), and Daniel Yankelovich (1981). It is no small thing to abandon conventional routines, relationships, and habits of mind; and the evidence from serious studies of new religious movements shows convincingly that young adults do not abandon themselves unthinkingly to experimental religion (see Barker 1984). Rather, they take a more or less calculated risk. By participating in a collective experiment—a movement—young adults share some of the risks with others and to some extent shelter under the patronage of people of presumably good will.

Let me make it absolutely clear that I am definitely not saying that people necessarily join new religious movements out of weakness or perceived powerlessness. On the contrary, my view is that the protection of new religious movements is sought for reasons having more to do with adventurousness and risk-taking than with weakness and retreatism. Ironically, some of the sources of power perceived in new religious movements are precisely the conditions of success in the major economic activities and professions of modern societies. Many of the goals of training in the various branches of the Human Potential Movement, for example, are indistinguishable from the goals of executive training schemes in industry, commerce, and the armed forces (see Tipton 1982). Similarly, the communicative skills and self-awareness techniques engendered in a wide variety of meditative movements are also cultivated in many training programs in the spheres of therapy, education, and social welfare (see Swanson 1980; Westley 1983). There is scope for a more intensive interpretation of the relationship between sources and experiences of power in the new religious movements and the distribution of economic, cultural, and social power in the wider society.

Religion and the Power Which Cures

I can illustrate this last point most economically by referring finally to the innovative work of Meredith McGuire who has clearly identified the centrality of power to the theory and practice of Roman Catholic Pentecostalists. Her book, *Pentecostal Catholics*, documents carefully the way in which "the discovery of a new source of power in their lives" (McGuire 1982:174) led the subjects of her research to an explicit practice of faith healing. Moreover, this practice is shown to be grounded in a coherent theory of disease and well-being. At its core is the notion of a desirable balance of power between good and evil to be achieved in an appropriate social setting. There is the added insight that "the practices of faith healing . . . may be a political statement—a counter-assertion of power—against the dominant medical system" (McGuire 1982:182). Her subsequent research on alternative healing groups in suburban New Jersey has shown that "power is a fundamental (if not *the* fundamental) category for interpreting healing. . . . The treatment of illness is essentially the restoration of the balance of power—by weakening the antagonist's (disease-causing) power or by strengthening the victim's power" (McGuire 1983:229). Ritual language is a particularly effective transmitter of healing power. In short, Meredith McGuire's work confirms my general argument about the importance of examining the relevance of power to the social dimensions of religion.

Conceptual Threads

Sensitivity to questions of power in all its diverse relations to religion is necessary for an adequate sociological understanding of religion. They can be likened to trace-elements which show up the crucial lines of sympathy and antipathy, affinity and rejection between the various models of man, blueprints for society, and visions of world order which are currently competing for support and power on so many different sociocultural levels.

Other examples of the newly apparent importance of the notion of power in religion could no doubt be added if space permitted. But enough has already been said to substantiate my main thesis that the sociology of religion is undergoing a reorientation of its main perspectives. What is urgently needed, of course, is a more careful analysis than I have provided here of the meanings denoted or connoted by power in relation to religion. Questions could then be asked about the bearing of discussions of power in general sociology on its specifically religious manifestations. In this way, a better integration might be achieved between sociological analyses of religion and of wider aspects of social structures and processes. The notion of power would then serve as a useful point of articulation.

Lest I be accused of completely ducking the matter of conceptual clarification, however, let me briefly sketch a general line of thought. The range of meanings commonly attributed to *power* include: *the capacity to produce effects; the actual production of intended effects; the probability that commands will be obeyed; the capacity of some persons to produce intended and foreseen effects on others;* and *the process of affecting policies of others with the help of severe deprivations for nonconformity with the policies intended.* These varied conceptualizations can be reduced to three main types: *dispositional, episodic,* and *relational.* No single approach has universal merit or acceptance, for all notions of power are contestable. Can we leave the matter there? On the one hand, this could be taken as a provisional solution while we awaited closer analysis of the conceptual issues that arise from the conjunction of religion and power. But, on the other, this would be unsatisfactory unless it could be shown that there was a prima facie case for investing time and energy in further analysis of the relationship between religion and power. I believe that the studies that have been reviewed in this chapter have made that case.

In my opinion, the orientation toward this notion of power in sociological analysis makes it possible to give greater attention to the *intentional* production of foreseen effects (see Wrong 1980). In contrast to the predominantly cognitive view of religion as both product and condition of normal processes of socialization and interaction, there is nowadays a sharper awareness of the deliberate attempts being made to bring about certain effects in the name of religion. Religion is no longer considered interesting solely as a part of the general apparatus of socialization and social control supplying meaning through culture. Some sociologists have stopped looking at religion as if it were the wallpaper of the social system. It has now acquired distinct importance in its own right as a sphere of activity where efforts are deliberately made to influence, manipulate, and control people's thoughts, feelings and actions in accordance with various religious values.

Conclusion

I must comment briefly on the relationship between the notions of *meaning* and *power,* for it may be objected that I have implied a contrast or opposition between them. It may also have seemed that I was advocating the abandonment of the perspective which has dominated the sociology of religion for the past fifteen years. But, in fact, my thesis is rather different. What I have proposed is that, in focusing on the capacity or function of religion to supply meaning, integration, and identity, the theoretical cart has been put before the empirical horse. The sociologists' interpretations of religious phenomena have been mistaken for their subjects' motives and intentions. In short, I agree that meaning and identity are important aspects of religion: but at the same time I dispute whether actors act out of consideration for them directly. Rather, I believe that actors respond to perceived sources of power, and their responses may or may not supply the meaning and identity of which we have heard so much. This is an empirical question: not something to be resolved by definition.

Doubt, despair, confusion, misgivings, rationalizations, agonizing indecisiveness, and evasiveness are no less common characteristics of the religious life than are meaningfulness and identity.[3] Present events connected with religion in many parts of the world have shown that the rumor of angels is a strident trumpet call to action in some believers' ears. (See, for example, Robertson and Chirico 1982; Dessouki 1982). But until very recently it was not much more than the background noise of the social system in the ears of many sociologists of religion. What I have therefore proposed is that empirical attention should, as a matter of priority, be focused on the reported experiences and the perceived manifestations of power and power struggles in religion. Until and unless this first step is taken, the meaning of religion for both individuals and societies cannot be adequately understood.

Notes

1. See, for example, the useful documentation published by the Center for the Study of New Religious Movements (1981); the sensationalist report by Conway and Siegelman (1982); the judicious theological critique by Webber (1981); and the balanced collection of commentaries edited by Liebman and Wuthnow (1983).
2. For interesting examples concerning the Roman Catholic Church, see Hanna (1979) and Vaillancourt (1980).
3. See Fabian's (1979) observations on the "terror" of sacred texts felt by some members of the Jamaa movement in the former Belgian Congo.

Bibliography

Barker, Eileen V. 1984. *The Making of a Moonie.* Oxford: Blackwell.
Beckford, James A. 1985. *Cult Controversies: The Societal Response to New Religious Movements.* London: Tavistock Publications.
_____. "Functionalism and Ethics in Sociology: The Relationship Between 'Ought' and 'Function.'" *The Annual Review of the Social Sciences of Religion* 5 (1981):101-31.
_____. "Politics and the Anti-cult Movement." *The Annual Review of the Social Sciences of Religion* 3 (1979):169-90.
Bellah, Robert N. "Civil Religion in America." *Daedalus* 96 (1967):1-21.
Berger, Peter L. 1969. *The Social Reality of Religion.* London: Faber and Faber.
Berton, Pierre. 1965. *The Comfortable Pew.* New York: Lippincott.
Brown, Peter. 1981. *Society and the Holy in Late Antiquity.* Berkeley: University of California Press.
_____. 1978. *The Making of Late Antiquity.* Cambridge, Mass.: Harvard University Press.
Burridge, Kenelm. 1969. *New Heaven, New Earth.* Oxford: Blackwell.
Capps, Walter H. 1982. *The Unfinished War: Vietnam and the American Conscience.* Boston: Beacon Press.
Center for the Study of New Religious Movements. 1981. *Resource Packet on the Christian New Right.* Berkeley: CSNRM.

Conway, Flo and Siegelman, Jim. 1982. *Holy Terror: The Fundamentalist War on America's Freedom in Religion, Politics and Our Private Lives*. New York: Doubleday.

Dessouki, Ali E. Hillel, ed. 1982. *Islamic Resurgence in the Arab World*. New York: Praeger.

Fabian, Johnannes. "Text as Terror: Second Thoughts About Charisma." *Social Research* 46 (1979):166-203.

Fenn, Richard K. 1981. *Liturgies and Trials*. Oxford: Blackwell.

Fitzgerald, Frances. "A Disciplined Charging Army." *The New Yorker* (18 May 1981):53.

Gilsenan, Michael. 1973. *Saint and Sufi in Modern Egypt*. Oxford: Clarendon Press.

Hadden, Jeffrey K. 1969. *The Gathering Storm in Churches*. New York: Doubleday.

Hadden, Jeffrey K. and Swann, Charles E. 1981. *The Prime Time Preachers: The Rising Power of Televangelism*. Reading, Mass.: Addison-Wesley.

Hammond, Phillip E. 1966. *The Campus Clergyman*. New York: Basic Books.

Hanna, Mary T. 1979. *Catholics and American Politics*. Cambridge, Mass.: Harvard University Press.

Hart, Roderick P. 1977. *The Political Pulpit*. West Lafayette: Purdue University Press.

Lasch, Christopher. 1980. *The Culture of Narcissism*. London: Sphere Books.

Liebman, R. and Wuthnow, R. eds. 1983. *The New Christian Right: Mobilization and Legitimation*. New York: Aldine.

Luckmann, Thomas. 1967. *The Invisible Religion*. London: Macmillan.

Lukes, Steven. 1974. *Power: A Radical View*. London: Macmillan.

McGuire, Meredith B. "Words of Power: Personal Empowerment and Healing." *Culture, Medicine and Psychiatry* 7 (1983):221-40.

_____. 1982. *Pentecostal Catholics: Power, Charisma and Order in a Religious Movement*. Philadelphia: Temple University Press.

MacIntyre, Alasdair. 1981. *After Virtue*. London: Duckworth.

Martin, David A. "The Sociology of Religion: A Case of Status Deprivation?" *British Journal of Sociology* (December 1966):353-59.

Mol, J.J. 1976. *Identity and the Sacred*. Agincourt: Book Society of Canada.

Niebuhr, Reinhold. 1940. *Christianity and Power Politics*. New York: Scribners.

Novak, Michael. 1974. *Choosing our King: Powerful Symbols in American Politics*. New York: Macmillan.

Radcliffe, Timothy. 1980. "Relativizing the Relativizers: A Theologian's Assessment of the Role of Sociological Explanation of Religious Phenomena and Theology Today?" Pp. 151-62 in D. Martin et al. eds. *Sociology and Theology: Alliance or Conflict?* Brighton: Harvester Press.

Robbins, Thomas; Anthony, Dick; Doucas, Madeline; and Curtis, Thomas. "The Last Civil Religion: Reverend Moon and the Unification Church." *Sociological Analysis* 37 (1976):111-25.

Robertson, Roland and Chirico, JoAnn. "Humanity, Globalization and Worldwide Religious Resurgence: A Theoretical Exploration." *Sociological Analysis* 46 (1985):219-42.

Robertson, Roland, and Holzner, Burkart, eds. 1980. *Identity and Authority*. New York: St. Martin's Press.

Schur, Edwin. 1976. *The Awareness Trap: Self-Absorption Instead of Social Change*. New York: Quadrangle Books.

Stark, Rodney et al. "The Sounds of Silence." *Psychology Today* 3 (April 1970): 38-41 and 60-61.

Swanson, Guy. 1980. "A Basis of Authority and Identity in Post-industrial Society." Pp. 190-217 in R. Robertson and B. Holzner, eds. *Identity and Authority.* New York: St. Martin's Press.

Tipton, Steven M. 1982. *Getting Saved from the Sixties.* Berkeley: University of California Press.

Vaillancourt, Jean-Guy. 1980. *Papal Power: A Study of Vatican Control Over Lay Catholic Elites.* Berkeley: University of California Press.

Webber, Robert E. 1981. *The Moral Majority: Right or Wrong?* Westchester, Ill.: Cornerstone Books.

Westley, Frances. 1983. *The Complex Forms of the Religious Life: A Durkheimian View of New Religious Movements.* Baltimore: Scholar Press.

Wilson, Bryan R. 1975. *The Noble Savages: The Primitive Origins of Charisma and Its Contemporary Survival.* Berkeley: University of California Press.

_____. 1973. *Magic and the Millennium.* London: Heinemann.

Wrong, Dennis. 1980. *Power, Its Forms, Bases and Uses.* New York: Harper and Row.

Yankelovich, Daniel. 1981. *New Rules: Searching for Self-Fulfillment in a World Turned Upside Down.* New York: Random House.

Yinger, J. Milton. 1946. *Religion in the Struggle for Power.* Durham, N.C.: Duke University Press.

3

Church-State Relations and
the World System

Roland Robertson

The tensions between church (a term which is here used very loosely) and state, and the crystallization of problematic relationships between religion and politics which have become evident in the U.S.A. in recent years are parts of a much larger—indeed a more-or-less global—pattern. Even when we allow for the possibility that recent American experience in a situation involving great sensitivity to such issues may involve America-based analysts projecting American problems onto other societies, the extensiveness of church-state and/or religion-politics tensions across the globe is very striking.

We have witnessed and continue to witness such tension in a considerable number of Central and Southern American societies, much of it resulting from the growth of the "Liberation Church" and its reversal of the more usual Catholic political quiescence (but more-or-less silent support of the status quo) in most Latin American societies. In some of those same societies there has also developed a not insignificant right-wing political presence among Protestant evangelicals and Pentacostalists. The intensification of various forms of Islamic—particularly, but certainly not only, Shiite—"fundamentalism" in the Middle East is well known and needs no further emphasis here; neither does the resurgence in Israel of forms of Jewish fundamentalism, nor do the political problems raised in the Middle Eastern conflagration with respect to Coptic Christians in Egypt, Maronite Christians in Lebanon, the globally oriented Bahai in Iran, and so on.

In Eastern Europe, Poland provides a particularly striking case of the thematization of church-state tension and the conflation of, as well as the conflict between, religious and political interests. However, not merely does the Soviet Union also appear to be experiencing problems with respect to a number of its religious groupings (ranging from Christian Baptists to Islamic ethnic groups), but so have the regimes in East Germany, Hungary and Czechoslovakia been faced recently with religious challenges to policies of "atheization."

In Western Europe the situation has been more subdued, with the exception of the Irish circumstance. Nevertheless a number of West European societies have experienced difficulties which parallel—but which have taken different form and been more muted than—those in the United States with respect to new religious movements such as the Unification Church, Hare Krishna, and so on (Beckford 1985). Spain and France have not been without recent problems concerning church and state, notably with respect to the education of children, while in England the debate about the liturgy of the established Church has raised significant questions about the relationship between religion and national identity. Moreover, in Western Europe (and elsewhere) there has emerged the so-called Green phenomenon, which while not religious in a traditional sense, involves considerable concern with human-existential questions of a kind which is challenging to the modern secular state.

Parts of Asia—notably Pakistan, Indonesia and the Philippines—have experienced waves of the Islamic politicoreligious fundamentalism which has been so conspicuous in the Middle East, while in the Philippines we have also witnessed trends which are concretely linked to the relationship between liberational-theological tendencies and the state to be found in Latin America. In China the problem of the relationship between the Vatican and indigenous Catholicism has arisen. In Japan the question has recently been raised as to the relationship between the Roman papacy and the Japanese state; while in the same society activities of the Soka Gakkai movement constitute yet another manifestation of the increasing involvement of religious movements and organizations in political matters. In India the violence involving the situation of the Sikhs, particularly in the Punjab, has dramatically focused problems concerning the relationships between political and religious activity and between religious and national allegiance.

In Africa, the types of occurrences I refer to in Asia, Europe, the Middle East and the Western Hemisphere, have not had highly tangible parallels. Nonetheless, leaving on one side predominantly Moslem North Africa (where Islamic fundamentalism has made some impact), it is clear that in recent years there has been an acceleration of interest in political activity within and among religious collectivities (much of it along "liberationist" lines), while in South Africa politicization has greatly increased in response to the racial conflict attendant upon apartheid.

Globally Oriented Movements

Some of the cases which I have just mentioned involve tension between a national government (or the legal or state apparatus of a national society) on the one hand, and a transnational religious organization or movement on the other. In that connection it should be emphasized that while, of course, a very large number of today's religious organizations and movements are multinational, operating in many societies, we are now apparently—and more significantly—in a phase of proliferation of religious movements whose leaders *are preoccupied with the concrete global-human circumstance as such.* By this I mean that they direct much of their organizational concern at the present and future of the world as a single, systemic entity. Moreover, they engage in concrete action directed at molding the world along their own preferred lines.

The Roman Catholic Church is, of course, by far the oldest and most thoroughly organized of these—but clearly under John Paul II it has become particularly concerned with the global-human "community" in the latter's empirical entirety, most notably with respect to its declared interest in the political policies of governments vis à vis the fate of the world; even though the Pope has, not unambiguously, prevailed upon Catholics as individuals to abstain from direct political action on the basis of religious commitment or via a synthesis of theology and ideology. That proscription, as is well known, has been directed particularly at Latin American liberationists—who, in doctrinal terms, are guided by a syncretism involving Marxism and Catholicism (as well, perhaps, as elements of populist magico-religion of pre-*conquistador* origins) and who operate politically in terms of populistic base communities. (In some East European countries—as well as in North America, western and southern Europe and elsewhere—base (or basis) communities of a more specifically religious form have developed in recent years, while certainly not all of the Latin American base communities are *politico*religious in orientation.)

However, the much debated question of the degree of conservatism of Pope John Paul II and its relationship to Latin American liberationism is probably of less significance than the *global* orientation of the modern papacy. Not merely has the Roman Church—and, even more specifically, the Holy See—become an increasingly significant actor on the global political scene in recent years, its leadership seems to have adopted a policy of concern with the global-human circumstance per se. Upon that orientation, many of the church's more specific policies and actions hinge. And it is worth noting that the most prominent explanation provided for the White House decision to resume full diplomatic relations with the Holy See in 1984 was the global significance of the modern papacy (as subsequently indicated by the abortive attempt of the Reagan administration to legitimate its policy vis à vis Nicaragua, by invoking alleged approval by the Pope).

The modern Roman Catholic Church is not, however, the only religious collectivity which has recently become specifically and explicitly occupied with the global-human circumstance (even though it may be the most powerful and effective). The Unification Church (and its many conferences, journals, welfare organizations, newspapers, academic organizations, industries, advisory groups, campaigns, etc.) is—notwithstanding journalistic and scholarly preoccupation with its methods of proselytization (which have not, in any case, been particularly fruitful, at least outside the Far East)—above all a globally oriented megaorganization. Its overriding concern, as its name suggests, is with the unification of the world; a development which is to proceed within the frame of a specific (if highly syncretic) set of "absolute" theological and mythological principles but which, at the same time, is to be nurtured by strategic principles of mobilization directed, inter alia, at the overcoming of racial and ethnic differences by miscegenation; the knitting together (in terms of absolute, but manipulable metaprinciples) of the major religious doctrines; the establishment of global media of communication and travel; and so on.

Of a somewhat different ilk—and in less crystallized form—is the series of international Christian Embassies which are being established around the world (notably but not only in the U.S.A.), following upon the setting-up of such an "embassy" by American-*Christian* Zionists in Jerusalem. Much more specific in its concern than globally oriented Catholicism or Unificationism—since it is centered on premillenarian prophesies having particular reference to the eschatological and apocalyptic significance of the congregation of the Jews in Israel and their probable conversion to Christianity—the Christian Embassy movement (and its broader constituency in Christian-fundamentalist support for the American backing of Israel) nevertheless shares with global Catholicism and Unificationism a direct, if highly selective, orientation to the condition of the modern world as a whole. In that regard it differs from the orientations of the more clearly sectarian kind of religious movement—for example, the Jehovah's Witnesses—which, while explicitly concerned with "the fate of the world," operates in a distinctively *introversial* mode. The difference may be highlighted in reference to the apparently half serious remark that Jerry Falwell is alleged to have made in reaction to the announcement of the restoration of the U.S.A.'s full diplomatic links with the Holy See—namely, that *he* might be asking for diplomatic recognition. That is not to say that Falwell was explicitly speaking in a global role; nor is it meant to indicate that his major concern is with the Christian Embassy movement (even though there is clearly overlap between the latter and Falwellism). Rather it is to consolidate the observation that a number of modern religious movements have established a position—or seriously seek to establish a position—that has some significant resemblance to the "old European" form of religious adjudication on political matters and (of more immediate significance) that a smaller number are doing this in terms of their interest in the *global situation*.[1]

Whether some of the explicitly globally oriented religious movements— and it should be stressed that some of the main Islamic traditions have definite conceptions of the world-as-a-whole—seek to go further than this in the direction of global *theocracy* (involving the coordinated subordination of the state to religious doctrine), is not an uninteresting question, but one which cannot be tackled here. Clearly, some of them have theocratic tendencies. In any case, globally oriented religious and quasi-religious movements are, in their different ways, addressing the problem of world order. They seek to give meaning and, in their own terms, stability to the idea of the world as a single place in relation to the world's cosmic context (as well—at least, in some cases—as engaging in strategic activity relative to such doctrinal work, on the one hand, and political and economic realities, on the other).

For reasons which should become apparent shortly, there is a series of constraints on modern religious collectivities to become concerned with the global-human circumstance as a concrete whole (the threat of virtually globewide annihilation of life during and/or in the aftermath of nuclear war being one of the major concerns). However, the proliferation of church-state tensions around the world cannot be fully understood, nor can they be accounted for, in sole reference to organizations or movements which are oriented explicitly to the global scene per se. In other words, many particular manifestations of church-state tension have—or at least appear at first consideration to have—a primarily *intra*-societal significance and do not involve an obvious degree of concern with the global circumstance. Nevertheless, I argue that most modern church-state tensions which do not involve overt concern on the religious side with global matters have arisen actually under essentially global-systemic constraints.

Globalization and Modern Societies

Why, then, are we witnessing widespread church-state tensions and the thematization—or, in historical terms, the *re*thematization—of the intimate relationships between religion and politics and between theology and ideology, regardless of the degree of explicitly global concern among the religious groupings involved? In the most general terms, I suggest that we identify the process of *globalization* as providing the most fruitful conceptual, summarizing key to that problem. By globalization I mean the process in terms of which, first, the world becomes *a single place* in which little can happen that does not have significant ramifications for the world as a whole and, second, there develops an acute sense (but certainly *not* consensual view) of the fate of humanity and its raison d'être. It is not possible here to sketch the various factors which have contributed over a very long period of human history to the contemporary crystallization of "globality."[2] It must suffice to emphasize that a mixture of trends in the direction of global implosion, on the one hand, and the "explosion" of societies, on the other, is very rapidly issuing in a global circumstance in which heavy constraints are imposed upon societies and their individual members to establish their identities vis à vis the world, perhaps the cosmos, in its entirety.

What are the major general features of this global entity? Probably the most specifically discussed in recent years is its increasingly high degree of economic interdependence. In other words it is the crystallization of the global economy—and its lack of legitimacy as far as the pattern of intersocietal inequality (notably as between North and South) is concerned—which has received particular attention among social scientists and other observers of and participants in the global scene. Another, much discussed feature of the contemporary global circumstance has to do with the trend, to use Marshall McLuhan's famous phrase, in the direction of "the global village," a trend which centers upon the globalization of the means of communication and travel and thus the global sharing of various forms of experience. However, the limitations of that popular characterization (which was not without religious connotations for McLuhan himself) are brought into sharp focus by Smart's (1981) use of the term *global city.* The contrast reflects old distinctions between different types of society, the most well-known of which is the *Gemeinschaft* (community) versus *Gesellschaft* (broadly, society) contrast. The latter was, of course, developed by Toennies to indicate the difference between premodern and modern societies. Subsequently many have come to agree that *Gesellschaft* does not totally replace *Gemeinschaft,* but rather that any given society manifests aspects of each (a line of reasoning which Durkheim largely initiated). The point is that the global system does not merely exhibit both aspects of *Gemeinschaft* and *Gesellschaft* but, even more important, that globality itself relativizes these concepts in such a way as to render them as competing images of the preferred character of collectivities. More specifically, religious (as well as other) movements oriented to the world-as-a-whole vary—and often compete—with respect to how the global system should be ordered (Robertson and Lechner 1985). *Gemeinschaft* and *Gesellschaft* constitute the major modalities of such, although, undoubtedly, a more elaborate typology is needed to capture the most salient variations among globally oriented movements. Here, however, I must concentrate on the factors that facilitate intrasocietal church-state encounters.

In the latter connection, particular attention should be drawn to the operation of *power* in global terms. Recent studies (Boli-Bennett 1979; Meyer 1980) have emphasized the extensive global legitimation of the strong centralized state as a primary feature of the world system. More specifically, one of the most significant attributes of the modern global scene is the fact that, in order for a society to be a legitimate member, it must exhibit certain characteristics associated with the strong, relatively centralized state. That means that the global political scene operates in terms which in important respects, run counter to the ways in which the internal political affairs of societies operate. National societies operate in terms of the centralization of political power, while the global system works—even though the superpowers limit the tendency—on the basis of the dispersal of political power.

The participation of national societies in the world system on the basis of globewide norms concerning statehood also involves the prescription that the state should be basically secular. In other words, global-political norms concerning national-societal participation in the world system do not in and of themselves allow for societal *identity* but only for the expression of national-societal *interests* in relation to other such interests and the world-as-a-whole. In this sense, then, the modern global system is highly secular in character, a secularity which is strongly reinforced by the perception of the secularity of the global economy. However, the global legitimation of the strong national state has been accompanied by the *de*legitimation of the world economy. The greater the generalization of the idea of the strong state, the less easy it becomes to justify, on a global basis, the existence of great economic inequalities between and among national societies. Moreover, the thematization of the phenomenon of intersocietal inequality in itself raises questions of a theodical nature about the world as a whole. By a "theodical" question I mean a question—or a series of questions—concerning the ways in which inequalities and disasters can be justified. It is not, however, merely the formal equality between states which exacerbates such questioning. It is the crystallization of the notion of *humanity*—not least because of the dramatization of the threat of nuclear annihilation—that may well form the centerpiece of the present global circumstance. For it raises an essentially eschatological question concerning the meaning and fate of collective human life.

Without claiming that the rise of the strong secular state on a globewide basis can be accounted for solely in terms of global-systemic pressures, nor that modern ethnic and religious nationalism can be explained in an equally monocausal manner, I argue, nevertheless, that the problem of global order and the crystallization of conflicts in defining the global-human situation are the main factors involved in solving the analytical puzzle as to why we have witnessed (and are likely to continue to witness in even more acute forms) a near-global proliferation of church-state tension.

The kind of national society encouraged by the process of globalization is at once secular and infused with a kind of religiosity. Its secularity resides in instrumental rationality at the level of the state and the forms of instrumental rationalization of various other spheres of life (about which, of course, Max Weber wrote at length). Secularity in these senses defines much of the internal life of modern societies and of their external, intersocietal relationships. On the other hand, societies are also constrained in religious and quasi-religious directions. The globally legitimated secular state has itself-in large part, because of the global-systematic pressure to do so—assumed a surrogate-religious form, in that it has taken unto itself various existential and moral issues concerning human welfare, psychic and physical well-being, the definition of life and death, and so on (Robertson 1979, 1981). These developments have also encouraged the politicization of religion. Lacking the aura of the genuinely sacred (or, better, the holy) and being constitutionally denied such in the United States and a number of other societies, the secular state has drawn—be it all, unintentionally—religious interests into it; that constituting a particularly problematic circumstance in a society such as the United States, where not merely is the state qua state supposed, officially, to be secular but where also elicited religious interests are likely to clash with each other.

However, there is a more directly global circumstance which encourages the politicization of religion and the "religionization" of the state. This has to do with the constraints upon modern national societies to formulate their own sociocultural identities—not only in relation to each other, but also in relation to the fate of humanity. The making of the world into a single human system does not, as we have seen, involve the worldwide concentration of political power in a single place. In fact, as I have argued, there has occurred—the superpower phenomenon notwithstanding—a *dispersal* of political power at the global level, "terrorism" and the potential "equality of nuclearity" being the major manifestations of such. This means that, in spite of the increase in significance of multi-, supra-, inter- and trans-societal agencies, the effective organization of life in the world as a whole remains at the national-societal level, even though affairs within societies—notably but not only economic affairs—*are* increasingly subject to global processes. Thus, in an increasingly globalized situation the constraint on the national society is to formulate an identity in relation to the global circumstance. Societies with sharp separations of church and state and of religion and politics (notably the United States as far as the former, if not the latter, are concerned), as well as those with major cleavages between religious or ethnic groupings, are at a disadvantage in some respects; for they are internally restricted in the degree to which they can strategically conflate material and ideal interests and make them cohere in the kind of religiopolitical identity which the global circumstance encourages. In contrast, caesaropapist societies can easily conflate the expression of material and ideal interests, for their internal structure encourages the use of religious or quasireligious imagery by the political regime. Communist societies, of course, fall into the latter category. Similarly theocratic societies—of which Iran is the outstanding contemporary example—can conflate religion and politics in terms of the subordination of the political to the religious. Much of the modern academic talk about civil religion has hinged upon observation of identity problems experienced by societies with church-state separation of varying degrees. My suggestion is that, whether acknowledged or not, "civil religion talk" has arisen under the particular constraint of a global situation in which the relationship between individual societies and the global system (as well as the general condition of humanity) demands expression.

It is little wonder that in the kind of situation that I have been describing we have witnessed so much religious and ideological fundamentalism. In the absence of a coherent, symbolically meaningful expression of the world in its totality and of a raison d'être for the continuation of the human species (even though nascent international communism, earlier in the century, attempted to provide something along those lines), one would indeed expect proliferation of fundamentalist movements inside societies, seeking to mold the society along *their* lines relative to the world as a whole, as well as movements oriented more directly at the global circumstance per se (Lifton and Falk 1982).

Interpretations

Individuals as different as Michael Harrington (1983) and Bryan Wilson (1982)—one an American socialist, the other an English conservative traditionalist—have recently contributed to the argument that religion as traditionally understood is dead. For both Harrington and Wilson the primary historical and sociological significance of religion (more specifically in Harrington's case, of belief in God) has inhered in its provision of solidarity, meaning and purpose to the politically organized and communally solidified collectivity (even though Wilson sees the shift from community to society—*Gemeinschaft* to *Gesellschaft*—as constituting in itself a process of secularization). As they see it, religion—at least in the West—is now marked by its inward significance (and thus is no longer really religion). Instrumental rationalization—notably that produced via the increasing salience of the economic domain in recent centuries—has been a prime mover in the disenchantment of the modern world, both within societies and in terms of the emergent global circumstance as a whole—although Harrington pleads, in effect, for a new "god" of global humanity; while Wilson wistfully speaks about the possibility of religion becoming once again the "ideology of community."

I mention these two theses not merely because they convey a flavor of some of the more important issues at stake in contemporary social-scientific discussion of religion in the modern world but, much more important, because they appear to me as reflecting—rather than as truly coming to analytical terms with—the world religious situation. Harrington's claim (expressed from the position of a "serious atheist") that God has died at the societal level but is now all the more needed at the global-human level constitutes an intellectual parallel to what is actually happening in the modern world. The fundamentalist movements concerned with the revitalization of their own particular societies—relative to other, culturally-alien societies and the secular humanism of the modern state—are indeed attempting to bring back the tribal gods of society or community, while those movements which are more explicitly oriented to the global scene are attempting to vitalize and establish a universal God for global humanity.

In the case of Wilson, it may also be said that his concern about the loss of religion as the "ideology of community" is deeply shared by Islamic, American and other fundamentalists. And his claim that the international system consists solely in instrumental-strategic relationships is more than matched by the activities of contemporary globally oriented religious movements—including those who, like the Unification Church or the Catholic liberationists, seek to establish a global Kingdom of God upon earth; the Christian Zionists who see the signs of "the last days" in the present configuration of international conflict (and are politically active in what they see as the preapocalyptic period); Shiite Moslems who also produce a (highly contrasting) symbolic image of intersocietal and inter-civilizational relationships (and who also are, to say the least, politically active); and, even the followers of Maharishi Mahesh Yogi, who attempt—via levitational "hopping"—to bring a new spiritually infused peace to the entire world.

One of the major recent sources of confusion which has arisen in attempting not merely to comprehend the particular topics of church-state and religion-politics relations but also general trends in the modern world as a whole has resided in the tendency to think that there is a basic incompatibility between the idea that the world is becoming more societally fundamentalistic and nationally protectionistic, on the one hand, and the perception that the world has, as I have put it, become a tightly knit single place, on the other. However, as I have been trying to show, not merely are these two sets of observations not at all incompatible, the phenomena to which they refer actually constitute two sides of the same coin. The problem of global order issues in large part from the societal and civilizational particularisms which themselves have been greatly encouraged by and are now "meaningfully" embedded in the world system. While, as I have emphasized, we certainly cannot account entirely for the character of the modern state in global-systemic terms (although there is a school of thought associated with the name of Immanuel Wallerstein which does make precisely that claim), the historical trends giving rise *within* societies to the modern state have been heavily accentuated and diffused under global pressure.

A significant contribution to this general problem has been made by Ernest Gellner (1983). Gellner argues that the modern state depends—largely, he claims, for economic reasons—on its monopolization of legitimate, high culture (as much as, perhaps more than, it does on its internal monopolization of legitimate violence). The modern societal economy relies upon communication and mobility in such a way and to such a degree that this cannot be accomplished without socialization of citizens into a dominant, high culture (which is, of course, the culture of secular humanism for American fundamentalists or the culture of satanic Westernism for Islamic fundamentalists). Gellner points out that modern high culture no longer resides, whatever its history, in a church or a faith. Its sustenance seems to need "the resources of a state coextensive with society . . ." (Gellner 1983:141). However, in spite of the perspicacity of Gellner's analysis, we could well say of him what has been said in the foregoing about Harrington and Wilson—namely, that his insight is widely shared by the church. In other words, it is in large part *because* of the (globally legitimated) state monopolization of culture that we are witnessing church-state tension within societies. Moreover, while Gellner's analysis may help us to comprehend some of the ways in which religion became privatized and of mainly personal therapeutic significance in the post–World War II period, it does not directly help in the explanation of the more recent outbreak of church-state tensions. Those can only be comprehended in terms of first, the reaction to the state monopolization of culture within societies (notably but only with respect to education)—which as I have repeatedly asserted—has a contemporary global underpinning; and second, the religious problem posed by pondering the fate of a single world, which is, nonetheless, divided not merely by differences in societal identities but also by conflicting conceptions of the meaning, purpose, and future of human life.[3] On the latter point it should be said that considerable and growing academic effort is being put into the program for a world theology (which parallels, and in some respects intersects with, one or more of the globally oriented religious movements to which I have referred).

In sum, religion is being politicized and politics (as well as economics) is being sacralized intrasocietally and globally. The prospect indicated by these new interpenetrations is, to say the least, daunting. Conflicts over ideal interests are often much more intense than those involving merely material ones; while, in any case, in this circumstance we have increasingly the fundamentalistic conflation of both sets of interests. Church-state entanglements—societal and global—are among the major institutional manifestations of contemporary global trends. They have enormous implications for the future of societies and for international relationships and foreign policy formation.

Notes

1. It must be emphasized that I am drawing an analytical distinction between religious movements seeking to *convert* (in the broadest sense of the word) the world, on the one hand, and those attempting to *organize* (as well, often, as convert) the world, on the other. Historically the former has been more evident than the latter; although clearly there have always been at least organizational implications of the conversion thrust. With rapidly increasing globalization, however, the constraint to think in terms of the organization of the world (if only in some cases in preparation for its demise) grows. The empirical cases which I mention in this essay are intended only as rather obvious examples. Detailed analysis of globally oriented movements would, undoubtedly, have to involve discussion, inter alia of the worldwide activities of the Mormons, one of the most—perhaps *the* most—successful conversionist movements of our time and their orientations to global organization, and Iranian type Shiism.

2. I have discussed various aspects of this issue in various publications, including Robertson (1977, 1981, 1982, 1983, 1984, 1985); Robertson and Lechner (1985) and, most generally, Robertson and Chirico (1985). I use the term *globalization* to refer in its primary sense to the making of the world into a single system. Its secondary sense has to do with the incorporation of local phenomena into the world system. Many recent authors use the term exclusively in my secondary sense.

3. However, Gellner's concern is not religion per se and thus my remarks here are not conceived in the form of criticism. Gellner (1983:140) maintains that the modern state "probably needs the homogenous cultural branding of its flock." This requires "a fairly monolithic educational system." It is, of course, upon the question of education that a number of church-state tensions center. Moreover, there is on the near horizon the possibility of church-state tension over teaching oriented to the global circumstance. In the United States there has been a remarkable flurry of interest in international education (or global education) in recent years, much of it directed at emphasizing the relativity of cultures and societies and the shared fate of humanity. There are already signs that fundamentalists—at least in Protestant America—regard this as an ugly extension of the secular humanism which the modern state seems to require, but which yet, in

their view, undermines national loyalty. For a diatribe against globalism, see Bowen (1984).

Bibliography

Beckford, James A. 1985. *Cult Controversies*. London and New York: Tavistock Publications.

Boli-Bennett, John. 1979. "The Ideology of Expanding State Authority in National Constitutions, 1870-1970." In John W. Meyer and Michael T. Hannan, eds., *National Development and the World System*. Chicago: Chicago University Press.

Bowen, William M., Jr. 1984. *Globalism: America's Demise*. Shreveport, La.: Huntington House.

Gellner, Ernest. 1983. *Nations and Nationalism*. Ithaca, N.Y.: Cornell University Press.

Harrington, Michael. 1983. *The Politics at God's Funeral*. New York: Holt, Rinehart and Winston.

Lifton, Robert Jay, and Falk, Richard. 1982. *Indefensible Weapons*. New York: Basic Books.

Meyer, John W. 1980. "The World Polity and the Authority of the Nation-State." In Albert Bergesen, ed., *Studies of the Modern World-System*. New York: Academic Press.

Robertson, Roland. 1985. "The Sacred and the World System." Pp. 347-58 in Phillip E. Hammond ed., *The Sacred in a Secular Age*. Berkeley, Calif.: University of California Press.

_____. 1984. "Interpreting Globality." In *World Realities and International Studies Today*. Glenside, Pa.: Pennsylvania Council on International Education.

_____. 1983. "Religion, Global Complexity and the Human Condition." In *Absolute Values and the Creation of the New World*, Vol. I. New York: International Cultural Foundations.

_____. "Societies, Individuals and Sociology: Intra-Civilizational Themes." *Theory, Culture and Society* 1, 2 (1982):6-17.

_____. "Considerations from Within the American Context on the Significance of Church-State Tension." *Sociological Analysis* 42 (Fall 1981):193-208.

_____. "Religious Movements and Modern Societies: Toward a Progressive Problemshift." *Sociological Analysis* 40 (Winter 1979):297-314.

_____. "Individualism, Societalism, Worldliness, Universalism: Thematizing Theoretical Sociology of Religion." *Sociological Analysis* 38 (Winter 1977):281-308.

Robertson, Roland, and Chirico, JoAnn. "Humanity, Globalization and Worldwide Religious Resurgence: A Theoretical Exploration." *Sociological Analysis* 46 (Fall 1985):219-42.

Robertson, Roland, and Lechner, Frank. "Modernization, Globalization and the Problem of Culture in World Systems Theory." *Theory, Culture and Society* 4, 1 (1985):103-17.

Smart, Ninian. 1981. *Beyond Ideology: Religion and the Future of Western Civilization*. New York: Harper and Row.

Wilson, Bryan. 1982. *Religion in Sociological Perspective*. New York: Oxford University Press.

4

When Will Revolutionary Movements Use Religion?

Leland W. Robinson

Activists in a revolutionary movement will use a variety of resources in attempting to reach their goals. Religion is often one of those resources. Revolutionaries may integrate religious symbols and values into their movement's ideology, make use of the leadership abilities of clergy and religious lay persons, and utilize the networks and organizational structures of religious groups for organizing the revolutionary effort.

This paper will examine six variables that influence whether or not a revolutionary movement will, in one way or another, use religion as a resource in promoting the revolution. The six variables are as follows:

1. a preponderantly religious world view among revolutionary classes
2. theology at variance with existing social order
3. clergy closely associated with revolutionary classes
4. revolutionary classes united in a single religion
5. revolutionary classes' religion different from dominant classes' religion
6. alternative organizational structures not available

I will argue that the first three variables are each necessary, and together they constitute a sufficient condition to insure that religion will, to some degree, be used as a revolutionary tool. The remaining three variables I consider neither necessary nor sufficient, but if present they increase the degree to which religion will be used in the revolution.

A Preponderantly Religious World View Among Revolutionary Classes

Individuals have what I refer to as a *preponderantly religious world view* if their view of the social and physical world about them is heavily influ-

This paper is a revised version of one presented at the annual meeting of the Association for the Sociology of Religion, San Antonio, Texas, 25 August, 1984. The author thanks James Davidson and Kenneth Westhues for their comments on that earlier draft.

enced by religion. When such individuals are involved in a revolutionary movement against a dominant class, their class consciousness will incorporate and be influenced by their religious perspectives. As Otto Maduro (1982:138) points out, "their awareness of their difference, subordination, opposition, and conflict vis-à-vis dominators, is necessarily a religious awareness." When the majority of participants in a revolutionary movement have a preponderantly religious world view, they will find it natural to incorporate their religious perspectives in the movement's ideology, and to channel their struggle against the dominant classes through their religious organizations.

A preponderantly religious world view is extremely widespread in subordinated classes throughout the Third World. Penny Lernoux (1982:376) writes concerning Latin America:

> Unlike the industrialized world, where religion has succumbed to materialism and a flexible social structure, Latin America is still profoundly influenced by the Church. Farming traditions, health, education, social mores, politics are all imbued with religious folklore. This popular religiosity is a genuine form of cultural expression and creativity—indeed, the only one for most Latin Americans.

A similar observation regarding the influence of religion could be made for much of the rest of the Third World, especially for South Asia and the Near East. Regarding Iran (admittedly an extreme case), Kai Bird (1979:427) has pointed out that "the masses of the Iranian people simply cannot be moved to any significant political action without the language of religion."

If individuals have a preponderantly secular world view, they will make use of secular rather than religious organizations and symbol systems in any revolutionary movement they might generate. A preponderantly secular world view is, of course, commonly found among the working class in the highly industrialized nations of Europe and North America. However, even here there are exceptions such as Ireland (Beach 1977; Carey 1983) and Poland (Kennedy and Simon 1983; Piwowarski 1976), and most industrial nations contain significant subcultures with largely religious outlooks.

Theology at Variance with Existing Social Order

Some religions simply are not appropriate tools for revolutionaries. If a religion is so used with the culture that religious action consists merely of conforming to social norms, revolutionaries will find it of little use. Primitive religions are often of this nature. On the other hand, if a religion stresses the total disjunction between itself and society, it likewise will not be a useful revolutionary tool. This was the case, for example, with early Buddhism (Bellah 1965:193).

For a religion to be useful for revolutionary purposes, it must have the potential to make people dissatisfied with the status quo. To do this, the religion must maintain what Robert Bellah (1965:194) calls "a creative tension between religious ideals and the world." Bellah describes this state as one in which "transcendent ideals, in tension with empirical reality, have a central place in the religious symbol system, while empirical reality itself is taken very seriously as at least potentially meaningful, valuable, and a valid sphere for religious action."

Though these three tendencies—fusion, disjunction, and creative tension—seem mutually exclusive, all three are found in some combination in most religions. Hinduism, for example, is a religion in which the tendencies toward fusion and disjunction have generally been stronger than the tendency toward creative tension. As a result, Hinduism has generally played a very conservative role in history. Nevertheless, even Hinduism has, at various times, displayed its potential for creative tension. The Hindu concept of a just society in which *dharma* (universal order) is embodied was not easily reconciled with British colonial rule (Bellah 1965:182). Thus, there was a potential for tension between the values of Hinduism and British colonialism, and the Hindu leadership of the Indian independence movement used those Hindu values to help mobilize the population. The movement was, from its very beginning, intimately associated with the Hindu Renaissance—a strong, assertive reaffirmation of ancient Hindu traditions and beliefs, combined with a condemnation of Western civilization. Although Mohandas Gandhi was not himself a Hindu fanatic, he was a Hindu, and he made use of and furthered the Hindu Renaissance. Gandhi inspired millions of peasants and urban poor with a vision of a new society characterized by the Hindu-based concept of *Sarvodaya* ("the welfare of all"). The concept of *Sarvodaya* suggested a society of self-sufficient peasant communes in which people would live together in cooperative harmony. Gandhi's use of this Hindu-based ideal was critical in turning the independence movement into a mass liberation struggle (Robinson 1982:6-8; Ulyanovsky 1974:223-25).

As this example shows, the relative influence of the three tendencies may vary significantly over time within any one religion. An important contemporary example of this is the case of Latin American Catholicism. Throughout most of its history it has played a very conservative role. However, in the past twenty years the Latin American Catholic Church has adopted a "preferential option for the poor," with the result that the Church's tendency for creative tension is now quite strong. The reasons for this change in policy have been explored in depth by a number of scholars (e.g., Adriance 1984; de Kadt 1971; Levine 1980; Westhues 1973). There is no need to examine these reasons here, but we should note that there were many factors leading to this change, and that they emerged both from the grass roots and from the very top of the Catholic Church's hierarchy. After the Second Conference of Latin American Bishops held in Medellín, Colombia, in 1968, the preferential option for the poor became a source of legitimation for the most progressive theologians and pastoral agents in Latin America. Ultimately, some of these people pushed the option for the poor far beyond the liberal reformist intentions of the bishops, and certainly beyond the wishes of the current Pope. As a result, liberation theology and the Basic Ecclesial Communities (CEBs) have both become extremely useful tools for Latin American revolutionaries.

The Protestant denominations in Latin America continue to play a more conservative role. Some scholars have argued that this is because Protestant theology has been so dominated by individualism that it hinders one from understanding social problems of a structural nature. Nevertheless, partly in response to competition from the reviving Catholic Church, and partly in response to the great suffering of the poor, some Protestant groups in Latin America are coming to accept the viewpoint of liberation theology (Montgomery 1980). Thus, Protestantism may also become, in the future, a potential tool for revolution in Latin America.

A religion may become a more useful tool for revolution in one country partly in response to events in another country. For example, the dynamic role of Shiah Islam in the Iranian revolution has led to a greatly increased role for Shiah Islam as a revolutionary tool in other countries, such as in Lebanon.

Sometimes there is a substantial degree of creative tension between a religion and the larger society of which it is a part. Then, as Kenneth Westhues (1976:311) points out, "the more at variance with a given social order is the theological tradition of a religious body, the more likely is it to assume an oppositional stance." The more a religious body assumes an oppositional stance, the more useful it will become to revolutionaries. This is especially the case when the religious body is critical of the economic and political institutions of the larger society and their effects on the distribution of wealth and power. This is why liberation theology is such a useful revolutionary tool in Latin America. It focuses on economic and political oppression and suggests ways of solving these problems.

Clergy Closely Associated with Revolutionary Classes

If the general membership of a religious organization consists primarily of members of the oppressed classes, and if these members possess a degree of revolutionary class consciousness, then the likelihood of prorevolutionary stance by the religious organization, and thus the usefulness of the organization to revolutionaries, is increased if there is a close association between the general membership and the clergy. Those clergy who are in close contact with the membership can communicate their concerns to the church hierarchy, and can promote organizational and theological changes within the organization to make it more supportive of the revolutionary effort. Furthermore, these clergy may themselves play important roles in grassroots organizing for the revolution. In such circumstances, the revolutionary movement is likely to use the religion's ideology and organizational structure in its revolutionary efforts.

In Latin America, it has been those Catholic leaders with the most day-to-day contact with the poor, such as parish priests and Catholic schoolteachers, who have been in the forefront in developing the growing Popular sector of the Church. Their contributions have been crucial in the development of liberation theology, and they are the ones who are helping to organize Basic Ecclesial Communities (Lernoux 1982:389-408). These CEBs, in turn, have become extremely important not only because they have been directly used by revolutionaries as bases for organizing the revolution, but also, as Madeleine Adriance (1984:22) explains, because the "CEBs would be the thread that would knit the hierarchy to the grassroots Church, and would hamper the continuation of previous alliances with the dominant classes. In providing a vehicle through which pastoral agents would be encouraged to work with the subordinated classes, the bishops were sealing the preferential option for the poor."

In Paraguay, where virtually the entire Church hierarchy is in opposition to the Stroessner regime, most of the key Church leaders are of local origin. The bishop most instrumental in bringing the Church to an oppositional stance was born in the rural interior, and at present most of the Paraguayan bishops are attached to rural, largely peasant, congregations (Westhues 1976:310).

In Iran, clergymen live simple lives among the people and are supported by their voluntary contributions. Claude van Engeland, a Belgian reporter, wrote during the revolution that "the Iranian clergy lives in a veritable state of symbiosis with the Muslim masses who are demanding the departure of the Shah" (quoted in Sweezy and Magdoff 1979:13-14). In such circumstances, revolutionaries will readily make use of religion.

If, on the other hand, the clergy has little daily association with the masses of the oppressed, the church will be neither available to the oppressed nor responsive to their needs. The clergy of the Cuban Catholic Church, before and during the Cuban revolution of 1956-1959, represents a good example of this. A 1957 survey of 4,000 agricultural workers throughout Cuba found that 53.5 percent claimed never to have even seen a parish priest, and only 7.8 percent admitted having any dealings with one (Crahan 1980:238). Instead of relating to the masses, the clergy allied itself with the Batista regime, and the Church came to be seen by the masses as a major bulwark of the status quo. With the Church being so unresponsive and unavailable, Castro's revolutionary movement made little, if any, use of religion in promoting its cause (Dewart 1963).

Revolutionary Classes United in a Single Religion

If the vast majority of the members of oppressed classes are united by a single religion, it will be much easier for them to use that religion as a tool in their struggle for liberation. For example, during the Algerian liberation struggle against French rule, the fact that almost all Algerians were Muslims made it easier for the leaders of the movement to mobilize the population by appealing to their Muslim identity and values (Vatikiotis 1979).

By contrast, the Vietnamese, in their struggle against the French and Americans, were internally divided into various religions—principally Buddhism, Taoism, Confucianism, and Catholicism. This made it much harder for them to use religion for mobilizing the population, and instead greater use had to be made of secular values. Nevertheless, even the Vietnamese liberation movement utilized religion to a degree. Religious leaders, particularly Buddhists, played a significant role in delegitimizing various U.S.-backed regimes, and the National Liberation Front made a special effort to cooperate with the Cao Dai and Hoa Hao Buddhist sects (Fitzgerald 1973:277-78). Furthermore, the secular values incorporated in the liberation struggle took on a quasi-religious character which ultimately allowed the different religious groups to form alliances (Maduro 1982:142).

Instances such as Vietnam demonstrate that religion can still play a role as a revolutionary tool even if the revolutionary masses are divided into different religions as long as the three variables discussed above are present. In such cases it will be necessary for the oppressed classes to develop a meaningful symbol that can unite, to a degree, the followers of the different religions in a common struggle. This, however, is difficult to achieve. Thus, when the revolutionary classes are religiously divided, religion will generally not play as important a role in the struggle.

Revolutionary Classes' Religion Different
From Dominant Classes' Religion

Religion may be more easily used as a tool by a revolutionary movement if the oppressed classes are not only largely united in a single religion, but if that religion is different from the dominant groups' religion. When this is the case, the involvement of the religion in a revolutionary struggle will typically stimulate in the religion a renewed vitality. This, then, makes the religion an even more effective tool for generating revolutionary effort. The Indian independence movement is an example, for it was intimately associated with the Hindu Renaissance (Wallbank 1965:99).

On the other hand, if the dominated and the dominators share a common religion, it will be more difficult to use religion as a revolutionary tool. In these cases, the dominated will be better able to so use their religion if they modify it and thus gain a certain religious autonomy vis-á-vis the dominating classes (Maduro 1982:140). As Otto Maduro (1984:129) has put it, the dominated must "reappropriate religious symbols and the means of symbolic production" so that their religion may serve their own interests rather than the interests of the dominators. An example of this is the development of the Popular sector of the Catholic Church in Latin America, with its liberation theology.

Alternative Organizational Structures Not Available

The degree to which subordinated classes channel their liberation struggle through religious organizations is increased if other organizations through which the revolutionary effort might be directed are eliminated by the police, military, and paramilitary forces of the dominant classes. This situation is quite common, especially in Latin American countries such as El Salvador, Guatemala, and Chile. Indeed, it tends to develop wherever dominant classes are significantly threatened.

Oppressive governments generally find it easier and safer to completely eliminate independent labor unions and other voluntary associations than to completely eliminate all local churches. Thus, when all other associations available to the revolutionary movement are suppressed, the movement will probably make even greater use of local church organizations. For example, Peter Marchetti (1982:45) writes that in Nicaragua, partly because the Somoza regime eliminated most alternatives, "the parish structure served as the organizational base—particularly for the youth who used the parish and the churches as their network for resistance against the Somozan guard. In a sense, the parish replaced Lenin's idea of a cell." The same can be said of the role of Basic Ecclesial Communities in the current revolutionary struggle in El Salvador (Krauss 1982:8).

Discussion: Religion and Revolution

Religion can be a powerful revolutionary tool, but it can also be a dangerous one. Where a revolutionary movement is making use of this tool, one will typically find that those forces resisting the revolution will also be making use of religion. When religiously motivated people are fighting religiously motivated people, the outcome is usually even more bloodshed than would otherwise be the case.

Religion can also be a revolutionary tool that is difficult to control. Gandhi used Hinduism as a revolutionary tool but was eventually killed by a Hindu fanatic, and the increased religious fervor set in motion by the Indian independence movement led ultimately to incredible bloodshed when independence was finally achieved.

One can find instances in which religion comes to totally dominate the revolutionary movement with the result that those in the movement with a more secular agenda end up being suppressed. A recent example of this is the suppression of the Iranian Communist Party (the Tudeh Party) after the Iranian Revolution had succeeded in overthrowing the Shah.

On the other hand, secular forces within a movement may also betray the religiously based goals of movement participants. As was pointed out earlier in this paper, Gandhi's Hindu-based concept of a new society characterized by *Sarvodaya* was extremely important in motivating mass participation in the independence movement. Independence, however, did not bring a society characterized by *Sarvodaya*, but rather a society dominated by the Indian national bourgeoisie. As Ulyanovsky (1974:225) points out, the Indian bourgeoisie never believed in *Sarvodaya*, but "made use of the ideology of Gandhism . . . both for nationwide and, primarily, its own class purposes." Once independence was achieved and the Indian bourgeoisie was firmly in control, the goal of *Sarvodaya* was publically rejected in favor of government-aided industrialization.

The Nicaraguan revolution seems to be one in which the mutually respectful relationship between the secular and religious forces within the movement has continued after the initial success of the movement, though not without tension and internal Church conflicts (Dodson and O'Shaughnessy 1984). At the time of this writing, in the current Sandinista government, the foreign minister, the minister of education, the minister of culture, and the ambassador to the Organization of American States are all priests, as is the chief architect of the Sandinista economic policy and the key adviser on agricultural programs (Woodward, Lantigua, and Nagorski 1984). However, this continued cooperation between the secular and religious forces, after the success of the revolutionary movement in overthrowing the previous elite, seems to be the exception rather than the rule. It remains to be seen how long this cooperative relationship will continue.

Some have argued that it is best that religion not be infused into movements for secular change. For example, one well-known and respected scholar in the field of the sociology of religion recently wrote, in a private letter to the author of this paper: "For my part, I've had enough. I've come to believe that God is best left out of those areas for which God has delegated responsibility to us mortal men and women. Religious language seems to me to be a powerful deterrent to negotiation, compromise, and openness of debate."

Others, however, have argued that religion must be used as a revolutionary tool not only because, in many societies, it is essential for motivating mass participation, but also because only a religious commitment can motivate people to work together in creating a new, more humane society once the dominant elite has been overthrown. Jürgen Moltmann (1969:40-41) has argued:

> The all-embracing vision of God must be linked with the economic liberation of man from hunger, with the political freeing of man from oppression by other men, and with the human emancipation of man from racial humiliation. It will thereby give these initiatives a power for prevailing over the world—a power which is necessary in order to go forward persistently against resistances and in face of disappointments.

Arthur McGovern (1980:327), also writing from a Christian perspective, has claimed:

> No social order will ever "produce" new persons. It can only remove obstacles and create a better environment in which human freedom and dignity can prosper. Christians thus must work not simply for social change, but for a social change that minimizes violence and hostility, that insists on respect for the dignity and freedom of every individual, and that accepts human limitations.

It would be nice to think that religion always does function in this way within a revolutionary context. However, cases such as the recent Iranian revolution leave one with doubts.

Given the nature of the major religions in the world today, and given the prevalence of a preponderantly religious world view among the oppressed classes in Third World countries, it would seem almost inevitable that, for better or for worse, religion will often be used as a revolutionary tool. Roger Garaudy (1966:32) has written: "Hundreds of millions of men find in religious beliefs the meaning of life and death, and the very meaning of the history of our race. . . . Thus it is an incontestable fact of our age that the future of man cannot be constructed either against religious believers or without them." Virginia Fabella (quoted in Palm and Bounds 1984:47) expressed a similar point of view when she wrote that we "cannot simply brush aside the world views, religious experience, and cultural aspirations which have given to countless millions the meaning, unity, wisdom, and strength of life as well as inspiration for their struggles for full humanity."

Suggestions for Further Research

It is far easier to find examples in which revolutionary movements against foreign or domestic elites have made use of religion than it is to find examples in which such a movement has taken an entirely secular form. Thus, if we are to broaden our understanding of revolutionary movements, it is important that we examine when and how they are likely to make use of this tool.

Further research might focus on finding examples to refute my contention that the first three variables are each necessary and together sufficient to insure that religion will be used as a tool in a revolutionary struggle. An adequate assessment will almost certainly require at least a rudimentary effort at quantification. For example, how preponderant must a religious world view be among the revolutionary masses? To what degree must a theological tradition be at variance with the existing social order? How closely associated must the clergy be with the revolutionary classes? How do you measure and quantify these variables?

As for the remaining three variables, it would be helpful to at least rank order their importance. It seems probable that future research will uncover other important variables to add to the list.

Bibliography

Adriance, Madeleine. "The Option for the Poor in Brazilian Catholicism." Paper presented at the annual meeting of the Association for the Sociology of Religion, 1984, San Antonio, Texas.

Beach, Stephen W. "Religion and Political Change in Northern Ireland." *Sociological Analysis* 1 (1977): 37-48.

Bellah, Robert N. 1965. *Religion and Progress in Modern Asia*. New York: Free Press.

Bird, Kai. "The Workers' Committees Are Pumping Iran." *The Nation* 15 (1979):426-28.

Carey, Michael J. 1983. "Catholicism and Irish National Identity." In Peter H. Merkl and Ninian Smart, eds., *Religion and Politics in the Modern World*. New York: New York University Press.

Crahan, Margaret. 1980. "Salvation Through Christ or Marx: Religion in Revolutionary Cuba." In Daniel H. Levine, ed., *Churches and Politics in Latin America*. Beverly Hills: Sage.

Dewart, Leslie. 1963. *Christianity and Revolution: The Lessons of Cuba*. New York: Herder and Herder.

Dodson, Michael, and O'Shaughnessy, Laura Nuzzi. "The Churches in the Nicaraguan Revolution." Paper presented at the annual meeting of the International Studies Association, 1984, Atlanta, Georgia.

Fitzgerald, Frances. 1973. *Fire in the Lake*. New York: Vintage.

Garaudy, Roger. 1966. *From Anathema to Dialogue: A Marxist Challenge to the Christian Churches*. New York: Herder and Herder.

Kennedy, Michael D. and Simon, Maurice D. 1983. "Church and Nation in Socialist Poland." In Peter H. Merkl and Ninian Smart, eds., *Religion and Politics in the Modern World*. New York: New York University Press.

Krauss, Clifford. "Religious Roots of Rebellion in El Salvador." *The Nation* 1 (1982):7-10.

Lernoux, Penny. 1982. *Cry of the People*. New York: Penguin.

Levine, Daniel H., ed. 1980. *Church and Politics in Latin America*. Beverly Hills: Sage.

Maduro, Otto. 1982. *Religion and Social Conflict*. Maryknoll: Orbis.

_____. "Is Religion Revolutionary?" *The New England Sociologist* 1 (1984):127-31.

Marchetti, Peter. "Church and Revolution in Nicaragua." *Monthly Review* 3 (1982):43-55.

McGovern, Arthur F. 1980. *Marxism: An American Christian Perspective*. Maryknoll: Orbis.

Moltmann, Jürgen. 1969. *Religion, Revolution, and the Future*. New York: Charles Scribner's Sons.

Montgomery, T. S. 1980. "Latin American Evangelicals: Oaxtepec and Beyond." In Daniel H. Levine, ed., *Churches and Politics in Latin America*. Beverly Hills: Sage.

Palm, James E. and Bounds, Elizabeth M. "Preparing the Soil: Notes on Liberating Theologies in Asia." *Monthly Review* 3 (1984):41-55.

Piwowarski, Wladyslaw, "Industrialization and Popular Religiosity in Poland." *Sociological Analysis* 4 (1976):315-20.

Robinson, Leland W. "Religion and Anti-Imperialist Movements." Paper presented at the Mid-West Marxist Scholars Conference, 1982, Bloomington, Indiana.

Sweezy, Paul M. and Magdoff, Harry. "Iran: The New Crisis of American Hegemony." *Monthly Review* 9 (1979):1-24.

Ulyanovsky, R. 1974. *Socialism and the Newly Independent Nations*. Moscow: Progress Publishers.

Vatikiotis, P. J. "What is an 'Islamic Revival'?" *New Society* 854 (1979):354-56.

Wallbank, T. Walter. 1965. *A Short History of India and Pakistan*. New York: Mentor.

Westhues, Kenneth. "The Established Church as an Agent of Change." *Sociological Analysis* 2 (1973):106-23.

_____. "The Church in Opposition." *Sociological Analysis* 4 (1976):299-314.

Woodward, Kenneth L.; Lantigua, John; and Nagorski, Andrew. "Nicaragua's Rebel Jesuits." *Newsweek* (September 4, 1984):74.

Part II

CHURCH-STATE TENSION IN THE UNITED STATES

5

Church-State Tension in the United States

Thomas Robbins

Church-state conflicts in the United States transpire within the context of a venerated constitutional tradition which prohibits Congress from making any law "respecting an establishment of religion, or prohibiting the free exercise thereof." Although the First Amendment speaks directly only to Congress, the Supreme Court has long since held that the bill of rights is *incorporated* into the due process clause of the Fourteenth Amendment, and is thereby binding on the actions of the states. In the context of this tradition and the increasing prominence of the Free Exercise clause in constitutional law in the last several decades, a very rough distinction can be made between two kinds of issues or conflicts involving the relationship between church and state in the United States today.

Church Autonomy Conflicts

Church autonomy conflicts are conflicts over what Leo Pfeffer terms religious exemptions. A potential church autonomy conflict is created when a branch of federal, state or local government proposes to impose some regulatory constraint on a religious group, a group member or an institution (such as a school or a business) connected in some manner to a religious group or organization. An actual church autonomy conflict arises when a claim is made by religionists opposing the regulatory measure that the measure burdens the "free exercise of religion."

A typical church autonomy issue was resolved when the Supreme Court decided in 1985 that the minimum wage and overtime provisions of the Fair Labor Standards Act were applicable to persons employed in church-owned enterprises. The case had been brought by the Alamo Foundation, a widely stigmatized cult. Most cases involving cults are church autonomy cases, an outstanding example being the prosecution of Sun Myung Moon for tax fraud, which is discussed in chapter 11. The same can be said regarding the bulk of the native American cases discussed in chapter 10. An example of a church autonomy case involving a more conventional organization is afforded by the ruling of a federal circuit court in 1981 that seminary personnel who were not directly involved in teaching or teaching supervision could not be considered ministers, and therefore, data concerning them must be filed by the seminary with the Equal Employment Opportunity Commission. The Supreme Court refused to hear the appeal of the Southwestern Baptist Seminary, which contended that a determination by the state as to which employees are performing "religious" roles burdens the free exercise of religion. In his essay, Dean Kelley indicates that he views *U.S.* v. *Bob Jones University and Goldsboro Christian Schools*, decided by the Supreme Court in 1983, as a church autonomy or "religious liberty" case, although the court majority did not seem to agree.

Church autonomy cases generally highlight the Free Exercise clause of the First Amendment, although the claim is sometimes introduced that in imposing a regulatory constraint on a certain church or class of churches, the state is discriminating against a church or churches such that other churches which are not affected by the proposed regulatory measure are being implicitly "established," i.e., the religious neutrality of the state is being undercut. When such a claim is raised, a case or issue arguably ceases to be purely a church autonomy conflict.

State Neutrality Conflicts

State neutrality cases involve either a proposed form of assistance which the state will provide to a religious group (i.e., aid to parochial schools) or the alleged expression of religious faith by a public institution. The controversy over prayer in the schools is an outstanding example of the latter subtype, although recent and pending Supreme Court cases involving religious displays (a Christmas creche) in a public place are also relevant here. Chapter 7 discusses these kinds of issues. Hammond shows that while opponents of prayer in the school perceive a threat to state neutrality in public religious expression, evangelicals and some other religionists retort that through measures such as banning school prayers, the Supreme Court has enshrined the religion of secular humanism. A similar issue arises in the debates over "creationism" vs. evolution in the teaching of biology in public schools. The Supreme Court has, at this writing, agreed to rule on the constitutionality of a Louisiana law that mandates the teaching of "creation science" alongside evolution in the state's public schools.

State neutrality disputes highlight the Establishment clause of the First Amendment, which is generally viewed as prohibiting state sponsorship of religion or public favoritism among competing religions. Sometimes, however, it is argued by religionists that the absence of a certain kind of public assistance to religious organizations will be crippling such that the free exercise of religion is jeopardized.

In the last two decades a certain formalism has developed whereby the outcomes of various Supreme Court cases have been extrapolated or synthesized in such a way as to produce tests which can be utilized to evaluate new state neutrality and church autonomy cases. Phillip Hammond describes in chapter 7 what has been called the "purpose-effect-entanglement test" to determine if a given statute violates the Establishment clause by straying into nonneutrality. Thus, in 1985 an Arkansas statute mandating a minute of silent prayer was struck down as lacking any semblance of a secular purpose, although the court hinted that similar laws might pass muster if they were worded differently. On the other hand, in church autonomy questions, "when a law or other act of government is challenged as a violation of the Free Exercise Clause, the burden, the Court says, is on the government to establish that it has a compelling interest which justifies abridgement of the citizen's right to the free exercise of religion" (Pfeffer 1979:2). In applying the "compelling interest" criteria, the courts also often inquire as to whether the religious beliefs pertaining to a religious practice which is deemed potentially regulable are sincere, whether the practice is central to the religion, whether a "substantial infringement" on the religious practice would ensue, and whether the regulatory initiative in question would constitute the "least restrictive means" of pursuing the state's compelling interest (Shepherd 1985:13). But neither the "purpose-effect-entanglement" test bearing on state neutrality issues or the "compelling interest" test applicable to church autonomy-religious liberty issues are really set in concrete for all time.

It is arguable that ultimately the distinction between church autonomy and state neutrality conflicts is spurious. Governmental regulations burdening churches are often attacked not only on the grounds that they infringe on church autonomy and thus negate free exercise, but also on the grounds that they discriminate against certain religions and thereby sacrifice the state's religious neutrality and contravene the Establishment clause. This was the barely successful claim of the Unification Church in the important 5–4 (1982) Supreme Court decision in *Larsen v. Valente*, a case which is briefly discussed in both chapters 6 and 11. In this connection it is also up for grabs as to whether tax exemption for churches entails positive state assistance to churches, or merely a negative regulatory exemption (In chapter 9, Dean Kelley expresses his opposition to the "subsidy" theory for churches and discusses the assumptions about it that were made by high court justices in the *U.S.* v. *Bob Jones University* case). Leo Pfeffer has written that religious freedom and separation of church and state (i.e., state neutrality) really constitute a unitary principle. "True understanding of the First Amendment would seem to impel the conclusion that the Establishment and Free Exercise Clause are two sides of the same coin" (Pfeffer 1979:7). Nevertheless, in some cases there appears to be a conflict of free exercise and separationist norms, e.g., would the government be unconstitutionally favoring a religion if it accommodated to the particularistic "free exercise" needs (e.g., Thursdays off in honor of Thor) of employees from a small religious minority?

There is validity to the argument that the distinction between church autonomy and state neutrality issues is ultimately not watertight. This distinction may be useful in allowing us to develop a typology of contemporary American orientations to church-state issues which does more justice to the complexity of the issues than a simple dichotomy or continuum of support versus antipathy to the separation of church and state.

Typology of American Church-State Orientations

There is a *separationist* agenda which "consists of the vigorous defense of the rulings made by the Supreme Court in the Establishment and Free Exercise clauses" (Pfeffer 1979:8). In effect "separationists" tend to be very hesitant about allowing the state to support a religion (e.g., by aiding parochial schools) and they also generally oppose enhanced state regulation of religious practices (e.g., allowing cults a lesser degree of protection than is accorded to recognized churches). The separationist view is that the state should neither positively support nor negatively constrain religious practices as a general rule. Separationists "are not happy about the *Walz* case [in which the Supreme Court permitted the exemption of churches from taxation—1970] although realistically they recognize that the chances of a determination in the foreseeable future against the constitutionality of tax exemption of church-owned property used for religious purposes or of tax deductions to churches are quite slim" (Pfeffer 1979:9).

The opposite of the separationist view is an orientation which is favorable to both enhanced regulatory constraints imposed by the state on religious practices and enhanced state support for religion. We will term such an orientation *statist* although it could be endorsed either by a caesaropapist or (conditionally) by a theocrat. For certain reasons it is arguable that this is the direction in which church-state court decisions and governmental policymaking will proceed. The options and prerogatives of the state are to be maximized. It will shape religion.

A strong "secularist" orientation approves enhanced state regulation of churches but would oppose greater state support for any religion or governmental religious expression. The opposite of the secularist orientation is a consistently proreligion or *supportive* orientation which demands greater state support for religion but rejects any collateral increase in governmental regulatory prerogatives. This is what Demerath and Williams refer to as a "take the money and run" attitude which accepts state support and belittles the risk of entanglement-establishment, and simultaneously guards church autonomy jealously and denies the state any augmented accountability to accompany the enhanced largesse for churches. This orientation characterizes the views of some politically conservative evangelicals as well as some social thinkers who value churches as *mediating structures* which intervene between potentially atomized individuals and the bureaucratic state (or other impersonal megastructures). To revitalize democratic pluralism and keep mass society at bay the state is urged to "encourage mediating structures as representing the best marriage of communal initiatives and public purpose" (Kerrine and Neuhaus 1979: 17-18). To further this goal we must be "more relaxed about 'no establishment' than is the present approach of the courts and more adamant about 'free exercise'" (Kerrine and Neuhaus 1979:14).

There is a partial contradiction here, in that the First Amendment must be simultaneously strengthened, to safeguard church autonomy and free exercise, and weakened, to defuse repressive nitpicking over the nuances of state neutrality and separation. Granted there is a proreligion tradition in constitutional scholarship which has favored a narrow interpretation of *establishment* and a broad interpretation of *free exercise* (Tribe 1978). Nevertheless, to judge from some discussions on televangelical talk shows, there may be an inadequate awareness of the implications of greater flexibility in interpretation of the First Amendment with regard to protecting church autonomy, granted its undoubted utility for "re-christianizing" America. Of course, the *secularist* problem is also one of strengthening the First Amendment to guard against the slightest whiff of state support of religion, while concomitantly weakening the First Amendment to give the secular state more latitude to clamp down on *religious abuses*.

Despite its practical contradictions, the supportive orientation is presently the orientation which is gaining strength and producing strident and provocative formulations. The sacralization of religious neutrality, it is argued, is in danger of producing a secularist substitute religion. Religious freedom has been perversely converted into freedom *from* religion. The republic is threatened by "the pervasive influence of ideas about a secular society and a secular state, ideas that have insinuated themselves into our religious thinking and that have been institutionalized in our politics" (Neuhaus 1984:32). Nonevangelical formulations of this perspective tend to be informed by functionalist sociology and its concern with legitimacy, meaning and alienation. "The American experience is not self-legitimat-

TABLE 1
American Orientations
to Church and State

ORIENTATION	GOVERNMENT SUPPORTS RELIGION	GOVERNMENT CONSTRAINS RELIGION
SEPARATIONIST	NO	NO
STATIST	YES	YES
SECULARIST	NO	YES
SUPPORTIVE	YES	NO

ing; it requires what it has until recently possessed, some sense of transcendent meaning" (Neuhaus 1984:32). The "exclusion of religiously grounded values and beliefs" from governmental policymaking and prestige media commentary "is at the heart of the outrage and alienation of millions of Americans" (Neuhaus 1984:29). The spectre of a prototolitarian state-promulgated civil religion is evoked as a possible consequence of further secularization, for "the naked public square cannot remain truly naked. The need for an overarching meaning, for moral legitimation, will not go undenied" (Neuhaus 1984:30).

The drive for clothing the naked public square with compelling spiritual garments may produce unintended consequences. It is arguable that court decisions and governmental policymaking are likely in the near future to move slowly in the statist direction. The increasingly conservative judiciary will probably tend to be more flexible in the future in their approach to the First Amendment. This is likely for a number of reasons, some of which may have little direct connection with church-state issues (e.g., crime control, tightening national security). A conservative emphasis on *"strict constructionism"* (Bork 1985) may discourage sweeping affirmations of principles deduced from the Bill of Rights as a basis for deciding both church-autonomy and state-neutrality cases. It may thus become easier for religionists to win state-neutrality cases but harder for churches to defend their legal autonomy and regulatory exemptions. The wall of separation between church and state may crumble a bit. The demand to respiritualize the *naked public square* and cease fetishizing state neutrality will reinforce this trend, but the consequences in terms of church autonomy and the defense of free exercise may be unanticipated. Increasing state control over and support of churches may also be consistent with a conservative drive to revitalize patriotic civil religion. The state will sponsor religion—but also control it more.

An assumption underlying our analyses is that legal perspectives and constitutional frameworks do influence policy outcomes, i.e., there are limits to cynical "legal realism." Eileen Barker's paper on discrimination against cults in Britain demonstrates that neither the American constitutional guarantee of religious liberty nor the contrasting British establishmentarian heritage are entirely meaningless or devoid of practical impact, although the Anglo-American differential with respect to the actual treatment of exotic fringe sects is not as great as the difference in legal traditions might suggest. In this connection, several years ago an analysis by James Beckford suggested that on the European continent quasimedical rhetoric about "mind-control" was less prominent in anti-cult campaigns compared to the United States, presumably because there is less necessity to evade civil libertarian norms by raising medical and mental health issues. Thus in France deviant groups could be directly attacked as antisocial and subversive of dominant cultural values (Beckford 1981).

Growing American Church-State Tension

Church state tension is presently growing in the United States. Several factors can be identified as contributing to this growth. The expansion of the apparatus and functions of the state is crucial in more than one way. Demerath and Williams note that the expansion of the state has made government a vital resource and locus of support for myriad social services such that churches and other private sector institutions become increasingly motivated to claim a share of these resources. This tendency contributes to the growth of state neutrality conflicts.

In his essay on marginal movements, Thomas Robbins argues that the proliferation of church autonomy disputes in the past decade is partly related to the interaction of two fundamental trends. The expansion of the authority and apparatus of the state and its regulatory mandate to hold organizations and professionals accountable for harmful and deceptive actions appears to clash directly with the expansion and diversification of the activities of religious organizations in the past decades. The latter trend embraces more than the rise of religiotherapeutic movements or totalistic cults and involves phenomena such as the growth of Christian Schools and current religious politicization, and arguably partly reverses the much touted secularization and privatization trends in religion in the twentieth century. The clash of governmental expansion and religious diversification in a context of constitutional protection for religious practices produces a plethora of disputes which test the boundary of church autonomy and free exercise.

While developing a global perspective on church-state conflict, Robertson (1981) has argued that church-state tension in both the United States and in the world is accentuated by the enhanced omnicompetence of the state. The state is increasingly expected to make decisions in arguably religious areas such as the actual definitions of life and death—the status of abortion and the cessation of life in terminal illness—and quality of life issues, including the care of seriously deformed and disabled infants. The state becomes a quasi-religious agency, and in pursuit of its religious functions it produces *sociodicies* or normative conceptions of life-in-society which "are at least potential rivals of the theodicies of religious groups. Indeed it is the autonomous production of these [by the state] which is the target of those who militantly decry the salience of 'secular humanism'" (Robertson 1981:201).

Finally, as Demerath and Williams note, the increasing role of the courts in American society as policymakers and conflict mediators encourages church-state conflicts. This dynamic may be particularly salient with respect to the increasing number of church autonomy conflicts as lawyers develop new modes of innovative litigation such as the 1985 clergy malpractice suit involving the alleged incompetent pastoral counseling of a suicidal youth which was dismissed in a California court.

As Robbins notes in chapter 11, in the context of the increasing functional diversification of religious organizations and the constitutional protection of church autonomy, diverse entrepreneurs and activists are motivated to declare their operations to be religious as a means of escaping governmental interference. To be "religious" in America is thus to be empowered. Chapter 2 has already highlighted the salience of the need to integrate a conception of power into the theoretical framework of the social scientific study of religion.

Our section on church-state tensions in the United States begins with a general historical overview by Demerath and Williams, who analyze how diverse factors such as the periodic extensions of American religious pluralism and the changing role of American courts have shaped and accentuated church-state conflict. Phillip Hammond follows with an overview of the state neutrality question and a discussion of changing conceptions of neutrality throughout American history and current popular misconceptions of the tendencies evident in court decisions. Leo Pfeffer discusses the status of church autonomy—so-called religious exemptions—in a number of key areas such as taxation, military service and standards for church schools; and Dean Kelley discusses the important *Bob Jones University* and *Goldboro Christian Schools* 1983 Supreme Court decisions involving the question of tax exemptions for schools practicing racial segregation or discrimination. Finally, Robert Michaelson and I discuss recent church autonomy disputes involving two embattled groups: native Americans and marginal religions or *cults*.

Bibliography

Beckford, James. "Cults, Controversy and Control." *Sociological* Analysis 42 (Fall 1981):249-64.

Bork, William. "Morality and the Judge." *Harpers* 270 (May 1985):28-29, reprinted speech.

Kerrine, Theodore and Neuhaus, Richard. "Mediating Structures: A Paradigm for Democratic Pluralism." *The Annals* 446 (November 1979):10-18.

Neuhaus, Richard. "The Naked Public Square." *Christianity Today* 28 (5 October 1984):26-32.

Pfeffer, Leo. "The Current State of the Law in the United States and the Separationist Agenda." *The Annals* 446 (November 1979): 1-9.

Robertson, Roland. "Considerations From Within the American Context on the Significance of Church-State Tension." *Sociological Analysis* 446 (November 1981):193-208.

Shepherd, William. 1985. *To Secure the Blessings of Liberty: American Constitutional Law and the New Religious Movements.* New York and Chico, California: Crossroads Publishing Co. and Scholars Press.

Tribe, Laurence. 1978. *American Constitutional Law.* Mineola, New York: Foundation Press.

6

A Mythical Past and Uncertain Future

N.J. Demerath III & Rhys H. Williams

One of social science's most important but thankless tasks is the continuing assessment of social mythology, particularly that potentially yawning gap between cultural conceptions of what ought to be and structural determinations of what is. The task is especially familiar to students of religion, many of whom sit squarely on the shifting boundaries between beliefs and reality. This paper concerns a belief that does not directly involve the supernatural, the transcendent, or the divine per se. It addresses an important aspect of the way American religion relates to its broader social context. American church-state relations are widely idealized and regarded an unique. But this is an area awash in stereotypes and clichés that have grown increasingly problematic. Following a quick-and-dirty historical review, we examine some of the reasons for the flurry of litigation since World War II then note the implications for religion, law, and society.

Historical Overview

For many Americans, the "separation of church and state" is one of the most familiar parts of the Constitution, notwithstanding that this language appears nowhere in that document. It was not until 1802 that Thomas Jefferson referred to a desirable "wall of separation" between the two domains. The First Amendment of the Bill of Rights mentions religion only in its opening sentence, "Congress shall make no law respecting an establishment of religion or prohibiting the free exercise thereof." As some historians have pointed out, this language is less restrictive than most of the subsequent court decisions that have invoked it. The framers of the Constitution were generally not averse to identifying the nation as religious—even Christian. What concerned them was a denominational hegemony that would deny standing and rights to those of other practices and persuasions. By the time the federal Constitution was framed, the nation's denominational pluralism probably already precluded the "establishment of religion," at least as the phrase was then understood. The nation's consensus on core religious beliefs made it unlikely that many "free exercise" cases would arise. In this sense, the language of the First Amendment did more to reflect reality than to create it. Of course, it did not apply to the states at that time (Massachusetts was the last to abandon a formal theocracy in 1833), since the religion clauses of the First Amendment were not ruled applicable to the states until 1940. The combination of religious consensus and churchly diversity produced few complaints or complainants.

For almost 200 years, judicial activity concerning church-state relations in this country had been relatively unexciting, though some, such as polygamous Mormons, would disagree. While no single church was established, religion was firmly ensconced as a matter of national principle. Our Christian and God-fearing rootedness was sometimes made explicit in actual court decisions. In *Church of the Holy Trinity* v. *United States* (1892), the Court upheld Congress's constraints on the importation of alien unskilled workers and noted: "These, and many other matters which might be noticed, add a volume of unofficial declarations to the mass of organic utterances that this is a Christian nation." In *United States* v. *MacIntosh* (1931), an application for United States citizenship from a man who refused to promise that he would fight in any and all wars in defense of the country was denied, partly on the following grounds:

> When he speaks of putting his allegiance to the will of God above his allegiance to the government, it is evident, in the light of his entire statement, that he means to make his own interpretation of the will of God the decisive test which will conclude the government to stay its hand. We are a Christian people, according to one another the equal right of religious freedom, and acknowledging with reverence the duty of obedience to the will of God. But, also, we are a nation with the duty to survive; a nation whose constitution contemplates war as well as peace, whose government must go forward upon the assumption, and safely can proceed upon no other, that unqualified allegience to the nation and submission and obedience to the laws of the land, as well as those made for war as those made for peace, are not inconsistent with the will of God.

Even as late as 1952—following several church-state decisions which presaged a major shift—Justice Douglas was responsible for this often quoted sentiment in his majority opinion in *Zorach* v. *Clauson,* allowing released time for religious instruction off the premises of the public school: "We are a religious people whose institutions presuppose a supreme being."

Similar to other nostalgic distortions of history such as the "extended family," the "melting pot," and the myth of "rags-to-riches mobility," the "separation of church and state" has been as much fancy as fact. Certainly it is fanciful to suppose that the state makes no provision for religion. As several scholars have pointed out, the nation's "civil religion" may be non-denominational, but it is hardly secular. Myths sometimes persist because they are useful in deflecting attention away from reality itself. In this case, the reality may have been a Protestant elite that controlled the symbols as well as the substance of power.

Much of this was to change following World War II. There is more "separation" today than at any time in the nation's history. Despite the persistence of godly trust on our coins, prayers before governmental functions, and recent court approval of chaplains in Congress, the so-called New Right is understandably vexed that the old tide has turned against it. Whether invoking the Constitution or going beyond it, the courts have drawn new lines around churchly activities in public space, on public time, and at public expense—especially concerning such vital functions as education. Even so, this is no strict separation. As endorsed by decisions from *Everson* (1947) to *Lemon* v. *Kurtzman* (1971), there is ample cooperation between church and state, as long as it is for secular purposes, neither "advances nor inhibits" religion, and avoids "excessive entanglements." This is another disconfirmation of the separation shibboleth and another set of ambiguous criteria for case-by-case decisions. The Reagan administration seems to be pressing for a reversal of recent direction in the positions it has taken on issues such as legislative chaplains, Christmas crèches, aid to private (parochial) school parents, and formal diplomatic representation to the Vatican. Questions of establishment and entanglement have been reopened like a Pandora's box.

"Establishment" cases have commanded headlines since the 1940s, but some of the recent "free exercise" decisions may have wider significance. Some forms of free exercise have been granted legislatively, including conscientious objector status to members of religious groups in 1864 and in 1917. There is also a tradition of denying free exercise to groups whose practices would jeopardize the welfare of adherents considered first as United States citizens and secondarily as church members. Such cases involve Mormon polygamy, religiously ordained snake handling or drug consumption, child labor, and the withholding of medical treatment to minors because of the religious convictions of their parents.

Several Supreme Court decisions have been particularly significant in giving more latitude to religious practices. In *United States* v. *Ballard* (1944), the Court decided that it could not deal with the alleged fraudulence of a minister who claimed to be in touch with God—a case somewhat similar to a recent New York state case involving the Unification Church. In *Wisconsin* v. *Yoder* (1972), the Court allowed a Wisconsin Amish family to educate their adolescent children at home for religious reasons. In the *Seeger* (1965) and *Welsh* (1970) decisions, the Court extended conscientious objector eligibility to those who are not members of a specific religious group and do not claim a belief in God. This was stated in the *Welsh* decision:

> If an individual deeply and sincerely holds beliefs which are purely ethical or moral in source and content but that nevertheless impose upon him a duty of conscience to refrain from participating in any war at any time, those beliefs certainly occupy in the life of that individual 'a place parallel to that filled by . . . God' (cf. Seeger, 1965) in traditional religious persons.

Insofar as the putative "separation of church and state" emancipates religious practice and observance from state intervention, the phrase has greater reality today than at any time in the past. As Canavan notes, the Supreme Court's implicit definition of religion, based on *Seeger* and *Welsh,* has become both more formalized and more individualized; that is, an individual's religion is defined not by the content of his/her beliefs, but by the formal place those beliefs hold in the conscience. Similarly, religion is considered an individual phenomenon, irrespective of any organizational or institutional commitments. The *Welsh* decision amounts to a reversal of the *MacIntosh* (1931) decision. This new position has been implicit in recent lower court decisions concerning groups such as the Unification Church.

This somewhat contentious historical overview raises several issues for more detailed attention. What accounts for the post-World War II rash of church-state litigation following a long period of relative quiescence, and what has been the response of society to these decisions? What does all of this suggest concerning the broader relationship between church and state, religion and the law, and culture and society? The challenge to explain any social change amounts to an intellectual Rorschach test since scholars from various disciplines are likely to invoke the various explanations with which they are most comfortable. So it is in accounting for a litigious orgy surrounding church-state relations since World War II. Students of religion pounce upon religious developments as the primary agent of change; scholars of the judiciary focus on the cumulative precedents and processes within the courts; students of politics and social structure examine the change from their vantage point, while many historians argue that the change has been exaggerated. We are convinced that changes have occurred, that they can only be adequately understood by combining several perspectives, and that it is useful to consider separately those developments that have concerned the church on the one hand and the state on the other.

Changes in the Churchly Scene

The term *church* is used for a wide range of phenomena, and even its relationship to *religion* is problematic. Cults, sects, denominations, ecclesia, civil religion, privatized religion—these represent more than semantic stations on a scholar's cross. Since World War II several developments have crescendoed to make religion a more contested area of American life.

Paradoxically, for more than a century the courts were able to sustain a principled opposition to any formal religious establishment partly because an informal religious establishment already existed. Despite various awakenings, reawakenings, and bitter interdenominational struggles, there was no question that ours was a WASPish hive until late in the nineteenth century. The nation's Protestant hegemony was so strong as to brook little opposition and encourage few grievances from those who were offended. The dominant focus in American legal history has not been on church versus state so much as sect versus state, especially if one broadens the term *sect* to include religious groups serving those on the margins of society. These are defined with reference to social class, ethnicity, and education—and include early American Catholicism. Far from being neutral, the courts have exercised considerable influence over the forms and functions of sectarian religiosity—even as its basic rights were protected—and the courts have been aligned with the churches in their struggles against the sects. The government's ample provision for religious symbols and observances endorses churchly forms and affords legitimacy to churches. Churches in the societal mainstream have needed little formal support because of their informal power and leverage. They could afford to spurn overt entanglements with the political establishment because of their covert ties and general security.

As Protestant dominance began to give way, potential disorder began to arise. In an increasingly secular society, churches begin to play sectarian roles, and the notion of mainstream religion becomes oxymoronic. As all religious groups compete for the shrinking resources of members, dollars, and influences, competition grows increasingly shrill and requires more formal resolution. This process was particularly exacerbated by the changing position of American Catholics in the years following World War II. No longer beyond the social and religious pale, their social mobility, organizational sophistication, and political aggressiveness made them increasingly threatening to Protestants and other religious groups. In a series of cases involving the conditions under which church and state might cooperate for secular purposes, many Protestants found themselves opposing any "entanglement" at all for fear that Catholics might become newly established and newly entrenched. Suddenly it seemed critical to examine all religious ties to the state for fear that one church in particular would gain sway. Developments in an increasingly pluralized and fractionated religious scene may have forced the Court's hand. Whereas previously the nation's religious roots had been acknowledged, it became necessary to draw a firmer line between the state and religion of any sort. This was symbolized most vividly in the school prayer decisions of the early 1960s (*Engel* v. *Vitale* and *Shempp* v. *Abingdon*). Most religious officials have now accepted such rulings as part of a trade-off in which each denomination retains autonomy while none attains preeminance.

Nowhere is it stipulated that a court's decisions must be consistent. There is now evidence that the Supreme Court may be backtracking on establishment. In the spring of 1983, the Court refused to rule as unconstitutional the employment of chaplains in the Nebraska legislature. The decision was based largely on historical grounds, as the Court noted that the same United States Congress that approved the First Amendment hired a chaplain only weeks later. The Court may take a similar stand in forthcoming decisions concerning town crèches and the moments of silence that are widely practiced in lieu of formal school prayers. Would such a shift signal another major change in the nation's religious situation? The answer depends in part on an evaluation of the much heralded surge of evangelicalism. There are reasons to question whether the numerical increase in religious conservatives represents a deep-seated renewal of spirituality. Although there has been undeniable growth among evangelical and fundamentalist churches, we are more inclined to credit recent findings suggesting that demographic factors offer more efficient explanations than do matters of doctrine or message.

There is little question that the Court is responding to a new religious configuration that has special political influence on the Right. If there was a paradox in the Bill of Rights' original disavowal of establishment at a time when an establishment already existed, there may be a double irony in the current relaxation of antiestablishment constraints. In the most extreme scenario, we may face the prospect of reestablishing religion at a time when the nation is arguably more secular than ever before in its history. This may be due in part to the influence of a "moral minority" upon one of the least personally religious presidents in the country's history. If the government can renounce a religious establishment in its presence and then accept one in its absence, this leads to some beguiling questions concerning not only church-and-state but, more generally, the relationship between cultural life and social structure.

Recent decisions concerning "free exercise" have a different history and a different set of implications. More than an arbiter between religious groups, the courts have increasingly mediated between religion, civil religion, irreligion, and even areligious interests. What is most remarkable about the recent period of church-state litigation is not the increasing recognition of the rights of peripheral religious groups, but the stretching of the concept of "religion" to cover a range of cases unimaginable 200 years ago. Following the putative religious revival of the 1950s, the period of the 1960s and early 1970s has been referred to as an age of religious experimentation. It is not simply that old-line sects and evangelical groups began to flourish (albeit for demographic as much as theological reasons). This was a time when new kinds of movements began to perform religious functions and claim religious license—some western, many nonwestern; some operating within previous religious traditions, and others as cultic entrepreneurs. Religious pluralism took on new dimensions; invisible religion became obtrusive; privatized religions came out of the closet. It remains debatable whether these developments were, in Robert Wuthnow's terms, a revolutionary bellwether or a cultural backwater. Again, changes in the cultural mood forced new set of issues on the courts. If the thrust of "establishment" decisions sometimes seemed antireligious (until very recently), the direction of "free exercise" judgments may have seemed tolerant to the point of an indiscriminate embrace. One wonders about the linkage between the two.

Changes in the Judiciary and the State

The argument has been that the judicial system's changing interpretation of church and state over the past forty-odd years was a response to developments within American religion. It is important to be cautious here. Courts are clearly affected by their legal, political, and cultural contexts. By the end of World War II, our society had grown exceedingly complex, teeming with special interests and considerations being brought to bear on even the simplest constitutional issue. The judiciary was especially sensitive to these social changes. Not only had it been politicized by events of the New Deal, but the world of politics had begun to suffer from power vacuum and immobilization of the center. Initiatives for change were increasingly either lost in the labyrinths of the executive branch's bureaucracies, or stalemated in the legislative process by the splintering of the old coalitions and the proliferation of interest-group politics. "Extremist groups" with single-issue agendas became agents of change, and the courts became a principal arena for the political fray.

The politicization of religion added to the pressure. This included not only the tendency for churches to become more overtly political as lobbying groups, but also the tendency for single-issue political movements to take on a religious guise. Nor is this restricted to the political Right and such celebrated cases as the Moral Majority and the right-to-life movement. Churches on the Left have a similar history of political lobbying, whether on behalf of race relations, the skirmish on poverty, ending the Vietnam War, or changing current United States foreign policy in the areas in which churches have accepted government money for dispensing relief and refugee services—e.g., Southeast Asia, the Middle East, and Central America.

A major change in the nation's political economy had an even greater triggering effect on church-state litigation after World War II. Just before the war the government became a major source of funding for such critical social sectors as education, health, and welfare. As public institutions discharged these functions at state expense, the private sector sought its own share of the resources. Inevitably, this led to new forms of church-state conflict. The question was not simply whether religious institutions qualify for direct public monies (and that is itself not a simple question, as noted in the *Walz* and *Lemon* v. *Kurtzman* decisions). Even tax exemptions can be seen as a form of state support for religion.

There are two models of tax exemption: a tax-base theory which holds that religious institutions are not taxed because they are exempt from the tax base to begin with, and a tax-expenditure theory which argues that every tax exemption is a form of subsidy expended on organizations performing some positive functions for society. The 1983 Supreme Court endorsed the expenditure model and specifically addressed exemptions as subsidies in revoking the tax exemptions of Bob Jones University and the Goldsboro Christian Schools on grounds of racial discrimination. This has made religionists uneasy, for it suggests a closer tie between the state and the church than may be acceptable in constitutional terms. From this anxious perspective, the Court may be preparing the churches for a considerable fall from exemptive grace. Some religionists, such as Dean Kelley, sensing this shift in the Court's attitude toward exemptions, have argued that churches deserve these "subsidies" because they serve secular, as well as sacred, functions. Aside from the potentially momentous implications that churches can no longer justify their status on purely sacred grounds, this argument suffers when pushed to its extreme. It suggests that if churches did not exist, the state would have to invent them (perhaps in the same way that secular wedding rituals were "invented" in the Soviet Union).

Tax exemption is an increasingly critical aspect of church-state relations, because of the pressure on financially strapped governmental authorities to find new sources of revenue. In a secularizing society, it is not surprising that public support should atrophy for exempting the local church from local taxes. Mainstream congregations with declining memberships have declining political support for the special considerations that tax exemptions entail. They are increasingly vulnerable to taxation, especially on those parts of their property that are not used exclusively for religious purposes—a criterion which is invoked more and more firmly.

Another possible fissure in the rock of tax exemption has emerged. The Supreme Court recently upheld the unconstitutionality of a ruling that would have required a religious group to receive more than half its funding from its membership in order to be exempt from filing tax forms. Such a ruling would have put mail-order, street corner, and electronic religious movements to considerable inconvenience and in some jeopardy. The court's decision was made by a narrow 5-4 vote. Since members of the majority included those justices whose replacement is most imminent, the tax status of these groups could soon be at issue again.

Mention of the Court's composition suggests yet another explanation of church-state litigation since World War II. The dam that broke in the late 1940s gushed cases which had been building up since the early 1900s, with a special infusion during the depression era. The Court changed its complexion drastically during the first half of the twentieth century. No longer were Holmes and Brandeis alone in their libertarian concerns. Once the Court became more inclined to hear First Amendment issues generally, a reinterpretation of church-state was not far behind. From this perspective, what is remarkable about the period after World War II is the change in the Court's posture toward the issues, rather than a change in the issues per se. It is perilous to infer what is going on in society from what is observable on the court docket or in court opinions. Not only can the Supreme Court prime the pump of litigation by what it is willing to hear, but it can be even more influential in what it ignores. Branches of government at every level are constantly acting in ways pertinent to changing church-state relations. These form a political climate that weighs heavily on the judiciary, especially when it is argued that even the Supreme Court tends to make a decision first and develop its justification later. We can add to the myths concerning church and state that the operative judicial decisions are all firmly grounded in a timeless Constitution as opposed to timely politics.

We must be especially wary of the fiction that once the Supreme Court decrees, society comes quickly to heel. Recent studies concerning compliance with court decisions have been primarily concerned with the *Engel* and *Schempp* cases dealing with school prayer and Bible reading. Some attention has also been given to the *McCollum* and *Zorach* released time decisions. In most cases compliance ranged from moderate to little, and each researcher speculates on possible causes and variables such as: the varying levels of regional religiosity; the enthusiasm with which local school superintendents called for compliance; the formation of local political coalitions that either facilitated or obstructed change; and the degree to which the community was religiously homogeneous without a strong dissident base. Dolbeare and Hammond are especially interesting for candidly dicussing their failure to confirm some specific predictions and their subsequent speculation on the full range of tensions affecting the local religious/political scene.

Whatever has occurred at the level of the Supreme Court in the past thirty years, there has been far less actual change in much of the nation's religious practices. The Court may be exercising considerable leadership, but it is questionable how many are following. Conservatively estimated, more than 25 percent of the nation's schools still begin their day with prayers or Bible reading and possibly end them with released time religious instruction in the school buildings. We know relatively little about the actual relationships that exist between church and state within local communities or in the daily routines of the citizenry. This points to another kind of church-state mythology. It is one thing to understand court decisions and court dynamics as a source of what the society ought to be doing; it is quite another to relate these to what is actually going on.

Implications for Religion, Law, and Society

There are a variety of models and theories concerning the relationship of legal institutions to society. Some portray the law as a passive reflector of prior change, a codifier of the passing scene and a crystallizer of consensus. Others, such as Clifford Geertz, suggest that the law can be an active agent in producing change, whether a political instrument on behalf of structural alterations or a cultural source of interpretive innovation. The history of church and state in the United States provides support for both of these models—and more. The Court has led, lagged, and languished—often in the same session and sometimes a single decision. The hobgoblin of consistency is not a household demon in the judicial manse. Church-state law invites inconsistency by the conflicts inherent within it.

Consider again the distinction between the proscription of "establishment" and the prescription of "free exercise." There is a conceptual tension between the two, and this has taken on historical reality. Recent Court decisions have been so generous in defining "religion" with respect to free exercise that they have created a possible monster for future decisions concerning establishment. Currently, the tension persists, as "free exercise" decisions present religion as broad and inconclusive, while the Court seeks narrower, stricter parameters, for "establishment" cases. Many cases could be dealt with under either rubric with opposite results, and legal scholars often question the Court on this basis. Some have suggested a middle ground in a single definition of religion for both purposes that contains explicit references to the transcendent, if not the supernatural. Others have suggested that the Court should be more forthright and adopt two quite distinct definitions, one broad for free exercise, and one narrow for establishment. (Still others suggest somewhat impishly that perhaps the best alternative would be to delete religion altogether from the First Amendment and trust the guaranteed freedoms of speech and assembly to produce the desired results on their own.) Most courts prefer to deal with cases under the establishment rather than the free exercise clause, although free exercise situations may be more common. The courts are no doubt aware that the free exercise of religion has been extended so as to potentially include far more than conventional churches, sects, cults, etc. Political groups, community associations, therapy circles, and other forms of voluntary associations may also seek the benefits of religious status.

If "religion" continues to be treated so broadly, "churches" are being increasingly circumscribed. As Sharon Worthing has pointed out, federal agencies such as the Internal Revenue Service (IRS) and the Department of Labor (DOL) have led this effort. Distinctions among categories such as "sacerdotal institutions," "integrated auxiliaries," and "church-related" groups raise profound constitutional questions of their own. Referring to new IRS criteria for tax exemption, Worthing points out:

> Christ and His band of disciples certainly did not meet these criteria. An examination of the relevant references indicates that the Biblical church which was in the home of Priscilla and Aquila would not qualify for tax exemption under these tests. It is perhaps never wise to define a religion based on its developed state, since its early state is not only its most fluid, but usually its most delicate and important. . . . If government can define what is a "church," it can also define what is not a church, and can do so in a manner which excludes religions which are not favored by government officials.

These are not idle academic matters. A great deal hangs in the balance of such definitional conundrums. Church-state relations are largely a matter of balancing what the self-styled religionists can get away with, on the one hand, with what an increasingly strapped and secular state can reasonably lay claim to, on the other. The problem is compounded in the case of religious groups who want to "take the money and run," that is, accept state support at the risk of entangling the issue of establishment while, at the same time, jealously guarding their freedom in all other respects.

The Court has neither the right nor the resources to aggressively seek out grievances; it must wait for cases to develop. Not only is there a considerable gap between what the Court has ordered and what society implements, but there are many other potential establishment and free exercise violations which are so institutionalized as to defy litigation. As Philip Gleason notes,

> Americans have attached so much importance to the juridical relationship between two highly formal institutions—the state and the traditional churches—that they overlook more diffuse social developments that actually move in the direction of amalgamating civic and religious concerns.

Legalists might shudder at the prospect of turning social scientists loose to uncover such matters. They might shudder even more if the social scientists were invited to use their own definitions of religion in the process. We wonder how far the founders were prepared to go in using the First Amendment as a warrant of moral diversity—not that this can be predeterminative, even if known. There is virtually no institution which cannot be said to have, in the words of the *Welsh* decision, some "deeply and sincerely [held] beliefs which are purely ethical or moral in source . . . but . . . impose . . . a duty of conscience." Every institution has a set of beliefs and rituals that confer a sense of sanctified singularity. If the constitutional objective is truly to guarantee the conditions of diversity, a number of institutions pose the possibility of a quasi-religious hegemony which may assume establishment standing at the expense of freely exercised alternatives. The schools are an obvious case in point. The courts themselves have been interpreted as "churches of the American civil religion." If the schools and the courts are religious, how is religion to be kept out of the classroom and separated from the state? This question may be a case of *reductio ad absurdum,* but it raises the issue of American civil religion.

From one constitutional standpoint, the notion of a civil religion is a contradiction. Recent Court decisions have provided the concept with considerable legitimacy, especially through broader definitions of religion. Recent decisions remind us that religion is not exclusively a denominational phenomenon, nor merely an expression of political nationalism, as many today interpret civil religion. The Court leads us back to Emile Durkheim's classic paradigm of religion at the core of society's integrating values and beliefs. While the Court does not go so far as to state that society is a religious phenomenon, which would require a leap of faith in doctrine, that would represent only another step down the rough path that the Court has been taking.

The special significance of church and state in contemporary America is that it directs attention to a range of larger cultural issues from which our attention has strayed. It invites us to study those issues on a more realistic basis. The conflicts and tensions revealed in this area remind us that no society's culture is ever a seamless web. Culture can be as divisive and dysfunctional as it may be integrative and beneficial, and there is always a potential gap between cultural conceptions of what society ought to be and what society is. Neither church nor state, let alone the relations between them, can be understood without reference to these issues.

The basic premise of this essay, like so many others, is that of a then-and-now comparison. "This is how things were then; this is how things are now; these are some reasons for the change." We argue that neither "then" nor "now" are accurately portrayed in our national mythology. Church and state have a long history of interactions, entanglements, and cooperations. The secular state, as we now understand it, was not the creation of the late eighteenth century. Although we have perhaps run the risk of oversimplifying the historical "then" to highlight the changes, we nonetheless maintain that World War II was something of a watershed.

Changes in church-state relations were the product of changes in American religious life and changes in American politics and polity. The major change in the churchly scene was the rise and mainstreaming of American Catholics. The societal mobilization produced by involvement in World War II not only helped to "deghettoize" Catholics and spread the suburban middle-class American dream, but it provided the training, exposure, and education (via the GI Bill) to make the dream more widely realized. Thus Catholicism lost its more sectarian status, and surging religious pluralism washed over and greatly diluted the dominance of a Protestant elite. More recently the rise of numerous new religions, from Eastern mysticism and privatized humanisms to resurgent fundamentalism, have made religious plurality all the more real, and cast the state even more in the role of a neutral mediator. There have been changes in American politics and the judiciary aside from these religious developments. The composition of the Supreme Court changed, rendering it more willing to hear church-state cases. The perception of the role of the judiciary also changed, becoming more assertive and less deferential to the legislative branch. All forms of public life, including the religious, became more regulated (and funded) by the government, opening new areas to potential conflict. Finally, the political process itself became less dominated by the center and more open to issues relevant to smaller political/religious factions.

These changes in American social life contain imperatives for changing the ways in which we study and interpret our society. There may well be a gap between the letter and the spirit of the law in every society, but there is a similar gap between the law and social reality. The "compliance" literature, for all its faults, demonstrates this. We believe that even our concepts for examining church-state relations are dated. Religion is no longer confined to the churches; law has wide-ranging implications that go beyond the apparatus of the courts or the theoretical constructions of the state. Traditional concepts of the separation of church and state are reliant on a social reality, both religious and political, that no longer exists. If we are to understand the present interactions between religion and government, we must expand our perspective on culture and social change.

Bibliography

Berns, Walter Fred. *The First Amendment and the Future of American Democracy.* New York: Basic Books, 1976.

Canavan, Francis S.J. "Impact of Recent Supreme Court Decisions on Religion in the United States." *Journal of Church and State* 16 (1974):217-36.

Dolbeare, Kenneth M. and Hammond, Phillip E. *The School Prayer Decisions: From Court Policy to Local Practice.* Chicago: University of Chicago Press, 1971.

Geertz, Clifford. *Local Knowledge: Further Essays in Interpretive Anthropology.* New York: Basic Books, 1983.

Gleason, Philip. "Blurring the Line of Separation: Education, Civil Religion, and Teaching about Religion." *Journal of Church and State* 19 (1977):517-38.

Kelley, Dean M. *Why Churches Should Not Pay Taxes.* New York: Harper and Row, 1977.

Worthing, Sharon L. "'Religion' and 'Religious Institutions' under the First Amendment." *Pepperdine Law Review* 7 (1980):313-53.

Wuthnow, Robert. "The New Religions in Social Context." In C. Glock and R. Bellah, eds. *The New Religious Consciousness.* Berkeley, Calif.: University of California Press, 1976.

7

The Courts and Secular Humanism

Phillip E. Hammond

Few Americans admit to being secular humanists. Yet the ideology they allegedly hold is blamed for society's ills. "Most of the evils of the world today can be traced to humanism," says Tim LaHaye, a Southern California pastor, in his book *Battle for the Mind*. "It is destroying our culture, families, country—and one day, the entire world." Mel and Norma Gabler of Longview, Texas, agree. They operate a textbook monitoring service to search out ideas that "undermine patriotism, the free enterprise system, religion, and parental authority." Most textbooks, they told *New York Times* reporter Dena Kleiman in 1981, are written from the perspective of "secular humanism, which permeates every aspect of contemporary society and teaches youngsters to lie, cheat, and steal." "Humanism is the religion of public schools," say the Gablers, who refer to public schools as "government seminaries."

Religious conservatives, especially those of the evangelical Protestant Right, are most likely to castigate secular humanism. More importantly, they are most likely to see secular humanism as a movement voluntarily adopted in preference to God's guidance through Christianity. Secular humanism is not merely an abstraction but an ideology which, because it is freely chosen, can just as freely be rejected.

According to the religious Right, among those choosing secularism are so-called mainline church leaders—theologians, administrators, and clergy affiliated with the National and World Councils of Churches, for example. To Francis A. Schaeffer, one of evangelicalism's current "theoreticians," the large, established denominations were "knocked down like a row of ten pins" by the wave of liberal theology early in this century. "Now if Christians had used their strength at that moment," Schaeffer said in a 1982 lecture:

> their influence could have stopped the drift toward the liberal theology in the churches, and it could have stopped the beginning of the slide toward a

humanist consensus taking the place of the Judeo-Christian consensus which had been the prevalent consensus previously, and upon which our country was founded.

Secular humanism in this discourse is an antireligious replacement for an earlier outlook congenial to religion and productive of good citizens and a moral society. The earlier outlook was broadly Christian, but individuals who today invoke the specter of its secular replacement do not have in mind an earlier idyllic theocracy. Those most vehement in their dislike of secular humanism are the chief heirs of the antinomian, egalitarian, nonconforming, and sectarian tensions that gave rise to the situation they deplore. Because of these tensions, the United States Constitution included provisions to assure religious freedom. Far from trying to promote secularism, the framers and ratifiers wanted to guarantee the free play of religion. To call the result "secular humanism"—and to believe, moreover, that it is a perspective voluntarily adopted in preference to some other ideology—is to seriously misinterpret the issues of church and state.

The Court as Agent for Secular Humanism

American courts are regarded by many as the chief agent for secular humanistic triumphs. Mainline churches may be blamed as primarily responsible for failing to stop the onslaught in time, but the judicial system—especially the United States Supreme Court, and especially its rulings on religion in the public schools—for some years has curdled the blood of those, such as LaHaye and the Gablers, who believe that secularism is being installed in place of righteousness in American culture. Even a centrist such as D. Elton Trueblood in a middle-American magazine, the *Saturday Evening Post*, in 1983 could write, "The zealots of separation have been most successful in persuading the Supreme Court to ban prayer in our schools."

The allegedly persuaded justices deny they favor either secular humanism or the decline of religion. The outlawing of state prescribed prayers, said Justice Black in *Engel* v. *Vitale* (1962) does not indicate a "hostility toward religion or toward prayer." A year later Justice Clark, in *Abington School District* v. *Schempp* (1963), explicitly denied that, by declaring devotional Bible reading unconstitutional, the Court was encouraging schools to teach "a religion of secularism." Many of the Court's religious critics think otherwise. Is it possible, they wonder, that writers of the Constitution intended to eliminate from American classrooms the religious influences they wanted so much to protect? How can it be that a school may sponsor an Evolutionary Biology Club but not a Bible Club? Is secularism not being promulgated, at least by default, when public schools are required to leave theism untouched? Such issues cause great anguish for some and considerable puzzlement for many others. When the law is interpreted as not permitting assistance to theism, is it not preferring secularism? Is the Supreme Court not an agent for secular humanism?

As plausible as this charge may sound, it is incorrect. At least three kinds of evidence might be offered in rebuttal. First, the Court has a record of protecting traditional religious interests. Second, the Court has a record of recognizing new religious possibilities, while acknowledging that these must be balanced against competing interests. Third, the Court is unfairly accused of promulgating secular humanism when it is merely employing neutral language, as it must when balancing competing interests.

The Court as Protector of Traditional Religion

Those who criticize the Supreme Court for its role in religion-in-public-school decisions would be surprised to realize how recently courts were criticized for ignoring, and allowing to persist, the *de facto* establishment of Protestantism in public school education. Just fifty years ago a report of the National Conference of Christians and Jews complained:

> In some places the school system is essentially still a Protestant school system: celebration of the Christian holidays is taken as a matter of course; "good character" in the appointment of teachers is interpreted as involving membership in a Protestant Church; . . . while there may be little open hostility toward Jews or Catholics, the teaching is imbued with an exclusive nativism that creates suspicion for everything that does not fit into the local tradition.

There is less *de facto* Protestant establishment today than in 1932 when those words were written. Nonetheless, one can look back during the interim and see instances in which the Court has acted to sustain, even encourage, traditional religious (if not just Protestant) influence:

* In *Pierce v. Society of the Sisters of the Holy Names* (1952) the right of churches to operate private, parochial schools was firmly declared. Public schooling could have a religious counterpart.
* In *Cochran v. Louisiana State Board of Education* (1930) a state's decision to fund the purchase of textbooks, even when used in parochial schools, was upheld.
* In *Everson v. Board of Education* (1947) public funds were approved for providing bus service to children attending parochial schools.

- In *Zorach* v. *Clauson* (1952) the Court allowed public school pupils to receive religious instruction during the school day, provided that it occur off-campus and involve no public tax money.
- In *Walz* v. *Tax Commission* (1970) the policy of allowing tax exemption for religious organizations was reaffirmed. Chief Justice Burger used this occasion to make explicit the Court's "benevolent neutrality" toward religion:

> The general principle deducible from the First Amendment and all that has been said by the Court is this: that we will not tolerate either governmentally established religion or governmental interference with religion. Short of those expressly proscribed governmental acts there is room for play in the joints productive of a benevolent neutrality which will permit religious exercise to exist without sponsorship and without interference.

In light of these cases and a doctrine of "benevolent neutrality," it hardly seems correct to charge the Supreme Court with being antireligious or prosecularist.

The Court as Balancer of Competing Interests

What the United States Supreme Court readily admits to being is the adjudicator of competing interests—the balancer between equally legitimate concerns that have the potential for conflicting. The free exercise of religion has never been understood as absolute, so considerations of time, place, and manner must be weighed against the presumption of freedom. The Court might have given short shrift to Mormons in the nineteenth century in finding polygamy "odious" and therefore illegal, but the record in the twentieth century is primarily one of ever expanding rights to exercise religion in diverse ways. Consider these cases of the past two decades:

- In *Sherbert* v. *Verner* (1963) a Seventh-Day Adventist was declared eligible for unemployment benefits after she was fired for refusing to work on Saturday, her Sabbath.
- In *Wisconsin* v. *Yoder* (1972) Amish children were permitted to drop out of school after eighth grade, since to continue beyond mastery of basic skills was, to the Amish, to become worldly, a danger to faith.
- In *McDaniel* v. *Paty* (1978) a Baptist minister in Tennessee was pronounced eligible to run for public office, thus invalidating a state law prohibiting such involvement of clergy.
- In *Thomas* v. *Review Board of Indiana* (1981) a Jehovah's Witness whose job required him to work on weapons contrary to his conscience, and who refused to work and was fired, was upheld in his right to unemployment benefits.

• In *Widmar* v. *Vincent* (1981) a Christian group of students wanting to worship on a University of Missouri campus was declared eligible to use state owned facilities in the same manner as any other recognized student group.

Considering these cases, it seems incorrect to charge the Supreme Court with being secular or antireligious. The Supreme Court seems to have an easier time upholding religious liberty than it does religion, though the first list, of "protector" cases, ought to prove that the Court is not hostile to religion per se. What the second list, of "balancer" cases, suggests is that balancing an individual's right to exercise his religion against society's right to restrain that exercise is easier than the parallel judicial task of balancing the government's right to act benevolently toward religion against the citizenry's right to object to such support.

Since 1970 the Court has applied three tests in deciding whether legislation that may benefit religion is, at the same time, an "establishment" of religion and thus unconstitutional. Governmental activity must pass all three tests in order to be legal. The "secular purpose" test asks about the legislative intent; is it to benefit religion, or is it to achieve a secular purpose which only coincidentally benefits religion? The "primary effect" test is similar to the secular purpose test, except it asks not about intent but about consequence; is religion either "advanced" or "inhibited"? If religion is neither advanced nor inhibited, it is not being "established," and the governmental action is allowable. If to insure that religion is neither advanced nor inhibited, government must monitor, or otherwise get entangled with religion, then such "entanglement" may be "excessive." This would indicate an unconstitutional establishment of religion.

The use of the first two tests is illustrated in *Stone* v. *Graham* (1980), declaring illegal a Kentucky law requiring the posting of the Ten Commandments in every public schoolroom. The Supreme Court said:

> We conclude that Kentucky's statute . . . had no secular legislative purpose, and is therefore unconstitutional. . . . The pre-eminent purpose for posting the Ten Commandments on schoolroom walls is plainly religious in nature. The Ten Commandments is undeniably a sacred text in the Jewish and Christian faiths. . . .If the posted copies of the Ten Commandments are to have any effect at all, it will be to induce the school children to read, meditate upon, perhaps to venerate and obey, the Commandments. However desirable this might be as a matter of devotion, it is not a permissible state objective under the Establishment Clause.

In applying the three tests for establishment, the Court can be thought of as weighing or balancing equally legitimate, but competing, interests. Government is expected to act to promote the general welfare, but in doing so it must not show religious favoritism and "establish" religion. In a similar balancing maneuver, government must allow religious freedom as much as possible without jeopardizing society. To do otherwise is to disallow the "free exercise" of religion. In balancing competing interests, the Court necessarily uses neutral language with respect to those interests. Consequently, when it is being benevolent to religion, the Court may sound secular. A second consequence is that when the Court declares a religious practice unconstitutional, the decision is vulnerable to misinterpretation.

The Court as Employer of Neutral Language

The United States Constitution does not require the Supreme Court to give reasons for its decisions. That it routinely does so, often in elaborate form, is easy to understand if we remember the Court's functions. Beyond the resolution of particular legal conflicts the Court, through its decisions, performs at least two other tasks. One is to educate society as to how similar conflicts might be resolved. In the Anglo-American, common-law tradition, in which precedents are vital in the determination of legality, this function is critical. The other function is to offer reasons for decisions which even the losers will accept as fair. That there remain disgruntled losers means that the Court is not totally successful in fulfilling this function. It would prefer all sides in a dispute to walk away gracefully, convinced that justice has been done. Because the Court performs these two additional tasks, its decisions necessarily employ neutral language.

In church-state cases, in which one party to the dispute can be considered proreligion and another party antireligion, the Court's decision will strive for a language that is neither pro- nor anti-. This may not be apparent to proreligion forces when they win because they do not care why they win. When they lose, even though the language used in the decisions will be neutral, the Court's reasons can be misinterpreted as hostile to religion and therefore secular. Consider the following cases which, from the proreligion standpoint, were lost:

- In *McCollum* v. *Board of Education* (1948) so-called released-time religious instruction in public schools was outlawed as "a utilization of the tax-established and tax-supported public school system to aid religious groups to spread their faith." We could interpret this statement of the Court's reasoning as an objection to the spreading of faith, whereas it is actually an objection to the utilization of the public school system for that purpose.
- In *Engel* v. *Vitale* (1962) the Court said "it is no part of the business of government to compose official prayers for any group of the American

people." We could interpret this statement as disdaining prayer, whereas the real objection is to governmental composition of prayers.

Contrast the language employed in two cases won by the proreligion forces:

- In *Cochran* v. *Louisiana State Board* (1930) the supplying of free textbooks to all school children, even those in parochial schools, was upheld. "The schools, however, are not the beneficiaries of these appropriations . . . . The school children and the state alone are." We could interpret this statement as approving parochial education, whereas approval is being given to a state's spending money to provide textbooks for its students.
- In *Zorach* v. *Clauson* (1952) the Court declared constitutional the released-time religious instruction that occurs off-campus and involves no tax money. "There is a suggestion that the system involves the use of coercion to get public school students into religious classrooms . . . . [but the record] tells us that the school authorities are neutral in this regard and do no more than release students whose parents so request." One could interpret this statement as favoring religious classroom instruction, whereas it is neutrality with respect to religious instruction that is being required.

The last case also contains the kind of gratuitous reasoning the Court tries to—and should—avoid if it is to remain neutral. Justice Douglas, who wrote the opinion in *Zorach* v. *Clauson*, went on to add the unnecessary reason that "we are a religious people whose institutions presuppose a Supreme Being." Cynics believe Douglas was motivated in this superfluous emendation because at the time he was angling for the presidential nomination of the Democratic party. Whatever the truth, the comment has since been overruled in conscientious objection cases, which find it unnecessary to believe in a Supreme Being in order to qualify for conscientious objector status. Good standing as a citizen entitled to protection of religious conscience does not depend upon having one's conscience informed by a Supreme Being theology.

A Look Backward

The legal system of America has regularly tried to maintain its neutrality. What changes is the religious makeup of American society and both the nature of the cases being litigated and the sensitivity of the judges toward religious questions. Change can be demonstrated by contrasting recent events with a school prayer case that arose in Georgia and was decided in 1922 by the Georgia Supreme Court in *Wilkerson* v. *Rome*.

Rome, Georgia, passed an ordinance requiring public school principals to see that each school day opened with exercises including a prayer to God and the reading of some portion of the King James Version of the bible. Suit was brought by citizens who contended that the ordinance was prohibited by three provisions of the Georgia Constitution: the right of all to worship "according to conscience," the assurance that no citizen of the state will be "molested in person or property" because of "religious opinions," and the declaration that no public tax money will "directly or indirectly" aid any religious groups or "any sectarian institution."

The state's supreme court heard the case and pronounced the religious exercises constitutional. Justice Gilbert wrote the opinion (with which only one court member disagreed), and it is, in retrospect, a remarkable and lucid document. Judge Gilbert begins by noting the resemblance between Georgia's constitutional provisions regarding religion and those of other states and of the nation. He then cites a Massachusetts case from 1859 that disallowed "sectarian" objection to public school exercises such as bible reading. "Those who drafted and adopted our Constitution could [similarly] never have intended it to meet such narrow and sectarian views. That section of the Constitution was clearly intended for higher and nobler purposes . . . the protection of all religions—the Buddhist and the Brahmin, the Pagan and the Jew, the Christian and the Turk." Diversity must be protected, but not "sectarianism."

How can we harmonize refusal to recognize a conscientious objection to devotional reading of the King James bible with support for the protection of religious diversity? A first clue to Gilbert's reasoning comes in his quoting of a legal scholar who said that "Christianity is the only religion known to American law." The Georgia Constitution "never intended to declare the policy of this state to be unreligious or unchristian." This easy equation of "religion" with "Christian religion" helps explain Gilbert's inability to see anything objectionable in public school devotions, for nobody suffers interference with the "dictates of his own conscience." "The mere listening to the reading of an extract from the Bible and a brief prayer . . . would seem remote from such interference."

How can he handle the charge that such religious exercises, state sponsored and supported, are sectarian because they specify the King James bible? Not so, says Gilbert. First, differences between the Douai (Roman Catholic) and King James translations, or between the "Rabbinical and Christian editions," are "not known to the ordinary lay reader" and therefore insignificant in the view of the law. Second, while it is true that teachers lead the exercises, and teachers are paid from state taxes, "no theological doctrines are required to be taught. The creed of no sect must be affirmed or denied . . . . No one is required to believe, or punished for disbelief, either in its [the bible's] inspiration or want of inspiration, in the fidelity of the translation or its accuracy, or in any set of doctrines deducible or not deducible therefrom."

What keeps the devotional use of the King James Version from being "sectarian"? The answer for Gilbert lies in the "real object" of the First Amendment to the United States Constitution, which is "to exclude all rivalry among Christian sects." To assert a difference between the Roman Catholic and King James versions of the bible "only shows, at the most, that the King James Bible is non-Roman Catholic, not that it is, of itself and necessarily in a constitutional sense, anti-Roman Catholic." Similarly, the Jew may not demand exclusion of Bible-reading or instruction in the Christian religion "merely because it is the Bible or the Christian religion." The Jew may seek relief in the law not as a Jew but "as a taxpayer just exactly when, and only when, a Christian may complain to a court as a taxpayer, i.e., when the legislature authorizes such reading of the Bible or such instruction in the Christian religion . . . as gives one Christian sect a preference over others."

It is a measure of our constitutional sophistication that such a judicial decision, just six decades old, seems hopelessly insensitive to the demands of justice in a religiously pluralistic society. Even in 1922, Justice Hines of the Georgia Supreme Court dissented. He believed the Rome public school exercises to be illegal on all three constitutional grounds brought by the plaintiffs. Religious freedom includes the right not to worship at all, he said, and yet the city is requiring "a system of worship for the schools of Rome." To be free of "molestation" for one's "religious opinions" is to be free of "anything which vexes, worries, or disturbs a person in body, mind, or soul," but required reading from the Protestant bible "offends and molests the Catholics and the Jews." Finally, giving public school approval solely to the King James Version "discriminates in favor of and aids the Protestant sects," but public schools are supported by taxation from all, and thus the practice is unconstitutional.

Nothing suggests that the dissenting Justice Hines saw himself as a secular humanist or his dissent as antireligious. So it is with his judicial successors, whose positions today are the law of the land. Those insisting on a neutral stance toward all religions in today's America claim to be "benevolently" neutral. It is not the case, as their critics charge, that a position of neutrality necessarily fosters secularism. To insist that creation-science be ruled out of the biology curriculum of public schools, for example, is not to elevate evolution to a metaphysical or religious construct which replaces the Genesis account of creation. Where such a construction is taught, it is not only unscientific but unconstitutional as well.

Individuals unhappy with Supreme Court rulings on church-state matters continue in their charges of secular humanism. That they persist in the face of repeated denials by the justices themselves, as well as ample evidence to the contrary, suggests some confusion on their part as to the real target of their indignation. They attack the Court for promulgating secular humanism, when what they want is what Justice Gilbert of Georgia erroneously believed still existed in this nation in 1922—an avowedly Christian America. Gilbert misinterpreted the situation then, and today's church-state discontents are even further off-target.

Nothing indicates the misinterpretation better than the latest effort to countermand the "secular" Supreme Court's position on prayer in public schools. Having tried in vain to enact legislation declaring this nation to be "Christian," and to change the Court's prayer rulings by legislation or repeated constitutional amendments, the evangelical Right now has President Ronald Reagan's endorsement of another attempt to amend the United States Constitution. In its entirety the amendment reads:

> Nothing in this Constitution shall be construed to prohibit individual or group prayer in public schools or other public institutions. No person shall be required by the United States or any state to participate in prayer. Nor shall the United States or any state compose the words of any prayer to be said in public schools.

The second sentence of the proposal has long been recognized as the law of the land. The third has explicitly been law since 1962 when the Court outlawed the New York regents' prayer in *Engel* v. *Vitale*. That leaves the first sentence. What does it make legal that is illegal now? The answer probably is: nothing. Religious free exercise has never been a license to do anything; government has routinely reserved the right to regulate time, place, and manner. What then prevents an "individual or group" from praying in public school today? Very likely nothing, providing that such prayer is not disruptive, and is not sponsored by any level of government.

Inasmuch as the evangelical Right is aware of the first provision— nothing, for example, now prohibits a student from offering grace before lunch in the school cafeteria silently to himself or unobtrusively aloud with others—we must suppose it is the second provision that is to be leapfrogged by the proposed amendment. It is, implicitly, government sponsorship that the amendment's supporters desire. What of sponsorship of "individual or group prayer"? That would violate the "benevolent neutrality" the Court has so painstakingly sought to enunciate; it would be preferring a Judeo-Christian style of worship over, for example, the meditating-chanting-fasting style of Eastern religions. America is not now a Judeo-Christian nation, whatever it once might have been; nor can it be said to worship secular humanism. There is no ideology of secularism voluntarily selected by judges in preference to Christianity. At most, we might refer to the "secular" outcomes of church-state issues raised by religious pluralism and resolved by the courts in humane ways. The courts show no religious favoritism and justify their decisions in language that all citizens are expected to accept. When any group of citizens fails consistently to understand and to accept that language, it misinterprets the real church-state issues.

8

Religious Exemptions

Leo Pfeffer

This essay considers the constitutionality under the First, Fifth, and Fourteenth Amendments of the practice of either according or denying to churches and their clergy exemption from duties generally imposed on community members. There are many instances of such exemptions, but the five selected—military service, taxation, fair labor law obligations, eligibility for public office, and educational standards—represent a fair cross section of possible constitutional conflict. I do not discuss nonclerical religious exemptions (such as military service accorded or denied to lay conscientious objectors, obligatory flag salute exercises, or compulsory jury service).

In considering clerical exemption, three alternatives are possible, and each has been urged and considered by the Court; they are: mandated, permissible and forbidden exemption. The first is predicated upon the claim that nonexemption would violate the First Amendment's free exercise clause; the second, on the claim that while exemption is not constitutionally mandated it is valid if accorded; the third, that exemption, if accorded, violates the establishment clause.

Tax Exemption

Exemption of churches and priests from taxation can be traced to biblical times. Scripture relates that after Joseph bought the Egyptians' lands for the food he had stored during the seven years of plenty, he "made it a law over the land of Egypt unto this day that Pharaoh should have the fifth part [of the produce]; except the land of the priests only, which became not Pharaoh's" (Genesis 47:26). Later, when Artaxerxes, king of Persia, authorized Ezra to levy a tax for the rebuilding of the Temple, he specifically directed that "touching any of the priests and Levites, singers, porters, nethinims, or ministers of the house of God, it shall not be lawful to impose toll, tribute, or custom, upon them" (Ezra 7:24). Exemption enjoyed by Christian churches goes back to the fourth century when Constantine, in the process of establishing Christianity as the state church of Rome, accorded this privilege to church buildings and to the land about them that was used for church purposes.

Thereafter, church exemption from taxation, as the exemption of priests from military service, became the norm in most countries, including England and its colonies. The practice continued uninterrupted in the United States after independence and the adoption of the Constitution and the First Amendment. Madison was certain of its unconstitutionality—even more than he was of the unconstitutionality of military chaplaincies. In his "Detached Memoranda" he cited (along with two bills he vetoed because he deemed them in violation of the establishment clause) an attempt in Kentucky to exempt houses of worship from taxes as another effort by ecclesiastical bodies to encroach upon the separation between religion and government.

In *Everson* v. *Board of Education* (1947) the Court spelled out the meaning of the establishment clause, and that decision appears to require a ruling that exemption is unconstitutional. The opinion in that case expressly forbids enactment of laws that "aid one religion [or] aid all religions." Exemption from uniform taxation appears to constitute such aid even though no funds are directly appropriated by the government to finance church activities. In countries in which all power rests in the sovereign, both taxation and exemption may be deemed incidents of sovereignty requiring no further justification. But our Constitution guarantees a republican form of government with powers limited to those necessary to effect the social contract between the government and the people. The purposes of that Constitution are expressly set forth in its preamble; they are to "establish justice, insure domestic tranquility, provide for the common defense [and] promote the general welfare." Both taxation and exemption must be justified as accomplishing these purposes. Section 8, Article I, expressly empowers Congress to impose and collect taxes in order—and only in order—to "provide for the common defense and general welfare of the United States." Churches, as all others, are benefited by the exercise of this power. Fairness and logic seem to require that they share, through taxation, the costs of financing such benefits as protection against crime, fire, and foreign enemies.

Efforts were made toward persuading the Supreme Court to pass judgment on the constitutionality of exemption, but it was not until the 1970 case of *Walz* v. *Tax Commission* that it accepted jurisdiction of a challenge by an objecting taxpayer. Three options were presented to the Court by the parties and *amici curiae* (friends of the court); it could rule that exemption was unconstitutional, permissible, or mandatory. Unconstitutionality was urged in Walz's brief and in the *amicus* brief submitted by the American Civil Liberties Union (ACLU). It was also originally urged in a brief *amicus* drafted by counsel for Americans United for Separation of Church and State (originally formed in 1948 under the name of Protestants and Other Americans United for Separation of Church and State in response to two events: the *Everson* decision upholding public financing of bus transportation to parochial schools, and President Truman's proposal to exchange ambassadors with the Vatican). Shortly before the case was to be argued, the decision makers in the organization directed counsel not merely to refrain from submitting a brief against exemption, but to prepare and submit one supporting it. One can only speculate as to what caused this complete turnaround; but it is a reasonable guess that the clergy and lay leaders in Protestant churches recognized that Protestants too enjoyed the benefits of tax exemption.

The argument in Walz's brief was based upon the mandate in *Everson* forbidding laws in aid of religion. The ACLU brief argued the same point, but also urged that to compel persons of one religion to subsidize churches of another through taxation, would violate the free exercise clause as well. In support of this, it cited Jefferson's *Virginia Statute for Religious Freedom*, which declared it sinful and tyrannical to compel a person to furnish contributions for the propagation of religious opinions that he disbelieves and abhors. The statute also declared it wrong to force a person to support a teacher of his own religious persuasion.

The free exercise clause was invoked in *amicus* briefs submitted independently by the National Council of Churches of Christ and the Synagogue Council of America, but only to reach a directly opposite conclusion. Their argument rested on the premise that the power to tax is the power to destroy, and since the free exercise clause forbids destroying churches, *ergo* it forbids taxing them. This argument is not without merit; imposition or enforcement of tax laws against unpopular sects or cults, such as Jehovah's Witnesses and Reverend Moon's Unification Church, was quite obviously motivated by an intent to destroy. Since the free exercise clause forbids destroying churches, it forbids taxing them. There is, however, a great difference between laws enacted and enforced uniformly and those aimed at particular unpopular faiths for the purpose of destroying or harassing them. Although the National Council of Churches, as well as the ACLU, later submitted or joined in *amicus* briefs in the tax evasion prosecution of Reverend Moon, neither the Synagogue Council nor any of its constituents were willing to go along.

In between the absolutist "may not" of the ACLU and the "must" of the National Council of Churches and the Synagogue Council was the position urged by the New York Tax Commission and in a brief *amici curiae* submitted by New York's attorney general in behalf of thirty-two state attorneys general. It did not argue that exemption was constitutionally mandated, but that it was constitutional to grant it. The *amicus* brief of the United States Catholic Conference took the same position.

At first glance, it is surprising that the states should take this position. No one who reads the newspapers can be unaware of the difficulties faced by the states and the federal government in attempting to balance their budgets through taxation, or of the never ending complaints by the people that they are being overtaxed. Were Walz to be successful in his suit, the legislatures would have been relieved to some extent of the unpleasant duty of taxing their constituents. While it would have been unwise for them to say openly to the Court, "for this relief much thanks," they could have mournfully placed the blame on the Supreme Court whose decision they had to honor whether they liked it or not. On the other hand, it was the function of state attorneys general to defend existing laws, and if a legislature deemed it financially necessary to tax churches, it could do so by repealing or modifying existing laws. In any event, the Court in *Walz* upheld religious exemptions, and only Justice Douglas dissented. (One can fairly speculate that were he alone the Supreme Court of the United States, he would have found some reason for ruling in favor of constitutionality.)

From the earliest days of our nation (Madison and the establishment clause notwithstanding), church exemption from taxation was an almost universally accepted part of our political system. It is fairly certain that the Supreme Court would not be rash enough to upset it. In upholding constitutionality, it went further than urged by some of the protagonists; it refused to base its decision on the "good deeds" argument, that is, that exemption is not really a forbidden subsidy of religious activities, but rather a recognition that many of the churches' activities (such as providing hospital care for the ill and homes for the aged or orphaned) relieve the taxpayers of burdens they would otherwise have to carry. Justifying exemption on the "good deeds" precept, the Court said, would require the state to become entangled in religious affairs in seeking to ascertain to what extent, if any, the budget of each church encompassed "good deeds." Such annual examination of the books and activities of churches would entail excessive governmental entanglement, and exemption could therefore be justified on that ground. Reliance upon excessive entanglement, rather than exclusively on precedent, was necessitated by the Court's protestation that "no one acquires a vested or protected right in violation of the Constitution by long use." This reliance seems not merely to justify but to impel exemption, reaching the result urged by the National Council of Churches and the Synagogue Council, although for a different reason. Exemption could logically be justified on the ground of excessive entanglement not merely for church properties used for worship but also for those used for commercial purposes. So long as all the income earned was used to practice or further religion, excessive entanglement would result from annual examination of books and activities.

In *Diffenderfer* v. *Central Baptist Church*, decided two years after *Walz*, the Court was offered an opportunity either to accept or reject that contention, but it elected to do neither. This was a taxpayer's suit challenging a Florida law which allowed exemption of all income earned by churches, including that from commercial enterprises. The Court accepted the taxpayers' appeal in the spring of 1972, and it was scheduled for argument after 1 October, when the Court resumed after the summer recess. Counsel for the taxpayer was provided by the ACLU, and in this case Americans United did decide to submit an *amicus* brief in support of the suit. During the summer, after the taxpayer's brief was served and filed, the Florida legislature amended the challenged statute so as to limit exemption to the extent that church property was used for religious purposes (in the *Diffenderfer* suit to the one day of the week in which the lot was used exclusively by persons attending religious services). When the appeal was called for argument, the Court dismissed it on the ground of mootness in that the plaintiffs had gotten what they wanted, and there was no longer a contested issue.

The *Diffenderfer* dismissal only postpones the day of decision, for legislatures in other states might elect not to discontinue exemption. The Court would have three options in passing upon the issue of constitutionality. First, it could decide what it refused to do in *Walz* and was unnecessary to do in *Diffenderfer*, that is rule that exemption is mandatory. Second, it might rule that while not constitutionally mandated, exemption is permissible. Finally, it might decide that at least with respect to income-producing properties, exemption is forbidden.

Support of the first alternative lies in the premise that governmental entanglement is an unseverable concomitant of taxation, and while the establishment clause does not forbid entanglement with museums and libraries, it does with churches and synagogues. Support could also be justified by acceptance of the argument rendered by the National Council of Churches and the Synagogue Council that taxation impairs the religious freedom guaranteed by the First Amendment. Were the Court to accept the entanglement argument for religiously owned commercial enterprises, the consequences would be aggravation of the serious financial burdens borne by many states and municipalities. Support for the second alternative— that exemption is permissible though not mandated—can be found in the *Everson* opinion. The Court went out of its way to note that it did "not mean to intimate that a state could not provide transportation only to children attending public schools," and thereafter consistently rejected appeals in suits by parents of parochial school children claiming that denial of secular auxiliary services, such as loans of textbooks or teaching equipment, violated their constitutional rights. Finally, the Court could decide, as it was asked to do in *Diffenderfer*, that exemption is not constitutionally permissible for income earned from secular profit-making enterprises engaged in by churches.

Military Service

Exemption of priests from compulsory military service can be traced back to biblical times. When Moses was commanded by God to number all the children of Israel that were "able to go forth to war," the Levites were not to be among them (Numbers 1:3, 5-15). The pragmatic reason for the exemption is found in 20:2-4.

> and it shall be, when ye are come nigh unto the battle, that the priests shall approach and speak unto the people, and shall say unto them, Hear, O Israel, ye approach this day into battle against your enemies; let not your hearts faint, fear not, and do not tremble, neither be ye terrified because of them; for the Lord God is he that goeth forth with you, to fight for you against your enemies, to save you.

Such exemption of priests from military service, emulated at least throughout western civilization, would seem to be constitutionally unacceptable in the United States. It accords religion a privilege not shared by other callings, preferring religion over nonreligion in violation of the establishment clause as interpreted in *Everson* v. *Board of Education* (1947). It also seems to violate the equal protection clause of the Fourteenth Amendment held applicable to the federal government through the due process clause of the Fifth Amendment.

The Supreme Court deemed such a contention so lacking in merit as not to warrant serious consideration. In the 1918 *Selective Draft Law* cases it said:

> We pass without anything but statement the proposition that an establishment of religion or an interference with free exercise thereof repugnant to the First Amendment resulted from the exemption clauses of the [Selective Service] Act to which we at the outset, referred because we think its unsoundness is too apparent to require us to do more.

The question of constitutionality merited more serious attention. The Court said in *Ex parte Milligan* (in ruling unconstitutional the trial of a civilian by a military court during the Civil War):

> The Constitution of the United States is a law for rulers and for people, equally in war and in peace, and covers with the shield of its protection all classes of man, at all times, and under all circumstances. No doctrine involving more pernicious consequences was ever invented by the wit of man than that any of its provisions can be suspended during any of the great exigencies of government.

The exemption accorded by the Selective Draft Law to "regular or duly ordained ministers of religion" was unconditional; unlike that granted to conscientious objectors, it did not empower the president to require them to engage in noncombatant services. This seems odd unless one considers what, I suggest, is the most likely basis for exemption. As the quotation from Numbers indicates, priests can be far more valuable to the nation's military effort by encouraging others to fight than by themselves fighting. There is an implicit quid pro quo understanding between church and state: exemption from service at the front in exchange for the spiritual encouragement of others to serve.

Not all ministers of religion have acceded to this agreement. Throughout our history there have been uncompromising pacifists among them who not only refused to encourage enlistment in the armed forces but urged others not to enlist and even to refuse to serve if drafted. On the whole, religion has been faithful to the bargain. In the eighteenth century, ministers, primarily Congregationalists, preached for the revolution, while their Anglican counterparts preached to the contrary. In the nineteenth century, the Presbyterian Church split because of the opposite position taken by northern and southern ministers with respect to the Civil War; while in the twentieth century, American ministers assured their congregants that "God is with us," while their counterparts in Germany were preaching *"Gott mit uns."* This function of ministers of religion is vividly illustrated in this item from the 1 May 1967 issue of the Jewish Telegraph Agency *Daily News Bulletins*:

> A U.S. Army private (Levy) who embarked on a "death fast" because he claimed his religious conviction as an Orthodox Jew prevented him from serving "an army practicing violence" in Viet Nam has been taken into custody and confined in a mental ward at Madigan General Hospital, Tacoma, Wash., military authorities revealed today . . . . Defense Department officials disclosed that the Army is trying to get rabbis to convince Levy that the war is righteous and his fast unjustified.

The government rewards ministers of religion who forgo their exemption and become military chaplains. The monetary compensation they receive, including living expenses, probably exceeds in most cases what they would have earned outside the military (although of course, they undertake risks not shared by nonmilitary clergymen). In addition, they are given the rank, pay, and retirement benefits granted to military officers.

Measured by the standards later declared by the Supreme Court, constitutionality seems less certain than was assumed in the opinion in the *Selective Draft Law* cases. Madison, who drafted the First Amendment, was not so certain. In his "Detached Memoranda" he expressed the view that "the appointment of chaplains to the two houses of Congress [was not] consistent with the Constitution, and with the pure principle of religious freedom." He recognized that in the case of "navies with insulated crews," salaried chaplaincies might be justified, but "not entirely so." "[We] are always to keep in mind," he said, "that it is safer to trust the consequences of a right principle than reasonings in the support of a bad one." At the time Madison wrote this, the two conflicts in which the nation was engaged were within its borders, and soldiers could have access to the spiritual services of civil clergymen. Today, this is not the case; the wars in which we have been engaged since the *Selective Draft Law* cases have been on foreign soil, and the soldiers were "insulated" from access to spiritual help and comfort. While the chaplaincies can perhaps make better soldiers of enlisted men, that is not their only function. They do often provide desperately needed comfort to millions of young Americans forcefully removed from their family churches to fight on foreign soil thousands of miles away. As Justice Stewart said in his dissenting opinion in *Abington School District v. Schempp* (1963), "a lonely soldier stationed at some far-away outpost could surely complain that a government which did *not* provide him the opportunity for pastoral guidance was affirmatively prohibiting the free exercise of his religion."

The selective service cases were decided before the borders of permissible governmental action on religion were spelled out in *Everson* and later decisions. Constitutionality with respect to both exemption of ministers from compulsory armed services and their employment as salaried chaplains is no longer in doubt. Evidence of this can be found in the 1983 decision in *Marsh v. Chambers* in which the Supreme Court upheld the constitutionality of employing paid chaplains to open legislative sessions with prayer on the sole ground that it was an accepted practice outdating the adoption of the First Amendment, and it continued uninterruptedly thereafter, clearly testifying to its validity. One is reminded of Justice Jackson's reference in his dissenting opinion in *Everson* to Julia who according to Byron's reports, "whispering 'I will n'er consent,' consented." The Court's reasoning is even more pertinent to military chaplaincies. Even Madison recognized that they might present a stronger claim to constitutionality than legislative chaplaincies.

Congress may discontinue military chaplaincies if it sees fit; its ruling in the selective service cases is still the law of the land. Clergymen may constitutionally be required to serve as soldiers in the armed forces since there are no constitutional limitations upon the power of the nation to defend itself from foreign enemies. Although religious exemption of clergy from military service is not mandatory, it is constitutionally permissible, and the same is true of their employment as military chaplains.

Fair Labor Practices

In *National Labor Relations Board (NLRB)* v. *Catholic Bishop of Chicago, Inc.* (1979) the Court was faced with deciding whether NLRB's exercise of jurisdiction with respect to demands by a union representing lay teachers in a parochial school would violate the religion clauses of the First Amendment. The problem was of recent origin. For the greater part of their history parochial school teachers were either priests or sisters, required by solemn oath to obey their church superiors in the performance of relevant duties. Because of Catholic proscription of contraceptive birth control and the tradition of giving at least one child to the church, there was no shortage of teachers. However, in the post-World War II period, many Catholics followed the mores of non-Catholics in limiting families through contraception. So sharp has the decline in church vocations become since the 1960s that, as reported in the *Wall Street Journal* of 10 October 1983, many bishops have found it necessary to accept applicants as old as seventy years for admission to seminaries in preparation for ordination. The resulting shortage of teaching brothers and sisters has also compelled the Church to employ lay teachers, most of whom have families to support. The Supreme Court's decisions barring use of tax-raised funds to finance parochial schools have impelled administrators of religious schools to offer salaries lower than those in the public schools. The result has been the increasing unionization of teachers and demands for collective bargaining. Rejection of these demands often resulted in proceedings before the NLRB under the National Labor Relations Act, and these were challenged by the church as violations of both the establishment and free exercise clauses.

The Court could have met the challenge to NLRB's assertion to jurisdiction in one of three ways: it could have ruled jurisdiction to be constitutionally forbidden, or permissive or affirmatively mandated. In support of the first alternative, the Court could have relied upon the principle first expressed in the *Walz* case that excessive entanglement in church affairs violated the establishment clause. It could have held that restrictions upon a church school's discretion in choosing faculty or in prescribing terms of employment infringed upon free exercise of religion. The Court could have cited support in the case of *In re Jenison* which held it a violation of the free exercise clause to punish a woman who refused to serve on a jury because the Bible commanded "Judge not that ye be not judged." In support of the second alternative, the Court could have relied upon the progeny of the *Everson* decision. In those cases the Court ruled that while state financing of transportation to parochial schools did not violate the establishment clause, refusal to finance did not violate either the establishment or free enterprise clause. By similar reasoning the Court could have ruled (as indeed the NLRB did) that while extending jurisdiction to parochial schools was not mandatory, it was nevertheless permissible. Finally, the Court could have held, as the minority in the *NLRB* case suggested, that inclusion of parochial schools was affirmatively mandated. The Court could have relied upon its decision in *Associated Press* v. *NLRB*, which rejected a challenge of unconstitutionality under the free press clause of the First Amendment. In light of that decision, rejection of NLRB jurisdiction in the present case would have violated the equal protection clause as incorporated into the Fifth Amendment.

The Court's majority selected none of these alternatives. Instead, it resorted to a rule traced back to John Marshall: where a statute can reasonably be interpreted in a way that does not require determination of constitutionality or unconstitutionality, this means of avoidance should be used. Since, in the present case, there was no express inclusion of church schools in the National Labor Relations Act, the Court would interpret it as excluding NLRB jurisdiction, until such time as Congress saw fit to expressly confer jurisdiction.

The Court's effort to avoid ruling on the constitutional issue may prove to be futile. Either in Congress or in some state legislature, labor union influence may be sufficient to impel the amendment of labor relations laws to do what the NLRB wanted, to authorize its acceptance of jurisdiction in controversies involving parochial school teachers. In such cases, it would be difficult for the Court to avoid deciding the issue of constitutionality.

Eligibility for Public Office

The Supreme Court decision in *McDaniel v. Paty* (1978) reflects the converse of the other decisions. The issue in this case was not the constitutionality of excluding clergymen or churches from obligations imposed upon others—such as taxation, military service, and collective bargaining—but of depriving them of rights universally enjoyed by nonclergymen, specifically, the right to be elected to public office.

The generation that adopted our Constitution was influenced by a strong wave of anticlericalism coming mostly from revolutionary France toward the end of the eighteenth century. An aversion to church involvement in the nonreligious arena prevailed. It was manifested in the last will and testament of Stephen Girard, who migrated from France shortly before the 1789 revolution and became quite wealthy in the United States. He bequeathed his estate for the purpose of establishing a school for orphans but added a proviso "that no ecclesiastic, missionary or minister of any sect whatsoever shall ever hold or exercise any station or duty whatever in the said college; nor shall any such person ever be admitted for any purpose, or as a visitor, within the premises appropriated to the purposes of said college." In *Vidal v. Girard's Executor* (1844) the Supreme Court upheld the validity of the will. Article VI of the Constitution forbids religious tests for public office, and thus prohibits exclusion of clergymen from eligibility for federal office. The states were not bound by Article VI, and, at the time the Constitution was adopted, a majority of them disqualified ministers from legislative office. Later, six new states, including Tennessee, followed suit. Over the years, these state constitutional or statutory provisions were repealed, abandoned or held unconstitutional by state courts. Not so in Tennessee, with the result that the United States Supreme Court found it necessary in the *McDaniel* case to determine the issue of constitutionality.

Considering the mandatory/permissible/forbidden trilogy, one should not assume that exclusion of clergymen from eligibility for state legislature service is not constitutionally permissible: indeed, it may even be mandatory. In 1778, no less a champion of religious liberty than Thomas Jefferson, the author of the *Virginia Statute for Religious Freedom*, drafted for that state a constitution that expressly barred ministers of the Gospel from holding political office. He did this because he believed that exclusion was required by the principle of church-state separation. It was only Madison's persuasive argument that exclusion would violate the principle of religious freedom that moved him to change his mind.

By the time the *McDaniel* case reached the Supreme Court there hardly seemed to be any question of how it would be decided. Surprisingly, while all the justices deemed the Tennessee law unconstitutional, the chief justice, who wrote the plurality opinion, could not muster a majority to agree on the reasoning to justify unconstitutionality. To him the provision violated the free exercise clause, but perhaps not necessarily the establishment clause. Justice Brennan, supported by Justice Marshall and in part by Justice Stewart, deemed it in violation of both clauses, while Justice White urged that invalidation should not be based on either clause but rather upon the Fourteenth Amendment's equal protection mandate, and Justice

Blackmun did not participate at all. Whatever the reason, all participating justices judged the Tennessee law to be within the forbidden area.

Educational Standards for Church Schools

Ever since the constitutional right to establish church schools was determined by the Court's ruling in *Pierce* v. *Society of Sisters* (1925), numerous questions have arisen concerning the states' power to regulate curriculum content, teachers' qualifications, or pupil eligibility in nonpublic schools. Many, perhaps most, states exclude from tax exemption schools which, even for religious reasons, discriminate on the basis of race (as in the *Bob Jones* case). The schools have, of course, constitutionally protected rights to require prayer, devotional Bible reading, or religious instruction; but can they be required to comply with minimum curriculum standards? Can imposed standards encompass inoculation against contagious diseases or the teaching of medical treatment for diseases, especially for those that are contagious? Can the schools bar the teaching of evolution and substitute Genesis-based creationism? In all these and many other instances, our courts, and ultimately the Supreme Court, must determine what is mandatory, what is permissible and what is forbidden.

9

The Supreme Court Redefines
Tax Exemption

Dean M. Kelley

One of the most intensely awaited decisions of the United States Supreme Court in recent years was announced on 24 May 1983: *Bob Jones University* v. *United States*. The case was controversial when it posed the question of whether private schools engaging in racial discrimination for religious reasons could be denied tax exemption. When the Reagan administration on 8 January 1982 sought to void the case as moot by restoring tax exemption to all private schools that had lost it because of discrimination, it became a *cause celèbre* overnight, and the controversy escalated several decibel levels.

The administration, which contended that Congress had never authorized withdrawal of tax exemption from schools for racial discrimination, quickly introduced legislation in Congress to give such authorization, and—assisted by a lower court order forbidding it to restore any exemptions—agreed to preserve the status quo until Congress had a chance to act. Meanwhile, the Supreme Court invited a black attorney, William T. Coleman, Jr., to argue as *amicus curiae* (friend of the court) the position the United States government had abandoned. Although the government had conceded the controversy, the Court reinstated it and called in a surrogate. The case was argued on 12 October 1982, with William B. Ball, a Roman Catholic attorney who specializes in religious liberty cases, arguing for Bob Jones University and Coleman arguing for the position relinquished by the government. By 24 May, *Bob Jones University* was the oldest outstanding case still unannounced, and some thought the Court might leave it until the end of the session, as it sometimes does with controversial cases.

On 23 May 1983, the Court handed down a decision in another case involving tax exemption that suggested the resolution of *Bob Jones University*. In *Regan* v. *Taxation with Representation*, a unanimous Court reversed the District of Columbia Circuit Court, which had struck down as unconstitutional the main section, 501(c)(3), of the tax code providing exemption for organizations whose purposes are "religious, charitable, scientific, testing for public safety, literary, education." An organization seeking exemption—Taxation with Representation (TWR)—had been denied by the Internal Revenue Service (IRS) because it had announced its intention to engage in substantial lobbying, an activity prohibited by the relevant section.

TWR contended that to make tax exemption conditional upon abandoning the right to "assemble and petition Congress for redress of grievances" was unconstitutional under several of the Court's earlier decisions. The circuit court maintained that Congress could place such a limitation on tax exemption if it wished. The circuit court declared Section 501 (c) (3) unconstitutional for another reason: its effect is to grant not only exemption but deductibility of contributions to organizations that meet its requirements. Another part of the same section, 501 (c) (19), permits veterans' organizations to engage in lobbying without losing deductibility of contributions, and therefore violates the equal protection component of the due process clause of the Fifth Amendment. The section does not treat similarly situated parties alike, but benefits one and not the other.

The Supreme Court unanimously reversed the circuit court decision in an opinion written by Justice Rehnquist, with arguments that foreshadowed how the Court was likely to rule on *Bob Jones University*. Projecting a pattern ominous for churches and other exempt organizations, the Court asserted:

> Both tax exemptions and tax-deductibility are a form of *subsidy* that is administered through the tax system. A tax exemption has much the same effect as a *cash grant* to the organization of the amount of tax it would have to pay on its income. Deductible contributions are similar to *cash grants* of the amount of a portion of the individual's contributions. The system Congress has enacted provides this kind of *subsidy* to nonprofit civil welfare organizations generally, and an additional *subsidy* to those charitable organizations that do not engage in substantial lobbying. In short, Congress chose not to *subsidize* lobbying as extensively as it chose to *subsidize* other activities that non profit organizations undertake to promote the public welfare. [emphasis added]

The Court observed that TWR's freedom of speech was not impaired by the limitations in Section 501 (c) (3). It could always set up a subsidiary to do its lobbying, as described in Section (501) (c) (4), so long as it did not use deductible contributions for that purpose. In any event, Congress is not obliged to "subsidize" TWR's freedom of speech:

> The issue in this case is not whether TWR must be permitted to lobby, but whether Congress is required to provide it with public money with which to lobby . . . we hold that it is not.

If tax exemption is not a subsidy, what is it? There is a significant body of opinion led by Boris Bittker of the Yale Law School, author of *Federal Taxation of Income, Estates and Gifts*, and Peter Swords of the Columbia Law School, author of *Charitable Real Property Tax Exemptions in New York State*. They insist that tax exemptions (at least the traditional non-profit and/or charitable exemptions) are not subsidies because the exempted bodies are simply not part of the tax base; they do not produce wealth, and their members already contribute their fair share of the costs of the commonwealth. They should not be taxed again for constructive activities from which they derive no personal pecuniary gain. That view was not the Court's in its current decision (except for intimations in Justice Powell's opinion), though it was clearly expressed with respect to churches in the Court's opinion in *Walz* v. *Tax Commission* (1970).

Given the unanimous acceptance by the Court of the idea that tax exemption is a subsidy, it seemed predictable that the Court would not approve what it considers a "subsidization" of racial discrimination to allow Bob Jones University and Goldsboro Christian Schools to be tax exempt. On 24 May 1983, the Court delivered its decision in that case, holding 8-1 that racially discriminatory schools—even religiously motivated ones—are not tax exempt.

In an opinion written by the chief justice, the Supreme Court gave a ringing repudiation to the administration's effort to roll back the IRS policy of denying tax exemption to racially discriminatory private schools. With an unusual solidarity reminiscent of *Brown* v. *Board of Education* (1954) and other historic desegregation decisions, the Court repaired what many viewed as a gradual erosion in the nation's commitment to the elimination of racial discrimination. In so doing, it ratified the full force of *Green* v. *Connally*, which had determined that nonreligious private schools discriminating on the basis of race could not be tax exempt. This was affirmed (under the name of *Coit* v. *Green*) in 1971 by a mere *per curiam* decision, and later slighted in a footnote in *Bob Jones University* v. *Simon* (1974) by a characterization of it as lacking "the precedential weight of a case involving a truly adversary controversy." The government had abandoned its view on the way to the Supreme Court and joined the defendant's position (reminiscent of the current case, only in the opposite direction).

The Court also resoundingly rejected the administration's contention that the IRS did not have congressional authorization for its policy of refusing tax exemption to private schools that discriminate. Congress had had a dozen years in which to amend the IRS's policy adopted as a result of *Green v. Connally,* said the Court, but had not moved to change it, and this "failure of Congress to modify the IRS rulings . . . make out an unusually strong case of legislative acquiescence in and ratification by implication of the 1970 and 1971 rulings." The Court added:

> During the past 12 years there have been no fewer than 13 bills introduced to overturn the IRS interpretation of §501 (c) (3). Not one of these bills has emerged from any committee. . . . Congress' failure to act on the bills proposed on this subject provides added support for concluding that Congress acquiesced in the IRS rulings. . . .

The Court concluded with reference to Section 501 (i) of the Internal Revenue Code (added by Congress in 1976 to prohibit tax exemption for discriminatory social clubs and with accompanying House and Senate reports referring to *Green v. Connally,* and remarking that "discrimination on account of race is inconsistent with an educational institution's tax exempt status").

All of this evidence persuaded the Court that Congress had in effect approved the IRS policy being contested in the current case. They did not persuade Justice Rehnquist, the lone dissenter, who trenchantly observed:

> In approaching this statutory construction question the Court quite adeptly avoids the statute it is construing. This I am sure is no accident, for there is nothing in the language of § 501 (c) (3) that supports the result obtained by the Court. . . .

> Perhaps recognizing the lack of support in the statute itself, or in its history, for the IRS change in interpretation. . . . the Court relies first on several bills introduced to overturn the IRS interpretation of § 501 (c) (3). . . . But we have said before, and it is equally applicable here, that this type of congressional inaction is of virtually no weight in determining legislative intent. . . .

> The Court next asserts [that Congress acted to ratify the IRS policy] "when it enacted the present § 501 (i) of the Code. . . ." Quite to the contrary, it seems to me that in § 501 (i) Congress showed that when it wants to add a requirement prohibiting racial discrimination to one of the tax-benefit provisions, it is fully aware of how to do it. . . .

> This court continuously has been hesitant to find ratification through inaction. . . . this Court has no business finding that Congress has adopted the new IRS position by failing to enact legislation to reverse it.

Occasionally in its history the Supreme Court has resolved difficult questions by resorting to discreet fictions, and this is evidently one such instance. Justice Rehnquist is correct that there is no supportive statutory language. The Court's majority did not contend otherwise, but contented itself with such phrases as "acquiescence" and "ratification by implication." Contrary to its frequent reluctance to impute nonenacted intentions to Congress, the Court did so in this instance.

In deciding for one adversary and against another, the Court often makes significant trade-offs, and sometimes the interests it rejects prove to be as significant in the long run as those it favors. In *Scott v. Sandford* (the Dred Scott decision of 1857, which held that Congress had no power to prohibit slavery in federal territories), the Court may have thought it was deciding for social stability, but its choice contributed to the precipitation of a bloody civil war. In the *Bob Jones University* case, the Court made a choice—the opposite kind of choice from that made in *Scott* or in *Plessy v. Ferguson* (which approved "separate but equal" accommodations for different races). It may help to correct the legacy of racial injustice that earlier decisions allowed. It may also contain significant trade-offs that will cause future problems for other important interests.

A worrisome aspect of the present case is the slippage in the doctrine of "unconstitutional conditions." The Court has long held that, even though the Constitution does not give anyone a right to a government job, unemployment compensation, welfare benefits, or tax exemption, once such benefits have been offered, the government cannot withdraw or withhold them from persons exercising a right guaranteed by the Constitution. Residence requirements for welfare are thus unconstitutional because they burden the constitutionally guaranteed right to travel (*Shapiro v. Thompson* 1969). A woman whose religion forbade her to work on Saturday could not be denied unemployment compensation because she refused to take jobs that entailed such work (*Sherbert v. Verner* 1963). In the current cases, the petitioners are required to choose between tax exemption and freedom of religion (or freedom of speech in *TWR*). In *Bob Jones University*, the Court admitted that "denial of tax benefits will inevitably have a substantial impact on the operation of private religious schools," then went on to reassure them, "but will not prevent those schools from observing their religious tenets." It may not prevent them, but it certainly will burden them—in a way and to an extent much greater than Mrs. Sherbert would have suffered for her Seventh-Day Adventist convictions had the Court allowed the state of South Carolina to impose a choice on her.

Taxation with Representation was reassured by the Court that it was not losing "any independent benefit" for exercising its freedom of speech by lobbying. It could always set up a subsidiary to do its lobbying with nondeductible funds. Thus the only thing it had to lose for freedom of speech was deductibility of contributions; it had to choose between deductibility and attempting to address its concerns to Congress, a right guaranteed by the First Amendment. Justice Rehnquist explained:

> Congress has merely refused to pay for the lobbying out of public monies. This Court has never held that Congress must grant a benefit such as TWR claims here to a person who wishes to exercise a constitutional right.

If one starts with the assumption that tax exemption is a government grant, then the Court's holding is logically consistent with its recent decision that poor women can be denied Medicaid payments for abortions. While they have a Constitutional right to abortion, Congress does not have to finance the exercise of that right (*Harris* v. *McRae* 1980).

If tax exemption were not viewed as a grant or a subsidy, then there would not be any reason to withhold or withdraw it to avoid "subsidizing" lobbying or racial discrimination. It is a benefit. Permitting it to be conditional upon the abandonment of freedom of religion or freedom of speech is a retreat from the Court's important opposition to "unconstitutional conditions." If the Court continues to say that people can be compelled to choose between tax exemption and the exercise of constitutional rights, everyone will be poorer.

Another significant aspect of the *Bob Jones University* decision is its endorsement of the IRS's grafting onto Section 501 (c) (3) the criteria of charitable trusts. The Court quoted from its opinions of 1861 and 1878 on charitable trusts to show that they have always been required to serve a public purpose and not violate public policy. No one disputes that. The tricky part is linking the law of charitable trusts with the basic exemption statute, which does not explicitly require all exempt entities to be charities. To be sure, "charitable" is one of the purposes eligible for exemption, but so is "religious." Must "religious" organizations also be "charitable"? The Court now says they do because that's what Congress intended, since it allows contributors to exempt organizations to deduct their gifts as "charitable contributions," under Section 170 of the Code, which the Court contends "explains" the charitable character of all Section 501 (c) (3) organizations. Again, Justice Rehnquist was not convinced:

> The Court seizes the words "charitable contribution" and with little discussion concludes that "[o]n its face, therefore, §170 reveals that Congress' intention was to provide tax benefits to organizations serving charitable purposes," intimating that this implies some unspecified common law charitable trust requirement. . . . Plainly §170 simply tracks the requirements set forth in §501 (c) (3). Since §170 is no more than a mirror of §501 (c) (3) and, as the Court points out, §170 followed §501 (c) (3) by more than two decades . . . , it is at best of little usefulness in finding the meaning of §501 (c) (3).

Instead, Justice Rehnquist insisted that Congress has already listed in Section 501 (c) (3) the qualities required of organizations exempt under it, and the Court is not entitled to add others.

What difference does it make? The justification for denying tax exemption to Bob Jones University is that it is violating public policy by engaging in racial discrimination, contrary to the law of charities. If the law of charities was never attached to Section 501 (c) (3) by Congress, then it is not a proper condition of tax exemption. Here again the Court resorted to the elaborate fiction that Congress intended to require such organizations to serve a public purpose, and not violate public policy. Justice Powell, who concurred in the Court's judgment and in part of its opinion, was troubled by the implications of this conclusion:

> With all respect, I am unconvinced that the critical question in determining tax-exempt status is whether an organization provides a clear "public benefit" as defined by the Court. Over 106,000 organizations filed §501 (c) (3) returns in 1981. . . . I find it impossible to believe that all or even most of those organizations could prove that they "demonstrably serve and [are] in harmony with the public interest," or that they are "beneficial and stabilizing influences in community life. . . ."
>
> Even more troubling to me is the element of conformity that appears to inform the Court's analysis. . . . Taken together these passages suggest that the primary function of a tax-exempt organization is to act on behalf of the Government in carrying out governmentally approved policies. In my opinion, such a view . . . ignores the important role played by tax exemptions in encouraging diverse, indeed often sharply conflicting, activities and viewpoints. . . . Far from representing an effort to reinforce any perceived "common community conscience," the provision of tax exemptions to nonprofit groups is one indispensable means of limiting the influence of governmental orthodoxy on important areas of community life. . . .
>
> I am unwilling to join any suggestion that the Internal Revenue Service is invested with authority to decide which public policies are sufficiently "fundamental" to require denials of tax exemptions.

The Court responded to Justice Powell's concern by adding footnote 23, which denies that the Court is permitting the IRS to make such determinations. Not everyone will be totally reassured by a footnote. Given several earlier attempts by the IRS to impose on other groups the "violation of public policy" criterion as a basis for denial of tax exemption (e.g., *Church of Scientology of California* v. *United States* 1980), it is conceivable that it might attempt to use that weapon to keep other unconventional or dissident groups in line.

Most troubling, none of the justices was disturbed by the Court's First Amendment analysis. The court casually disposed of claims to religious liberty by asserting that the petitioner can still practice "religious tenets"— without a tax exemption—and by pointing out that the free exercise of religion can be burdened if it is "essential to accomplish an overriding governmental interest." The Court announced that the governmental interest in eliminating racial discrimination is compelling and that it can be served in no other way ("no less restrictive means . . . are available to achieve the governmental interest"), even though there are few intensely religious schools such as Bob Jones University and not too many black people clamoring to attend them. The specter of the proliferation of "segregation academies" professing to be "for whites only" because of religious convictions, inhibited the Court from seeking any "less restrictive means" of eliminating racial discrimination in education.

In an effort to delimit the scope of its decision, the Court clearly confined it to education. Without weighing the trial court's findings that Bob Jones University is more a religious than an educational institution, the Court treated it as an educational institution. In footnote 29, the Court stated:

> We deal here only with religious *schools*—not with churches or other purely religious institutions; here, the governmental interest is in denying public support to racial discrimination in education.[emphasis in original]

This suggests that the Court may be moving toward a separate category of tax exemptions for churches, reflected in its statement in *Walz* v. *Tax Commission* (upholding property tax exemption of churches):

> Obviously a direct money subsidy would be a relationship pregnant with involvement . . . , but that is not this case. . . . The government does not transfer part of its revenue to churches but simply abstains from demanding that the church support the state.

It is true that there are various kinds of tax exemptions, including "incentive" exemptions intended by the legislature to subsidize certain behavior—such as housing renovation—that it wishes to encourage. Perhaps within Section 501 (c) (3) there are exemptions to which the decisions on *Bob Jones University* and *Taxation with Representation* apply more than to others. Insofar as the quid pro quo rationale for tax exemption (that it benefits nonprofit organizations providing services to the community that the government would otherwise have to provide) does not apply to churches, since government cannot constitutionally provide religious services (except perhaps in prisons and military outposts), then tax exemptions of churches may be of a constitutionally different character than exemptions of other organizations. The Court has not explicitly said so, and there is some danger that a footnote is a weak barrier to the seepage of the Court's logic to all exempt organizations, including churches.

How many churches will be disposed to risk their tax exemptions by violating public policy by counseling young people to refuse to register for the draft, by giving sanctuary to refuge seekers from El Salvador, by engaging in secondary boycotts against banks doing business with South Africa, or by otherwise dissenting from an incumbent administration's ideas of proper conduct? There is also the possibility that the IRS will be under some pressure to deny tax exemption to churches that discriminate against women in the clergy. Will the Supreme Court consider that such discrimination is also contrary to public policy and uphold the denial of tax exemption? If, as all of the justices seem uncritically to assume, tax exemption is a subsidy, then eventually may the Court not be likely to conclude that churches are not entitled to it at all?

What can be done by churches and other nonprofit organizations that wish to attempt to influence legislation? A suggestion was offered by Justice Blackmun in a concurring opinion in *Regan* v. *TWR*, joined by Justices Brennan and Marshall. He observed:

> Because lobbying is protected by the First Amendment . . . , §501 (c) (3) therefore denies a significant benefit to organizations choosing to exercise their constitutional rights. The constitutional defect that would inhere in §501 (c) (3) alone is avoided by §501 (c) (4).

Blackmun described how a Section 501 (c) (3) organization may create a §501 (c) (4) affiliate to carry on lobbying activities, the distinction being that the latter may not use deductible funds. At times in the past, when that has been done, the two organizations have drifted apart, as did the National Association for the Advancement of Colored People (NAACP) and the NAACP Legal Defense Fund, Inc., so this has not been a promising solution to the lobbying problem. Justice Blackmun insisted that the IRS must permit the main organization to exercise complete control over its affiliate, merely keeping their deductible and nondeductible finances separate. That is the only policy that will save the constitutionality of Section 501 (c) (3):

> Should the IRS attempt to limit the control these organizations exercise over the lobbying of their §501 (c) (4) affiliates, the First Amendment problems would be insurmountable. It hardly answers one person's objection to a restriction on his speech that another person, outside his control, may speak for him. . . . In my view, any such restriction [on control of the affiliate] would render the statutory scheme unconstitutional.

Should churches and other organizations claiming exemption set up wholly owned and controlled subsidiaries to do their lobbying, financed by nondeductible funds? That seems to be the prudent course, but churches have long resisted bifurcating their mission into what might be viewed as "high road" and "low road" branches. That might reinforce the all-too-prevalent notion that something is inferior or not quite nice about mixing in politics. Churches have been trying to upgrade the political realm as an important arena of God's action in history, and they will be reluctant to downgrade it.

What other option is there? One possibility is to proceed on the tenuous assumption that churches are legally a unique entity under the religion clauses of the First Amendment: they have been speaking and acting on moral issues that affect the well-being of society since before there was a United States, a Constitution, or a First Amendment; it is their duty to God, their faith, the nation, and the world, to continue to do so to the best of their ability, with or without deductibility or tax exemption. They may take a little encouragement from the possibility that the Supreme Court may be treating churches as a unique category of exemptions.

Churches have survived under many different political systems and tax structures, and they will continue to do so. More vulnerable will be the many nonprofit citizens' organizations of which Justice Powell spoke. Even if they set up a lobbying subsidiary and find nondeductible funds to run it, they will be anxious not to lose their exemption for offending against the "public policy" of the moment. They will thus fail in their important function to help formulate the public policy of the future rather than merely to conform to the public policy of the present. Then democracy will be weaker than it otherwise would and should have been, as the result of a trade-off in the never ending tension between justice and freedom.

10

Civil Rights, Indian Rites

Robert S. Michaelsen

Religious freedom is a fundamental right in America. The urgency of the Founding Fathers' concern to protect it is seen in that it is the first among the rights guaranteed in the Bill of Rights. The First Amendment to the United States Constitution begins: "Congress shall make no law respecting an establishment of religion or prohibiting the free exercise thereof. . . ." However, freedom of religion was actively denied to American Indians for a century and a half following the ratification of the Bill of Rights. Only in recent years has the government given attention to the subject. In 1968 and again in 1978 the United States Congress formally acknowledged that the constitutional guarantee of religious freedom extends to American Indians. Encouraging as this might be, however, American Indians still experience difficulties in freely practicing their religions.

In 1968 the United States Congress extended many of the provisions of the Bill of Rights and the Civil Rights Act to Indians living under tribal jurisdiction. The "Indian Bill of Rights" formally protects Indians from tribal interference in their religion. While this act marked an advance of sorts, Indian tribes are scarcely the most formidable obstacles to the free exercise of religion by Indians. The chief culprit is the United States government itself. Congressional recognition of this fact gave rise to the passage of the American Indian Religious Freedom Act (AIRFA) in 1978.

The American Indian Religious Freedom Act

The AIRFA affirms that religious freedom is "an inherent right" for all people; it also recognizes that religious practices form the basis of Indian identity and value systems and hence are integral to Indian life. The heart of the act is a congressional resolve: "that henceforth it shall be the policy of the United States to protect and preserve for American Indians their inherent right of freedom to believe, express, and exercise [their] traditional religions . . ., including, but not limited to access to sites, use and possession of sacred objects, and freedom to worship through ceremonials and traditional rites."

Congressional hearings and other governmental consultations held in connection with AIRFA revealed the nature and extent of the abridgment of Indian religious freedom by governmental agencies. An impressive list of details is given in a twenty-nine-page appendix to the Department of the Interior's *American Indian Religious Freedom Act Report* (1979) under the headings of land, cemeteries, sacred objects, border crossings, museums, and ceremonies. Following are some examples.

Sacred sites have been destroyed by governmental action. Cherokee burial grounds in the Little Tennessee Valley were flooded by the completion of the Tellico Dam. Sites regarded by the Navaho as sacred, and even as deities, were inundated by the impoundment of Lake Powell. According to Navaho belief, the deities were drowned by this action. Sacred sites have also been desecrated, and access to sites has been denied or severely limited. Hopi and Navaho have persistently protested that the erection and proposed expansion of ski resort facilities on sacred sites in governmentally owned areas of the San Francisco Peaks in northcentral Arizona not only interferes with their religious practices—many of which entail secrecy— but also destroys the sanctity of the sites.

Federal legislation designed to preserve wilderness areas and to protect endangered species sometimes adversely affects important Indian religious practices by preventing access to sacred sites and objects. Congress sought to rectify this situation through AIRFA. Nevertheless, government agents continue to have or to create problems concerning Indian access to sacred objects such as bald eagles and bald eagle feathers. The full list of complaints continues. For example, the sacredness of medicine bundles has been repeatedly violated by the probing of customs officials, and Indian remains have been removed from sacred ground for public display in museums.

The implementation of AIRFA relative to these and similar complaints has been disappointing. While AIRFA contains praiseworthy affirmations, it is basically a toothless resolution. It calls upon federal agencies to reform but provides no way of assuring that reform results. The implementation section of the act called upon the president to direct the relevant federal agencies "to evaluate their policies and procedures in consultation with native traditional religious leaders in order to determine appropriate changes necessary to protect and preserve Native American religious cultural rights and practices." Results of these evaluations were to be reported to the Congress within a twelve-month period along with a report on administrative changes made and a list of recommendations for possible legislative action.

Under the chairmanship of the secretary of the interior a federal agencies task force was formed which, following relatively extensive consultations, produced, within the required time frame, the *American Indian Religious Freedom Act Report*. This report includes some thirty-seven pages of recommendations for federal agency action, uniform administrative procedures, and possible legislation. An executive order was also prepared to facilitate federal implementation of the congressional resolution. Very few of the recommendations for administrative action have been implemented; uniform administrative procedures have not been developed; none of the proposals for legislation have been followed, and the executive order has not been signed. Noting this massive inaction, a frustrated spokesperson for Native American rights called upon the House Subcommittee on Civil and Constitutional Rights to hold oversight hearings regarding Indian religious freedom and the implementation of AIRFA. That was in June of 1982, and nothing has happened since. American Indian religious freedom has apparently moved off the public agenda once again.

The Continuing Problem

Like the characters in Jean-Paul Sartre's *No Exit*, Indians and agents of the federal government have been thrown together in an intimate, continuing, and frustrating relationship from which there is apparently no escape. Each has sought a way out. Congress and various administrations have repeatedly sought to solve "the Indian problem" through one form or another of "the final solution." Despite high (or low) hopes, none of these proposed solutions has worked. Indians, the weaker party in the encounter, have recently sought redress through the courts, and some, giving up on the American system entirely, have appealed to international agencies. Results of Indian freedom-of-religion appeals in the United States courts have been mixed. The effects of appeals to international forums are more difficult to assess.

Some recent governmental approaches to Indian affairs have given increasing prominence to input from Indians. This was intended in AIRFA. It is even more clearly prescribed in such acts as the Indian Education Act of 1972, the Indian Self-Determination and Education Assistance Act of 1975, and the Indian Child Welfare Act of 1978. These acts extend the degree of tribal control over tribal affairs, including tribal education. Control over education of the young can be of critical importance to the free exercise of religion.

Resort to the Courts

Failing to achieve desired results through legislative or executive chan-
nels, many Indian groups and individuals have turned to the courts in
search of protection of their religious freedom. These efforts have been
more successful than results achieved through the other branches of government but less successful than desired. It is most significant that the
United States Supreme Court has yet to pronounce directly and decisively
on American Indian religious freedom. Therefore, one must look entirely
to lower court decisions.

Over the past two decades the Native American Church, an Indian religious group, has achieved increasing judicial and legislative recognition of
the legitimacy of the sacramental use of peyote in that church. While
peyote is one of the substances subject to control under the Federal Comprehensive Drug Abuse Prevention and Control Act of 1970, federal regulations for the enforcement of that act provide an exempt status for "the
nondrug use of peyote in bona fide religious ceremonies of the Native
American Church" (21 C.F.R. § 1307.31 [1971]). Nine states also legislatively exempt the use of peyote for religious services from their controlled
substance laws: Iowa, Minnesota, Montana, Nevada, New Mexico, South
Dakota, Texas, Wisconsin and Wyoming. Case law in three additional
states supports such an exemption: Arizona, California and Oklahoma.

In *People v. Woody* (1964) the Supreme Court of California reversed, on
free exercise grounds, the conviction of several Navahos for illegal possession and use of peyote in a service of the Native American Church. The
Woody decision has been cited in similar cases in California and in other
states. With *Woody*, and subsequent decisions, and following the exemption clause to the federal act, Native American Church use of peyote in
services has been relatively free of prosecution. However, there have been
many court cases involving possession of peyote in contexts other than a
Native American Church ceremony.

In *Whitehorn v. State* (1977) the Oklahoma Court of Criminal Appeals
significantly extended free exercise protection beyond the sacramental use
of peyote in a religious service of the Native American Church to "the
practice of 'carrying' peyote by members" of that church. If this view were
shared by other courts, prosecutions of Native American Church members
for illegal possession might be sharply reduced.

Problems remain in the peyote area. Avoiding the consequences of anti-
peyote legislation typically entails membership in the Native American
Church. But what constitutes such membership? Further, what about the
sacramental use of peyote by people who are not members of the Native
American Church? Exemption clauses do not include them, and court

doctrine has ordinarily required that in litigation they must demonstrate good faith as religious practitioners.

Debate also continues concerning the long-range effects of peyote. Is it (or is the mescaline in the peyote cactus) a dangerous drug? Is it addictive? Does persistent use result in adverse long-range effects? Edward F. Anderson has provided a thorough and useful summary of the results of research on these and related questions in *Peyote: the Divine Cactus*. The evidence is nonconclusive. A layman might well conclude that since peyote is relatively scarce in the United States, since its use is thus quite limited, and since it is apparently used chiefly for religious purposes, it does not pose a serious threat to public order. Therefore, as an act of good public policy, peyote could even be decriminalized. Such a move would certainly enhance the free exercise of religion.

Another area of considerable litigation involves other objects regarded as sacred which, at the same time, have been given protected status by legislation. These include a variety of game animals, such as deer and moose, species designated as endangered, such as bald eagles and golden eagles, certain species of whales, and selected plants. Here too court results have been mixed, and this continues to be a source of tension between Indians and federal agents. Perhaps the most significant positive developments from the standpoint of Indian religious freedom have been those by which Indians have been exempted on free exercise grounds from certain game laws. For example, following a case in which a Winnebago Indian was exonerated by an appellate court from a conviction for violating a Wisconsin game law concerning deer, the Wisconsin legislature adopted a provision which exempted the taking of deer by Winnebago Indians for religious purposes. The Supreme Court of Alaska noted that provision and recommended a similar one for that state in a case in which it reversed, on free exercise grounds, the conviction of an Athabascan Indian for violating the game laws of Alaska concerning moose. (The case is *Frank* v. *Alaska* 1979.) In both of these instances the importance of religious practices to particular Indian tribes was clearly acknowledged.

Relationships between life-style and American Indian religions have been a central concern in a number of court cases. Indians seeking to wear long hair in keeping with their religious beliefs or traditions have been prevented from doing so by institutional regulations in schools and prisons. Several have sought relief through the courts on free exercise of religion and other grounds. Appellate court decisions have given mixed signals on this issue. Some have seen sufficient connection between life-style and Indian religion to grant claimants' relief; others have not. The most significant case of the former type is *Teterud* v. *Gillman* (1975), in which a federal district court in Iowa upheld the claim of a Cree prisoner in an Iowa penitentiary that the prison's regulations concerning hair violated his First Amendment rights. Teterud maintained that wearing long hair in braids was integrally related to his religion and hence was entitled to First Amendment protection. Both the Iowa district court and the court of appeals supported his claim.

Recent litigation has focused on access to and control of sacred sites. This is the most significant area for measuring the progress of equal protection for American Indian religious freedom. It is the area in which the stakes are the highest as far as public interest is concerned. Furthermore, sacred sites are often critically important to Native American religions and culture. Typically, specific geographical areas are understood to be the places in which the people originated and the loci of other significant events in tribal life. They may also be thought to be points of origin of the world and life in general and axes upon which the world turns. In these locales people relate in a sacred manner to ancestors and relatives, including, perhaps, animal and plant as well as human relatives. Here one relates to all of the most significant sacred powers.

Special relationship to place is essential to the continuing vitality of traditional Indian religions and cultures. This became evident in the most significant and successful access-to-site claim yet to receive public attention—the return in 1970 of Blue Lake and its environs to the Taos Pueblo. As national forest land since 1906 this area had been open to various uses—recreational and commercial, for instance—by nonmembers of the Taos Pueblo as well as by tribal members. The argument that led to the congressional decision to restrict the area to use by the Taos Pueblo was (1) that religion is central to Taos life generally, (2) that Blue Lake and the surrounding areas are crucial to Taos religion, and hence (3) that continued denial of protected access to that lake threatened the very existence of the culture.

Most Indian claims involving sacred sites on governmentally controlled land have not been successful. These include: Cherokee seeking to block the flooding of the Little Tennessee River Valley by the Tellico Dam (*Seqquoyah* v. *TVA* 1980); Navaho seeking to have the water level of Lake Powell lowered and tourist traffic restricted in the Rainbow Bridge area (*Badoni* v. *Higginson* 1981); Hopi and Navaho seeking to prevent the expansion of a ski resort in the San Francisco Peaks area of northwestern Arizona (*Wilson* v. *Block* and *Navaho Medicinemen's Association* v. *Block* 1984); Lakota (Sioux) and Tsistsistas (Southern Cheyenne) seeking more protected access to Bear Butte in western South Dakota (*Frank Fools Crow* v. *Gullet* 1983); and Inupiat seeking to preserve an area in the Beaufort and Chuckchi Seas from oil exploration (*Inupiat Community of Arctic Slope* v. *United States* 1982). The free exercise clause has also been appealed to by the Sioux in their claim to the Black Hills of South Dakota, but that appeal has played no role in court decisions in the cases which have been generated by this claim.

The central issue for the courts in dealing with these free exercise claims involving sacred sites has been the nature and extent of access required to protect the Indians' religious rights. Sincerity of view has not been an issue of weight, nor, for the most part, has been the question of whether the contested areas are of some importance to the religious practices of the complainants. The question has been one of degree: *How* important are the sites to those practices? In answering this question the courts have come to rely upon the criteria of *centrality* and *indispensability*. These are the controlling criteria which were first set forth by the Sixth Circuit Court of Appeals in *Sequoyah* v. *TVA*, and they have become precedential for other court decisions in sacred site cases. The sixth circuit acknowledged the historical importance of the Little Tennessee Valley in the life of the Cherokee people and its significance for the "personal preference" of the individual complainants, but it did not see the area as being central and indispensable to the practice of Cherokee religion or in the life of the Cherokee people.

Court imposition of the criteria of centrality and indispensability raises questions of equity. Satisfaction of these criteria is not a simple matter in any religious system, but it may be especially difficult in one in which there are neither formal definitions of orthodoxy nor formally sanctioned promulgators and interpreters of the faith. Such an imposition may require more of Indian free exercise claimants and less of the state than has been required of other free exercise claimants. Nonetheless, these criteria have assumed a significant role in sacred site cases in particular.

Even when these criteria can be satisfied in a court case, the free exercise claim must compete with state interest. Constitutional free exercise doctrine affirms the absolute character of the protection of religious belief but the relative character of the protection of religious practice. For example, even though professedly grounded in religion, practices which seriously threaten public health or safety may be denied the protection of the free exercise clause. Further, even in free exercise cases in which such a threat is not evident and it has been established that certain state actions do impose a burden on claimants' free exercise of religion, the courts must balance the free exercise right against state interest. If that interest is found to be "compelling," and if it can be achieved through no other means, the court may decide for the state.

State interest has been generally well treated in Indian sacred site cases. Indeed, as the Circuit Court of the District of Columbia commented in one case, some courts have even implied that "the Free Exercise Clause can never supercede the government's ownership rights and duties of public management." On the contrary, that court continued in a statement that is both obvious and necessary: "The government must manage its lands in accordance with the Constitution" (*Wilson* v. *Block* 1984).

Sacred site cases typically entail a confrontation between the right to protect property of religious significance and the right to regulate property in the interest of the public. The law for dealing with this confrontation is not well developed in this country, possibly because we are a nation of movers and hence do not tend to invest particular areas with sanctity. The sacred sites of the major religions of the United States are, for the most part, at some distance from this country. The courts have faced the challenge in Indian sacred site cases of balancing constitutional free exercise rights against governmental claims to manage public property in the interest of the larger public. Therefore, representatives of the federal government have argued successfully that the flooding of the Little Tennessee Valley and the Lake Powell areas brought benefits to the larger public which overrode the free exercise claims of the Indians. Similarly, representatives of the state have successfully maintained that public lands such as the San Francisco Peaks and Bear Butte areas should be managed in such a way as to benefit both Indians and non-Indians and to serve recreational and commercial as well as religious interests.

There is one significant case in which the trial court held that the interests of the state were not sufficiently compelling to override Indian free exercise claims: *Northwest Indian Cemetery Protective Association* v. *Peterson* (1983). In this case the United States District Court of Northern California supported the free exercise claims made by and on behalf of the Yurok, Karok, and Tolowa Indians regarding an area in the Six Rivers National Forest. The Indians and various supporters, including the State of California through its Native American Heritage Commission, challenged decisions by the United States Forest Service to complete construction of a paved road—known as the "G-O Road"—and to allow the harvesting of timber in an area known to the Indians as "the high country." The Indians contended that the area is central to their religious beliefs and practices in its present pristine condition and that the construction and use of a road in it would so change the area as to violate their freedom of religion. The district court held that the evidence supported a conclusion that access to and use of "the high country" in its pristine state is "central and indispensable" to the religion of the Yurok, Karok and Tolowa Indians. Indeed, the court concluded that the projected National Forest Service changes in the area would actually pose a "very real threat of undermining" not only the religious practices of the Indians but the tribal communities themselves. Hence, the court concluded that the interests of the federal government in the development of the area were not sufficiently compelling to override such weighty free exercise claims. The Forest Service is appealing this decision.

In general, having examined the status of the free exercise of religion by American Indians through a survey of recent legislation and litigation, public policy and practice have clearly improved since the ratification of the Bill of Rights, especially in recent years. While the effects of the American Indian Religious Freedom Act of 1978 have been disappointing, the fact that it is on record continues to be of some importance. Cases such as *Woody, Whitehorn, Teterud, Frank* and *Northwest* have brought significant advances in selected areas. Still, the United States Supreme Court has yet to pronounce decisively and directly on any aspect of the subject. Failed cases such as *Sequoyah, Badoni, Wilson, Inupiat,* and *Fools Crow*, as well as a host of continuing conflicts over such matters as sacred objects and ceremonies, indicate that the current situation is far from a complete success.

11

Church-State Tensions and Marginal Movements in the United States

Thomas Robbins

In the United States, the traditions of religious liberty and separation of church and state create a unique context for conflicts between religion and public authority. The growing tension along the increasingly ambiguous boundary of church and state can be related to two current trends: the phenomenal expansion of the modern state with permeation of governmental prerogatives through nearly all socioeconomic and cultural processes; and the consequent increasing fragility of the state and the precariousness of its provision of both services and legitimation. A third key trend, the expansion of the activities and functions of churches, is partly a consequence of the fragility of the overexpanded state. The convergence of diversifying "religious" operations and an expanded scope of public authority with a mandate to regulate organizations operates to maximize the potential for conflict. The upshot is a proliferation of church autonomy conflicts involving allegations that social values such as racial equality, organizational financial accountability or the prevention of child abuse, which the government is seen as responsible for enforcing, are being violated by churches conducting social service, healing, commercial, financial or educational operations. Church autonomy conflicts ensue when counter-claims are registered affirming that the state regulation is inadmissible because the separation of church and state would be violated and/or the free exercise of religion would be unduly burdened (Laycock 1981).

The consequences of what might be termed the "regulatory gap" between church-related and secular enterprises are mitigated to the extent that religious groups are highly specialized in their functions and do not compete with other institutions and groups. The phenomenon of secularization in the twentieth century and the much touted privatization of modern religiosity have entailed the specialization of religion and its detachment from other social realms. This inhibits the potential for conflict

135

in the interface of privileged churches with an increasingly expanded, centralized state. Some aspects of the much touted secularization and privatization of American religion are arguably now being reversed, and, in consequence, the boundaries of the religious specialization are becoming less distinct. Religious organizations frequently appear to be seeking to expand the scope of their functions and authority. They come into conflict with both the state and other institutions and groups such as family, businesses, medical practitioners, teachers, social workers, and minorities. Dean Kelley (1982) of the National Council of Churches notes, "The churches are let know that [if] they venture out of their hallowed precincts of chapel, croft and chantry into the 'real' world, they will have to brave the rigors that their 'secular counterparts' (supposedly) have to meet."

The heavily regulated and bureaucratic nature of American society, particularly its social service processes, encourages the functional diversification of religion as a means of evading regulatory constraints. In their introductory essay to *Religious Movements in Contemporary America* (1974), Irving Zaretsky and Mark Leone argue that today's religious ferment is typically American in its entrepreneurial quality. "As a people we have a built-in incentive toward individualism and innovation, and we are reaping the consequences of that tradition today in religion. If it is gone from the small businessman in the economy, it is alive and well in religion." In America, according to Zaretsky and Leone, religion is "the only place where social experimentation is possible. It is the folk answer to a system that is overdiplomaed, overcertified, and too specialized, and too conscious of where one receives certification."

An observer sympathetic to religion may be uncritically enthusiastic over the innovative and entrepreneurial quality of today's religious esotericism. Perhaps it was innovative and dynamically entrepreneurial for the Reverend Jim Jones to have his followers adopt children who were wards of the state of California and thus become eligible for welfare benefits to be paid to the church (Wooden 1981). The religious claims of the Church of Scientology and Synanon might be viewed as end-runs around the constraints of accreditation and professional standards for psychotherapists. Such evasions provoke resentment and movements to expand state authority to protect the "religious consumer." These movements crack down on alleged fraud, deception, and malpractice by gurus and others said to be practicing therapy without a license by promising specific psychic benefits for established fees. Such demands are met by arguments affirming the priority of religious freedom and the inadmissibility of state intervention in this realm. The diversification of religious entrepreneurship, protected by the First Amendment, conflicts with trends toward broader public regulation of organizational behavior and increased liability of professionals for harmful practices.

Fragility of the Expanded State

The expansion of the apparatus and regulatory mandate of the state has contributed to church-state tensions. Paradoxically, the same can be said of the fragility of state authority and operations, which is now increasingly apparent, and which is perhaps in part a consequence of the state's overexpansion. The state's ability to manage the economy and mitigate both inflation and unemployment is more and more in doubt. The conflict between containing fiscal deficits and enhancing military preparedness is particularly acute. The contraction of public services may imperil key social values such as equal opportunity or the elimination of poverty. The foundations of public revenue may be seriously threatened by tax revolt. The ability of the state to cope with crime and terrorism, with or without an erosion of civil liberties, has been questioned. The state cannot deliver the goods, services, and meanings essential to an elevated quality of life. The Great Society motif of the 1960s, as well as the dissident sociopolitical currents of that period, entailed a demand or promise that the state should or would create an elevated quality of life for the general populace, that what Hubert Humphrey called "the politics of joy" would actualize fraternal harmony and the social equity. A widespread skepticism has now crystallized regarding the ability of state power to solve social problems and bring about the good life for all.

As the state falters, social movements and groups attempt to fill the vacuum. The Guardian Angels claim to be combatting crime and are resented and allegedly persecuted by the police. Religious groups are particularly adept at seizing opportunities arising from a vacuum. Religious symbols and mystiques of fellowship provide broad and unbounded legitimation for expanded activities and services; constitutionally grounded church autonomy provides a barrier to the intrusive state and its constraining regulatory apparatus, which is prohibited from becoming entangled with ecclesiastical affairs. The communal provision of diversified services by totalistic cults such as the Unification Church is an extreme example of this development. On a more mundane level, some Protestant parents send their children to Catholic parochial schools because they believe that the teaching is superior and drug use and knife fights are less frequent than in public academies. Other Protestants send their children to evangelical Christian schools where parental values will be transmitted and interracial contacts minimized. The growth of religious surrogates for public services such as public schools produces conflicts with both traditional providers of services—such as licensed doctors, teachers, or social workers—and with groups that feel dependent upon public services. Those groups—often disadvantaged—fear that nonpublic services will not be accessible to them and that the surge of private surrogates will diminish the resources available for public services.

These tendencies contribute to the increasing range, intensity, and salience of issues involving churches and religious groups in public, legislative, and judicial debates. Stigmatized movements such as Scientology and the Unification Church are at the cutting edge of church-state boundary disputes because they are so highly diversified and multifunctional. Their religious shield against state regulation enables them to consolidate what Richard Ofshe (1982) calls *protected empires*. Many issues involving cults are closely related to broader issues of church autonomy versus public prerogatives in various areas including labor and employment, health, education, commercial practices, and financial accountability. With the notable exception of the mystified "mind control" issue, the conflicts in which cults are involved are similar to conflicts and controversies involving less stigmatized religious groups. The esoteric beliefs and rituals of cults, their frequent messianic intolerance, and their lack of community and grassroots support, render them particularly provocative and vulnerable. However, the broader reality is the ongoing diversification of religious activities conflicting with the expansion of the state's regulatory mandate.

Religious Diversification and State Regulation

In the fall of 1983, the Reverend Sun Myung Moon appealed his conviction for tax fraud. The appellate brief written by Laurence Tribe notes that the prosecution relied heavily on the assertion that Moon has expended funds for personal and business, rather than religious, purposes. This established that they were Moon's taxable personal funds, not tax-exempt church funds. Tribe's brief argues that the distinction between *the religious* on the one hand and the *economic* or *the personal* is "itself a constitutionally protected religious distinction" such that "the jury was bound to accept the Unification Faith's *own* definition of what was religious." The judge allegedly erred in empowering the jury "to decide, on whatever basis it wished, whether various expenditures 'were' religious." Moon was also the beneficiary of an *amicus curiae* (friend-of-the-court) brief filed by the National Council of Churches, the United Presbyterian Churches, and other mainline church groups. The *amicus* brief complains that evidentiary rulings by the trial court prevented the defendant's attorneys from eliciting testimony indicating the relationship between the defendant's commercial enterprises and the financial needs of the church's spiritual mission. The *amicus* brief expresses "sharp distress" at the horrendous "breach of religious liberty" (Trent 1982).

The question of who determines what economic involvements or financial allotments are for religious or nonreligious purposes is of crucial importance to highly diversified movements with far-ranging operations and investments. Cults are egregious but not unique in their diversification, hence the support given to the claims of the generally detested Mr. Moon by more respected religious groups, which may also have investments and commercial enterprises. Interestingly, the prosecution sought to characterize Rev. Moon as "merely a businessman" and seemed to view the case as essentially a simple case of white-collar crime.

A second issue which concerns the broader church community which has rushed to the defense of Moon is the authority of the government to specify the organizational structure of tax-exempt religious entities. The account into which the monies arising from Reverend Moon's investments flowed was in his rather than the church's name. But if this is held against him, argues the *amicus* brief, free exercise of religion is curtailed and the government is "entangled impermissibly in the movement's internal affairs."

Joey P. Moore (1978) argued that the economic diversification of some movements is so extreme that organizations such as Synanon "further secular purposes which are not enumerated by Section 301(e) of the Internal Revenue Code." "An examination of the economic enterprises admittedly affiliated with the Unification Church provides justification for its being characterized as a multi-national corporation . . . . A pattern emerges revealing a structure manned by interlocking directors, officers, and stockbrokers who freely funnel corporate funds back and forth among the various enterprises to maximize investment potential" (Moore 1978: 688-89). Like the prosecutors in Reverend Moon's trial, Moore is really maintaining that the organizational economic rationality of Moon's and other cultist operations is so preponderant that the ultimate spiritual goals which may be tenuously served cannot preclude regulation.

Much of Moore's concern is directed at the sociopolitical programs of esoteric movements such as the Unification Church, Scientology, the People's Temple, Synanon, Hare Krishna and the Children of God. Moore doubts that the underlying goals and policies of these movements are truly religious. The agendas of the movements, he argues, include altering the nature of the family, creating a utopian society, revolutionizing sexual mores, fighting communism, or promoting socialism. He suggests that the efforts of Synanon and other groups at securing formal recognition as religious organizations are merely efforts to conceal their social programs.

"Cultist programs of this nature . . . have uncertain, if any, religious import" and should be carefully scrutinized.

Moore's implicit definition of an authentic religion is narrow and would exclude, for example, millenarian sects, which attempt to create visions of a better world and whose members often try to live in accordance with such visions. More interesting are the implications for the expanding social programs of conventional churches, for example, the Catholic bishops' agenda on arms control, conservative sociopolitical activism of evangelicals, Jewish support for Israel, and Catholic agitation against abortion and gay liberation. As James Beckford (1983:18) recently noted, the protests within churches against American involvement in Vietnam in the late 1960s and early 1970s were relatively low-key compared to "today's religiously inspired campaigns against abortion, euthanasia, and the teaching of evolutionary theory in public schools."

The conflicts in which both conventional and esoteric groups are enmeshed seem similar. Fundamental issues cut across the sometimes ambiguous line separating reputable churches from stigmatized cults. The general issue of state interference in the internal processes of churches, which surfaced in the Moon prosecution, has also arisen in the Worldwide Church of God receivership, which, like the Moon case, appears to have traumatized the mainline churches.

The Worldwide Church of God was founded almost fifty years ago. Until recently under the leadership of its eldlerly prophet and founder, Herbert Armstrong, the movement may be on the borderline of respectability. Acting on complaints from church dissidents of serious financial mismanagement, the attorney general of California began an investigation and sought to examine the church's books. To prevent the records from being destroyed, the attorney general obtained a court order appointing a receiver, who was forbidden to interfere with so-called ecclesiastical affairs. The receivership lasted for nearly three months in 1979 until loyal church members raised a $2 million bond and obtained a stay of the court order. The theory under which the attorney general acted is that church finances constitute a public trust. The status of a church as a charitable trust or corporation gives the state a special mandate to investigate mismanagement and to ensure that tax-exempt funds are spent in accordance with the stated purposes for which the exemption was granted. Under this doctrine, church funds are "public funds" and the attorney general, who represents the public, has a greater regulatory mandate regarding church finances than for the affairs of private businesses. This theory is anathema to officials of the National Council of Churches and other groups, who insist that what is essential is not that a given church is also a charitable trust, but that a particular charity has a special status as a church. This severely limits the power of the state to interfere since the First Amendment as interpreted broadly gives churches a greater protection from the state regulation than is afforded private companies. Concerned denominational spokespersons also repudiate what appears to them as an overly facile distinction between financial and ecclesiastical affairs of churches. According to Breiterman and Kelley (1982), this is a dichotomy that religious bodies cannot afford to concede. "How a religious body raises, invests and expends its funds cannot be divorced from its religious purpose, ministry and mission, and Government cannot intervene in the one without affecting the other." The *religious freedom lobby* appears to want to cover diverse financial and commercial endeavors under the blanket protection of freedom of worship.

The concern of conventional church leaders over both the public trust doctrine and the financial/ecclesiastical dichotomy is not mitigated by the likelihood that the state will apply these doctrines primarily to esoteric groups with charismatic leadership, which, as Richard Ofshe (1980) has noted, tend not to have developed built-in bureaucratic mechanisms to promote financial accountability. But the implications may still be substantial for more stable groups. Protestant and Catholic church groups collaborated in a successful campaign to amend the California statutes to nullify the power of the attorney general to take future action similar to that taken against the Worldwide Church of God.

Certain social values such as equal opportunity and racial non-discrimination are now viewed as partly enforceable by the state on institutions linked to churches. An example is afforded by the Southwest Baptist Theological Seminary case. This case does not involve an esoteric movement, but does illustrate how the expansion of the regulatory mandate of the state is increasing the number and range of church autonomy conflicts.

In 1977, the Equal Employment Opportunity Commission (EEOC) sued the Southwestern Baptist Theological Seminary in federal district court to compel the seminary to file form EEO-6, which seeks to obtain data on the number and duties of several categories of employees concerning their compensation, tenure, race, sex, and national origin. According to regulations of the EEOC, submission of this form is mandatory for all institutions of higher learning with fifteen or more employees. The commission's authority in this area is ultimately grounded in Title VII of the 1964 Civil Rights Act.

The government's contention regarding the applicability of the EEOC rules was disputed by the seminary, which argued that there was never any congressional intent to apply the Equal Employment Opportunity Act to religion or religious activities. The seminary is wholly owned and operated by the Southern Baptist Convention, and it has the exclusive purpose of training people to serve the denomination. The district court agreed with

the defendant and in January 1980 issued an opinion denying EEOC jurisdiction over the seminary, which has a right to make what it views as
"divinely guided assessments of each employee's suitability" without state
interference. The district court opinion also argued that an unconstitutional burden on the free exercise of religion is presented by the application
of Title VII to any aspect of the seminary's employment practice or policy.
In July 1981 the circuit court of appeals partly reversed the decision of the
district court and ruled that administrators and support personnel of the
seminary, who are not ministers, are subjected to the regulatory jurisdiction of the EEOC. While the Baptist seminary was entitled to the status of a
church, only personnel directly involved in teaching could be viewed as
ministers and be excluded from the EEOC's jurisdiction. The circuit court
rejected the opinion of the district court that a determination by the state
as to which employees are performing religious roles threatens the separation of church and state and burdens the free exercise of religion. In the
spring of 1982, the Supreme Court declined to review the circuit court's
decision.

EEOC v. *Southwestern Baptist Theological Seminary* presents a clear
conflict between claims of religious liberty/church autonomy and the expansion of the scope of state regulation in pursuit of a key social value—
equal opportunity. The substantive area of labor and employment policies
is also one in which cults are under attack. The multifunctional diversification of some religious movements may render participants highly dependent upon the group, which provides a range of services for the participant,
who is relatively powerless to affect group policy. There are implications for
exploitation of the participants, who may derive more spiritual than material benefit from their labor in church owned enterprises. In a recent case
involving a controversial group, the Alamo Foundation, the Supreme
Court affirmed that the minimum wage and overtime provisions of the Fair
Labor Standards Act are applicable to commercial enterprises tied to the
Foundation. Other issues involve implicit contracts in which the participant surrenders his own property in return for a nonenforceable promise
of lifetime care, which is conditional upon the whim of a guru or prophet.
There are also questions arising from the training of professionals and
paraprofessionals in religiotherapeutic movements. The alleged noncer-
tification of the trainees renders them dependent upon the movement,
outside of which they cannot practice their trade. There are allegations that
labor patterns in exploitative totalistic cults constitute instances of slavery
in violation of the Thirteenth Amendment. To what extent can the state
interfere in so-called religious practices involving labor and employment?
This question bears upon churches as well as cults.

There are numerous allegations of fraudulent practices and substandard care with respect to a range of social services operated under the auspices of religiotherapeutic movements. Particularly likely to be affected are quasi-medical institutions such as baby clinics or nursing homes, as well as facilities for delinquents or drug addicts. Fierce controversies over licensing have erupted. In this respect excoriated cults are often in the same position as born-again groups, although the latter have considerably more political clout and grassroots support. Several years ago, the attorney general of Texas made strenuous efforts to subject to a licensing requirement homes for incorrigible girls operated by Brother Lester Roloff, an ally of erstwhile Governor Clements. Although corporal punishments and one attempted murder (of an inmate by other inmates) allegedly transpired in these establishments, the state's nominal victory was nullified by a formal transfer of ownership to a church.

In the recent landmark Supreme Court decisions involving Bob Jones University and the Goldsboro Christian Schools, the Supreme Court rejected the claim that withdrawal of a tax exemption from church-linked schools practicing racial discrimination unconstitutionally burdens the free exercise of religion. Justice Burger's majority opinion represents a broad and sweeping application of the "public policy doctrine" whereby tax exemptions are conditional upon the exempt organization's conformity with public policy. This doctrine has also been used by the Internal Revenue Service (IRS) against the Church of Scientology. In arguing for the withdrawal of Scientology's tax privileges, the IRS produced a lengthy list of transgressions against public policy, ranging from theft of public documents (for which several Scientologists have been convicted) to brainwashing. The litigation continues, but an appellate court has drastically reduced the list of actionable transgressions.

Burger's opinion affirms that all tax exemptions are fundamentally granted in consideration of the charitable quality of the organization's activity. The petitioning schools had claimed that an institution was entitled to a tax exemption if its purposes were religious or charitable or educational—i.e., there are three alternative, coequal qualifications. Justice Burger rejected a literal reading of the Internal Revenue Code and affirmed that all tax-exempt organizations must be "charitable" in the common law sense of the term, serving a public purpose and not contravening public policy and community standards. Logically, a charitable interpretation of religious tax exemptions should strengthen the activist public trust doctrine. This would affirm the government's responsibility for overseeing church finances, as claimed by California in placing the Worldwide Church of God under receivership. Additional implications of the

Burger opinion may include claims that exotic cults have jeopardized their tax privileges through authoritarian, antisocial, and antifamily practices which contravene community standards (for example, the IRS cites brainwashing as one of many reasons for challenging the tax exemption of the Church of Scientology). Alternatively, politically active church groups may risk their tax privileges in challenging public policy (e.g., the Sanctuary movement). In a concurring opinion, Justice Powell expressed unease with the sweeping nature of Burger's public policy emphasis, and reminded the court that one aim of our system of tax exemptions is to subsidize diversity and dissent.

We have agued that the diversification of activities transpiring under so-called religious auspices, arguably reversing previous secularizing trends, constitutes one key factor, underlying the current proliferation of church-autonomy disputes. An interesting attempt to curb the unregulated expansion of religious fundraising is afforded by the Minnesota Statute amended in 1978 to impose an obligation on religious organizations that obtain less than half of their funds from membership contributions to file a comprehensive financial report from which other churches would be exempt. "Such a ruling would have put mail-order, street corner, and electronic religious movements to considerable inconvenience and in some jeopardy" (Demerath and Williams 1984:7). The statute was challenged by the Unification Church. It was pointed out that under the statute a small church which obtained a majority of its funds from nonmembers would be subject to disclosure while a large church which obtained more than half of its funds from members would not, although the latter might draw a much greater absolute amount from the public through a far more extensive public solicitation-commercial operation. The federal district court and the Eighth Circuit Court of Appeals held that this differential treatment of religious organizations violated the Establishment Clause of the First Amendment. The Supreme Court's 5-to-4 decision in *Larsen* v. *Valente* upheld the circuit court; however, there were several dissenting opinions. Justice Rehnquist's dissent suggested that it was unnecessary for the Court to probe the constitutional issues as it had not been clearly established that the Unification Church was a legitimate church.

The *Larsen* case raises another crucial issue. Attorney Sharon Worthing (1979) has argued that religious organizations, because they are *ideological* organizations, are highly susceptible to selective repression and discriminatory law enforcement. Therefore, it is argued, the protection afforded religious organizations should be on the level of the protection afforded individual faith (and greater than the protection granted businesses). Churches are finding it increasingly difficult to rely on individualistic and pietistic rationales such as freedom of religion and the sanctity of private

conscience to legitimate the legal autonomy of formally organized structures which operate in a context of economic rationality but are linked to
churches. The state, in endeavoring to extend its regulation to such organizations, easily appropriates these individualistic-pietistic rationales by affirming that private conscience is indeed private and so deeply personal
that it cannot be embodied in rational formal organizations such that the
latter cannot be viewed as (sacred) vehicles of the consciences of the congregation. In this connection the Minnesota statute struck down in *Larsen*
proposed in effect to regard churches which draw most of their funds from
members as vehicles of the consciences of those members, while regarding
churches which draw most of their support from the public as essentially
businesses. Similarly, the prosecutors in Reverend Moon's trial affected to
regard the defendant simply as a businessman and to interpret the case as a
simple matter of white-collar crime.

It should be noted that new religions are unlikely to have a large con-
gregational base for internal fundraising and thus tend to be dependent
upon public solicitation as well as the unpaid labor of totally committed
activists. They are therefore particularly vulnerable to regulation and
highly dependent on favorable public policy.

In another public solicitation case the Supreme Court unanimously upheld a Minnesota regulation restricting religious solicitation at state fairs to
assigned booths (*Heffron* v. *International Society for Krishna Consciousness*). The court relied on the government's right to regulate the time,
place and manner of expression in public places, which requires a lesser
standard than substantive infringements on constitutional liberties. The
language of the court's opinion would appear to restrict its applicability to a
public fair (Fisher 1982).

The Issue of "Mind Control"

There is one respect in which conflicts over the alleged use of "mind
control" by cults are continuous with conflicts embroiling less esoteric
religious groups. Presently the range of groups that are alleged to use brainwashing methods and attempt physical abduction and "deprogramming"
is expanding. Increasingly, born-again, fundamentalist, and Pentecostal
groups are being targeted. An aspect of what Robert Wuthnow (1978) has
called today's "religious populism," is the diffusion of religious patterns
such as fundamentalism, glossolalia (speaking in tongues), and faith healing—once associated with rural, southern, or lower-class persons—among
the educated middle classes. New Christian fellowships are arising and
developing campus ministeries. Such groups, as well as older fundamentalist or Pentecostal groups, appear alien and antimodern to many parents

of converts, who are prone to call these groups cults and apply to them a conceptual framework developed by the opponents of groups such as the Unification Church and Hare Krishna. The growth of these latter groups has leveled off. Consequently there appears to be a cadre of professional deprogrammers and auxilliaries that cannot be supported merely by operations against the classic "destructive" cults. Recent deprogrammings have involved supposedly Christian groups such as the Maranatha Fellowship, the Champaign-Urbana Fellowship, Hobart Freeman's Faith Assembly (which rejects modern medicine), Jews for Jesus, and even the respectable and rapidly growing Assemblies of God. As Ted Koppel was told during an airing of a "Nightline" television program (1983) by a deprogrammed ex-member of the Faith Assembly, "it is not only the Moonies or the Krishnas wearing orange robes who brainwash people, it is also the groups which are so close to Christianity that no one wants to fight them, but they're the real danger" [approximate quote]. The line separating stigmatized mind controlling cults and acceptable high-commitment groups is becoming increasingly indistinct.

Integral to debates about church and state is the traditional distinction between religious *belief*, which is generally interpreted as receiving an absolute constitutional protection, and religious *action* or behavior, which receives a more limited protection. The degree of protection afforded verbal behavior involving direct expression or acting out of beliefs is generally viewed as substantial, since freedom of belief must entail affirming and teaching beliefs, praying, chanting, and performing other rituals.

The belief/action distinction is currently under attack by both proponents and opponents of enhanced state regulation of churches. The defenders of church autonomy fear that diminishing the sanctity of religious behavior relative to the sacred subjectivity of belief will lead ultimately to effective state control of religion via control of religion's practical implementation. "'Exercise' is an *action* word, used expressly in the First Amendment solely to characterize freedom of religion" notes Breiterman and Kelley (1982). A rigid adherence to the belief/action dichotomy will "render the free exercise clause a dead letter, conferring no independent rights to act or practice and no collateral sanctions where beliefs were unpopular enough to incur the wrath of repressive legislation." However, some of the opponents of cults have questioned whether the belief/action dichotomy is applicable to the context of cultist religiosity in which religious beliefs are allegedly inculcated by coercive persuasion and are thus not held voluntarily. The constitutional guarantee of free exercise of religion may be inapplicable to cults, in which religion is supposedly not "free." *Coerced*, i.e., "unfree" religion is allegedly not legally protected (Delgado 1984). This perspective differs from the conventional view that perceives a constitutional proscription of *any state interference with re-*

ligious beliefs, notwithstanding how those beliefs are generated (Shapiro 1978).

The radical quality of the concepts of *brainwashing* and *mind control*, which are used to legitimate public or private action against cults, elevates the challenge to church autonomy *from the level of religious action to religious belief.* Cultist brainwashing syndromes are said to include as key components repetitive chanting and the teaching of converts that loss of faith will result in eschatological harms such as being reincarnated as a worm or being cast into a lake of fire. (Both ritual chanting and eschatological warnings figured in a recent trial in which the Hare Krishnas were ordered to pay an ex-devotee and her mother $9.5 million largely for "false imprisonment" through brainwashing of a fourteen-year-old girl). Elements of sectarian ideologies such as abolutist and polarized thinking are interpreted as aspects of mental impairment produced by cultist mind control. Attributions of mind control often entail transvaluations of items (for example, indifference to nonreligious matters, suddenness or apparent irrationality of conversion, dualistic thinking, stereotyped discourse, chanting) that might otherwise by viewed as simply demonstrating the intensity and dogmatic quality of the devotee's faith (Robbins 1984; Shapiro 1978). The convert's belief is used as a sign of incompetence or victimization.

Some *remedies* for cultist mind control appear to involve constraints on religious belief, teaching, and ritual. A pervasive remedy has been coercive deprogramming, toward which the courts have often been permissive. The process involves forcible confinement of a devotee who receives counterindoctrination, which often entails direct attacks on the convert's beliefs. Legislation has been introduced in several states to directly legitimate and facilitate such procedures through court-ordered guardianships or conservatorships. Such proceedings will directly implicate the state in the deconversion of minority believers. Arguably, the introduction of *mind control* into legal discourse has radical implications for shifting the focus from religious action to religious belief.

Mind control claims additionally shift the focus of inquiry and control to the murky area of individual consciousness of which reliable knowledge is lacking and interferences are highly susceptible to subjectivity and bias. Even though *free will* is a metaphysical concept, the legal system has generally assumed that individuals are autonomous and responsible. If peer pressure, perhaps accompanied by repetitive chanting, rituals, intolerance, dogmatism, and fire-and-brimstone intimidation, is treated as a demiurge that inundates free will, the result will be a radically innovative reinforcement of a disturbing trend to erode the assumption of personal autonomy as a premise of legal action.

Conclusion

The interface of the diversification of putatively protected religious activities and the expanding regulatory mandate of the state is presently heightening the tension between church and state. Cults such as Scientology and the Unification Church are egregious (though hardly unique) in their diversified aggrandizement and are thus on the frontier of church-state conflict. The conflicts in which stigmatized cults are enmeshed are not qualitatively distinct from the conflicts involving more reputable groups. The basic conflict can be conceptualized as a claim of church autonomy clashing with a claim that public authority is responsible for enforcing a certain value (for example, racial equality) which is allegedly contravened in a commercial, financial, educational, healing, social service, or political operation linked in some way to a church. The most absolutist defenders of church autonomy would cover all manner of enterprises with the shield of the First Amendment, thereby equating with freedom of worship the right to pursue profitable activities without public accountability. Not only can one make money for God, but that process must be deemed a religious one. At the opposite extreme is the doctrine of the California attorney general in which the state may interfere with the finances of a bonafide church more freely than it can intervene in the affairs of a private corporation because church money is held by church officials as a public trust. The traditional proscription of governmental entanglement in the running of churches is alleged to pertain mainly to ecclesiastical affairs, not to church finances.

In our view, hostility is directed toward authoritarian cults particularly because of their extreme diversification and aspiring omnicompetence. These tendencies can also be seen somewhat in more reputable groups. Cults have provoked various groups such as clergy, parents, and mental health workers whom they compete with or seek to displace. Legal constraints on religious movements should be developed within the framework of the duality of action and belief. Substantial constraints can be imposed on abusive movements without undermining the protection of religious belief and verbal expressions of belief.

Bibliography

Beckford, James. "The Restoration of 'Power' to the Sociology of Religion." *Sociological Analysis* 44 (1983).

Breiterman, Marvin and Kelley, Dean. 1982. "When Is Government Intervention Legitimate?" Pp. 194-200 in *Government Intervention in Religious Affairs.* Dean Kelley, ed., New York: Pilgrim Press.

Delgado, Richard. "When Religious Exercise Is Not Free." *Vanderbilt Law Review* 37, 5 (1984).

Demerath, N. J. and Williams, Rhys H. "A Mythical Past and Uncertain Future." *Society* 21, 4 (1984): 3-10.

Fisher, Barry. 1982. "Current Issues in Government Regulation of Religious Solicitation." Pp. 129-40 in Dean Kelley, ed., *Government Intervention in Religious Affairs*. New York: Pilgrim Press.

Kelley, Dean. 1982. "Introduction," in Dean Kelley, ed., *Government Intervention in Religious Affairs*. New York: Pilgrim Press.

Laycock, Douglas. "Toward a General Theory of the Religion Clauses." *Columbia Law Review* 81 (1981): 1372-1917.

Moore, Joey P. "Piercing the Religious Veil of The So-called Cults." *Pepperdine Law Review* 7 (1978): 655-710.

Ofshe, Richard. "Regulating Diversified Social Movements." Presentation to the Seminar on Law and The New Religions," 1982, Graduate Theological Union, Berkeley.

_____. "Shifts in Opportunities and Accountability and the Regulation of Religious Organizations." Paper presented to the Association for the Sociology of Religion, August 1980, Boston.

Robbins, Thomas. "Constructing Cultist 'Mind Control.'" *Sociological Analysis* 45 (1984): 241-56.

Shapiro, Robert. "Mind Control or Intensity of Faith." *Harvard Civil Rights-Civil Liberties Law Review* 13 (1978): 751-97.

_____. "Of Robots, Persons and The Protection of Religious Beliefs." *Southern California Review* 56 (1983).

Trent, Earl. 1982. (Counsel for Amici Curiae). *Brief for the National Counsel of Churches of Christ*, et al.

Tribe, Laurence et al. 1983. (Counsel for Appellant). *Brief for Appellant Sun Myung Moon* (*U.S.A.* v. *Sun Myung Moon*, 2d Circuit).

Wooden, Kenneth. 1981. *The Children of Jonestown*. New York: McGraw-Hill.

Worthing, Sharon. "The State Takes Over a Church." *The Annals* 446 (November 1979): 136-48.

Wuthnow, Robert. 1978. *Experimentation in American Religion*. Berkeley: University of California Press.

Zaretsky, Irving and Leone, Mark. 1974. "The Common Foundation of Religious Diversity." Pp. xvii-xxxvi in I. Zaretsky and M. Leone, eds., *Religious Movements in America*. Princeton, New Jersey: Princeton University Press.

Part III
COMPARATIVE PERSPECTIVES

12

Church-State Relations in Comparative Perspective

Roland Robertson

This section consists of a series of papers on aspects of the church-state theme in a number of different societies. Exceptions to this context include Hamid Dabashi's analysis of religious and political authority in a religiocultural tradition (Islam), Roland Robertson's focus on the Latin American continent and the survey by John Markoff and Daniel Regan of religion in the national constitutions of the world. The overall thrust of the papers is in the direction of enhancing our sense of variation in church-state and religious-authority/political-authority relationships. Since some of the essays do not engage directly in comparison per se, it is necessary to indicate at this point some of the more salient issues involved in church-state relations.

There is a vast literature on church-state relationships extending back at least to the beginning of the fourth century A.D., when Constantine began to promote Christianity as the state religion of the Roman Empire, but much of it is of little direct use to the sociologist. Not merely is a vast proportion of that literature exclusively concerned with Christian conceptions of religious collectivities and Western conceptions of the state, it is also problematic from a sociological standpoint in its tendency to be concerned with narrow ecclesiastical and/or constitutional matters, rather than with objective relationships holding between religious and political authority. That is not to say that sociologists cannot learn from such approaches—for in some respects they constitute an essential part of the raw material which the social scientist must use. Nonetheless, the sociologist must reach for less culture-bound and legalistic approaches.

The Western experience of the emergence of the civilizational problem of church and state occurred between the Edict of Milan (313 A.D.), granting Christians unrestricted freedom of worship in the Roman Empire, and Justinian's promulgation in the sixth century of what became known as *caesaropapism* (the domination of the church, and of religion generally, by the state). In important respects, this experience has been misleading. For in societies other than the entirely preliterate, the most common circumstance is that in which religion is "neither state-controlled nor yet a state in itself," one in which the dominant religion generally "harmonizes with its society without being entirely dominated by it" (Strayer 1958:43). Religion becomes politically important only in exceptional circumstances. Otherwise it operates as a diffuse moral force.

More than any other factor, the Christian distinction between an earthly and a heavenly kingdom has given rise to the church-state theme in its most circumscribed sense. In fact the distinction between church and state is an extension of that basic Christian theme. However, as Martin (1978:279) emphasizes, even though the differentiation of church and state is invariably maintained symbolically and more often than not organizationally, "Christianity encounters a vigorous Durkheimian pull towards a total unity of Church and State." When the unity is broken there still remains "a pull towards collusion between fundamental social and religious values." We cannot enter here into the very complex problem as to when and where *the state* first emerged; however, it is clear that any serious discussion of church-and-state must address the general issue of the ways in which and degrees to which different world views, more often than not embodied in religiocultural traditions, express the relationship between worldly and supra- or extra-worldly spheres and the worldly manifestations or vehicles of those spheres.

In such terms we may, by way of an important example, contrast the Christian with the Buddhist world view. In its very earliest phase—as best we can tell from unclear records—Buddhism was not concerned with *society* as we nowadays use the term, however loosely. Monks and nuns were regarded as having departed from everyday social life, while lay Buddhists were enjoined to accept society passively. Certainly, neither monastics nor lay Buddhists in the incipient phase of Buddhism attended in any significant respect to the structural contingencies or normative requirements of the social order. Dumont (1982) argues, to all intents and purposes, that there were some remarkable parallels between that circumstance and the incipient phase of Christianity, insofar as the very earliest Christians were expected to be indifferent to the world and consolidate a charismatic community of the faithful in preparation for Christ's return. However, the founding of the Church per se seriously altered the Christian situation. From the fifth to the third century B.C. Buddhists were enjoined only to consolidate the Buddhist community; the conversion of King Aśoka to Buddhism in India changed things—but not in the same direction as early Christianity after the founding of the church.

Aśoka took the view that the state was not only of sociopolitical significance but also a soteriologically significant phenomenon (Kitagawa 1980:
91). From that point, Buddhism became embroiled in an Asian equivalent
of the Western church-state problems, a circumstance which continues to
the present day in the Theravada Buddhist societies of Sri Lanka, Burma,
and Thailand, where there is currently religious strife. Throughout this
long period (and not just in its Theravada branches) Buddhism has greatly
differed from Christianity (in spite of the fact that in comparison with
other major religious traditions they have shared the characteristic of having relatively differentiated religious structures) in the small degree to
which it has developed social teachings. Buddhism is said to lack what in
Christianity has variously been called middle principles, social teachings,
explicit practical-ethical applications of doctrine, or lay social ethics. One
of the most important consequences has been that Buddhism has frequently—and continuously in parts of South East Asia—become involved
in political matters and has indeed been adopted as the religion of a
number of nations, while at the same time sustaining what S.J. Tambiah
calls "a basic distinction that ideally the *sangha* (the monastic order) and
political authority are separate domains" (1976:521). While the king or
head of state has always needed the *sangha* in order to legitimate his
authority and was traditionally accorded the right of purifying the monas-
teries, the domains of religion and state politics have been kept intact. One
particularly significant aspect of that phenomenon is that it has been quite
common for individuals to move from one domain to the other and in the
process effect a rupture in their patterns of behavior. Traditionally kings
made "the passage from violence to piety" which is echoed more generally
among young people today, while also in modern times it is possible and
"politically feasible—first to be a monk and then later to become engaged
actively in this world" (Tambiah 1976:522).

Notwithstanding similarities, in the sense that there have been over the
centuries many situations of ambiguity, tension and conflict, the Buddhist
case contrasts sharply with the Christian in the degree to which in predominantly Christian contexts church and state have frequently claimed jurisdiction over the same domains. As the Christian church developed in the
Western world it became increasingly a rival to the state, to the point that
in certain periods of European history there were in effect two states—that
of the church and that of the secular governmental domain. This meant
that the church was an estate in parallel to the king's and resulted eventually in the *sacerdotium* acquiring "an imperial appearance and the *reg-
num* a clerical touch."[1]

The major contrast between Christianity and Buddhism (particularly in
its Theravada form) is captured succinctly in Dumont's conception of the

principle of *hierarchical complementarity*. Deriving from a world view which regards society as sui generis and the individual as very secondary to it, the Indian conception of hierarchy emphasizes the relation between priestly and royal functions as having a double aspect, with the priest being superior in a spiritual respect but, at the same time dependent "from a temporal or material point of view" (Dumont 1980:290). (In Dumont's analysis the major focus is Hinduism and the Indian caste system, rather than Buddhism. I will find it necessary in a moment to draw a line between Hinduism and Buddhism.) In contrast the Western world view, in spite of Dumont's claim that early Christianity was world-denying, has stressed the notion that society is basically made up of individuals (which, it should be remembered, was precisely Hobbes' starting point in his highly influential formulation of the strong, centralized and secular state in the sixteenth century). Thus hierarchy is seen as the stratification of individuals, not as a functional necessity of an organically united society. In that perspective there is no natural delineation of societal domains. Domain delineation and the ranking of domains is an essentially contestable matter—hence the odyssey of attempts to arrive at concordats between church and state in Christendom, which finally issues in the separation principle in the U.S.A.

Having established a general contrast between Christianity and Buddhism, it becomes necessary to repeat that in comparison with other major religiocultural traditions, they share the characteristic of having been largely embodied in distinctive structures. Christianity has been concretized in the structure of the church (which in its widest reach refers to a number of different types of religious organization, including sects and denominations), while Buddhism's major (and less "formidable") organizational vehicle has been the *sangha*. Using the work of Smith (1974a) as a guideline, we can contrast both Islam and Hinduism with Christianity and Buddhism by noting that the former pair share, in a broad sense, the characteristic of not having distinct structures. Islam and Hinduism have promoted an organic connection with society, in the sense of more or less equating the religion (which itself is a problematic term in this immediate context, most acutely in the case of Hinduism) with the society or civilization in which it is objectively located. In both cases "church-state" problems do not truly emerge until something like the self-consciously secular state has been installed. This is clearly true of Hinduism in India, in that it was not until India's political leaders explicitly attempted to establish a secular state in the late 1940s that there arose problems about defining religion. In Islamic societies the historical significance of Islamic law—in the form of *Shari'a*—has meant that everyday life, including political and social aspects thereof, have been directly subject to religiocultural regulation; while rulers in both the Shiite and Sunni traditions (although more in the former than in the latter) have been subject to that same constraint.

Thus we arrive at a typological format—in slight revision of Smith (1974a)—which distinguishes between Christianity, Buddhism, Hinduism and Islam in terms of two main variables: on the one hand, the degree to which the religiocultural tradition has been promoted in the form of relatively distinct structures; on the other, the degree to which the tradition is innerworldly or otherworldly (innerworldliness involving an emphasis upon making or remaking the world along the lines of the doctrinal tenets of the tradition; otherworldliness involving the view that the world is largely to be accepted in its existing form). Christianity is thus characterized by innerworldliness and structural distinctiveness; Islam by innerworldliness and relative lack of structural distinctiveness; Hinduism by otherworldliness and relative lack of structural distinctiveness; and Buddhism by otherworldliness and relative structural distinctiveness.[2]

Thus far I have focused on the church-state problem in a particularly broad and general way, which is clearly not specific enough to deal with many of the thornier issues in the areas of church-state relations and the connection between political authority and religious authority. One of the most well-established frames of reference with respect to these problem areas is that provided by Max Weber in his typology of caesaropapism, hierocracy and theocracy. Addressed broadly to the theme of legitimation, Weber's delineation specifies caesaropapism as the domination of religion by secular powers; hierocracy as the legitimating oversight of the political realm by religious functionaries; and theocracy as the fusion of political and religious authority (the priest who is also king). Actually in Weber's original formulation theocracy is defined as an extreme form of hierocracy (Weber 1978:1159-60). Thus it might be an improvement on Weber's typology to suggest that there are weak and strong forms of hierocracy (the stronger form being theocracy) and a form of domination of the religious realm by the central-political realm which is weaker than the extreme case of caesaropapism. That weaker form has often been called erastianism— namely, the subordination of religion, often in the form of an established church, to the state, but not the actual domination of the former by the latter.

Thus we can stipulate that as far as the theme of religious legitimation of the state is concerned there are four limiting types: *theocracy*, which involves union of church and state, with emphasis, however, on church autonomy; *hierocracy* which involves separation of church and state, with a high degree of church autonomy; *caesaropapism* which involves union of church and state, with a low degree of church autonomy; and *erastianism*, which involves separation of church and state, with a relatively low degree of church autonomy.[3] No matter what the basic world view, there is always, however minimally, the potential for religion-state conflict, which makes this typology of legitimation patterns applicable in principle to all of the types of religion-society relationships discussed previously. We have seen, however, that this potential for conflict is most pronounced in the sphere of Christian culture.

In attempting to be yet more specific—moving, that is, toward very concrete circumstances—it becomes necessary to pay particular attention to what may be called objective patterns—or *frames*—of religion-society relationships (Martin 1978:15-18). In this perspective the crucial factors are the number and variety of religious confessions in a society, on the one hand, and the degree to which that circumstance is, as a matter of degree, *rigid or flexible*, on the other (Robertson 1970:101-2). In those terms we may isolate four major tendencies.[4] First, we have the *monopolistic rigid* situation, exampled by most Christian Orthodox, as well as Iberian Catholic, societies. Second, we have the *monopolistic flexible* situation, in which one religious confession dominates a small number of other forms of religious commitment, as in France. Third, we may identify the *competitive rigid* situation, as seen in very different ways in the Netherlands (at least until very recently) and Lebanon. Finally, we may isolate the *competitive flexible* circumstances, best exemplified by the United States, but approached by Britain and, even more so, by Australia, Canada and New Zealand. Each of these patterns is greatly affected in its operation by state-governmental policies, which vary from either attempting to alter the pattern or strenuously maintaining it, at one extreme, to being indifferent toward it, at the other. In any case, any particular society that one examines can best be understood in the first instance by considering both the church-state pattern in "socioconstitutional" terms, as indicated previously, in conjunction with the religion-society pattern, as just outlined.

The foregoing suggests only some basic considerations and guidelines as to what is involved in the comparative study of church-state relations and cognate matters. In the following chapters some of the themes which have been raised here are pursued in depth.

Markoff and Regan, in a preliminary report on a larger study, indicate the extent to which national constitutions are converging in a general sense, but vary—may even be diverging—on religious matters. The difference is attributed to the national identity-conferring aspect of religious tradition. They show, moreover, that religion remains an important ingredient of ostensible modes of legitimation in many societies.

Dabashi's survey of Islamic traditions emphasizes the contrast between the theological emphasis upon the unity of "piety and polity" and *actual* tensions between religious and political forms of authority. In the modern era, he argues, the claims of "universal truth" of Islamic traditions begin to lose validity in the face of modernity—a tension which he expresses in terms of the relationship between truth and ideology.

My own discussion of Latin American liberation theology traces the latter's emergence and explores the options available to the Catholic Church in relation to the liberationist movement. Also discussed is the complexity of relationships between religion and ideology. Ewa Morawska's essay on Poland is particularly concerned with Polish civil religion, which has crystallized and persisted not so much in spite of but because of the virtually unique historical pattern of the partitioning and "on-off" sovereign status of Poland. Of particular importance is Morawska's emphasis upon the romantic motif in modern Polish history—a motif which includes, indeed gives prominence to, the idea of Poland as the embodiment (particularly when oppressed) of suffering on behalf of mankind, and carrying mankind's potential for redemption.

Bryan Turner locates his discussion of Australia within the analytical frame of the legitimation problems of the modern state and the empirical frame of the old (British) Commonwealth, white-settler societies. In advancing the importance of the state in forging the collective identities of the latter, Turner emphasizes the degree to which the modern, so-called secular state is in fact reliant upon religious modes of legitimation. In Australia, state-owned broadcasting plays a particularly important role in the promotion of moral-oriented civil religion centered on the family.

In his discussion of church-and-state in Ireland, John Fulton concentrates, unlike most analysts, on the situation in the Republic of Ireland. Developed to serve a Catholic state, the constitution of the Republic is a vital but neglected aspect of the church-state religion-politics issue in Ireland. Fulton is particularly concerned about connecting the constitutional situation in the Republic to that of the Northern Irish "statelet."

Finally, Eileen Barker addresses the issue of religious freedom in Britain, mainly in terms of contrasts between the latter and the United States. She notes the contrast between the legal distance between Britain and the U.S.A. as far as the protection of religious rights is concerned, on the one hand, and their de facto proximity, in the exercise of religious freedom, on the other. The low degree of salience of religion in Britain is a major factor in this regard.

Notes

1. Kantorowicz (1957:193). Quoted in Tambiah (1976:7).
2. There are, of course, societies (apart from the primitive) not comprehensively covered by this typology, notably China and Japan.

3. Each of these types can move in a highly secular direction. Martin (1978) offers many relevant insights. My typology in effect combines Weber's delineation with Vallier's (1970:35) attempt to depict the range of church-state relationships in Latin America.
4. See also Martin (1978:18-24).

Bibliography

Dumont, Louis. 1980. *Homo Hierarchicus: The Caste System and Its Implications.* Rev. English ed. Chicago: Chicago University Press.
———. "A Modified View of Our Origins: The Christian Beginnings of Modern Individualism," *Religion* 12 (1982):1-27.
Kantorowicz, E.H. 1957. *The King's Two Bodies.* Princeton: Princeton University Press.
Kitagawa, Joseph M. 1980. "Buddhism and Social Change: An Historical Perspective." Pp. 84-102 in *Buddhist Studies in Honour of Walpola Rahula.* Somaratna Balasooriya et al., eds., London: Gordon Fraser.
Martin, David. 1978. *A General Theory of Secularization.* New York: Harper and Row.
Rahman, Fazlur. 1982. *Islam and Modernity.* Chicago: University of Chicago Press.
Robertson, Roland. 1970. *The Sociological Interpretation of Religion.* New York: Schocken.
Smith, Donald E. 1974a. "Religion and Political Modernization: Comparative Perspectives." Pp. 3-28 in *Religion and Political Modernization.* Donald Eugene Smith, ed., New Haven: Yale University Press.
———. 1974b. "Patterns of Secularization in Latin America." Pp. 116-31 in *Religion and Political Modernization.* New Haven: Yale University Press.
Strayer, Joseph R. "The State and Religion: Greece and Rome, the West, Islam," *Comparative Studies in Society and History* I (1958):38-43.
Tambiah, S.J. 1976. *World Conqueror and World Renouncer: A Study of Buddhism and Polity in Thailand Against a Historical Background.* Cambridge: Cambridge University Press.
Vallier, Ivan. 1970. *Catholicism, Social Control and Modernization in Latin America.* Englewood Cliffs, N.J.: Prentice Hall.
Weber, Max. 1978. *Economy and Society.* Edited by G. Roth and C. Wittich. Berkeley: University of California Press.

13

Religion, the State and Political Legitimacy in the World's Constitutions

John Markoff and *Daniel Regan*

Introduction

Our themes are simple: the richness and diversity of religious expression in the world's societies and the range of variation in what is problematic in the relations between religion and politics. Our source to explicate these themes is unlikely: the constitutions of the world's nations.

Why should national constitutions represent improbable templates on which to gauge and locate religious aspirations and to chart the ways in which religion enters into political conflict? To answer this question, consider a typical process of constitution drafting. The procedure which led to Thailand's 1978 document serves as a convenient example. Thirty-five members composed a Constitution Drafting Committee, of whom 25 were chosen from the membership of a National Legislative Assembly; 10 were nominated by the government from among the heads of major political parties, leading jurists, and noted political scientists. This assemblage, typical in its apparently secularist composition, was locked in debate for some five months. Owing to divisions among committee members, according to a first-person account (Tongdhamachart 1979), it took a long time to compromise on the wording of some proposed clauses; others were settled by majority vote. At times heated and emotional and at others businesslike, the sessions appear to have resembled an extended faculty meeting more than a religious or even political revival meeting.

Such a process—same scene and players, with appropriate local modifications—has been enacted in many countries around the world. It seems the very apex of a society's attempt to achieve rational-legal legitimacy—one particular form of legitimacy that Max Weber proposed was becoming dominant in association with the rise of strong and effective central bureaucracies. Rational-legal (or bureaucratic) legitimacy is the belief that one owes obedience to a body of rules which have been promulgated in what is held to be the proper manner. Such a belief implies that it is the laws of humankind, not those of the divine, to which one defers. Thus a search for rational-legal legitimacy, and the process of constitution-making which appears to exemplify it, would seem to provide an uncongenial vehicle for religious expression.

We take the nineteenth century Latin American jurist, Justo Arosemena, as a reasonably representative, if unusually articulate, enthusiast for constitutionalism. In addition to actual participation in constitution-writing, Arosemena edited two important collections of constitutional texts. In doing so, he sought to provide data that would advance the day when politics would be rational and the study of politics a science (Arosemena 1870; 1888). In his introductions and commentaries on specific examples, Arosemena makes plain that he favors a clear-headed, systematic and modern approach to rational government, the intellectual paternity of which he traces back to Aristotle (as opposed to the dreamy and emotion-rich aspect of Platonic pedigree). This sensitive and highly self-conscious champion of the modern is nowhere as consistently critical of the Latin constitutions he devoted himself to improving as in their religious aspects. Their propensity for involving the state in religious life he found both backwards and worthy of condemnation. And yet, as we shall show, the documents which secular jurists such as Arosemena actually produce deviate wildly from what one might expect from a knowledge of the makers and the process of making.

Besides the ardently secular composition of most constitutional drafting committees, and the character of the rational-legal process in which their members participate, there is also to be considered the nature of the document itself. First of all there are but a handful of styles of writing constitutions, most of which have either drawn upon American, French or Soviet constitutions (or Roman Catholic documents) as models or have been heavily influenced by the juridical traditions of the colonial power (especially England and France) when they have not been literally drafted by jurists from the metropole. By now each style has been internationalized and is well imitated among the world's more than 150 independent nations, nearly all of which possess written constitutions. (The proportion with written constitutions has increased since 1870, when only 39 of 47 nations had them.) As a result of all this borrowing, it would appear that constitutions are documents which leave scant leeway for particularistic religious concerns to find expression.

In addition, as Ivo Duchacek (1973a, 1973b) reminds us, most national constitutions are alike in that they contain similar elements: a preamble; a description of various governmental procedures, along with the structures and agencies which perform them; articles which stipulate procedures to be followed in case constitutional revisions are sought; and an enumeration of citizen rights and duties. Thus, exoterically, constitutions are rather similar. When it comes to their styles and to some extent their contents, there is a considerable degree of convergence. Scholars may debate the question of whether cross-societal convergence or divergence is a product of modernization; on the whole the debate would seem to be settled for modern constitutions. Although, for example, life in the Republic of China (Taiwan) and in the People's Republic of China is assuredly different for the average citizen, their constitutions contain many surprisingly similar elements. (When we quote from or paraphrase constitutions, the reader is referred to the third edition of the English-language Peaslee collection (1965-70) unless we indicate otherwise.)

Such generic resemblances are not merely the case for ideologically contrasting pairs; interregional or other comparisons would yield similar results. A recent quantitative study of the changing contents of constitutions over the past century (Boli-Bennett 1976) finds them to be not merely more numerous but increasingly similar. This finding raises the question of whether the institutions of the modern state are converging on a common pattern—the author's view—or whether the public self-presentation of national states in their constitutions is converging regardless of institutional differences. Such a perplexing question may incline some readers to reject constitutional documents as a fundamentally gratuitous and hence invalid source. We do not think so, and explain why below.

Amidst this overall pattern of convergence, however, there is significant contrast and divergence. Where these otherwise similar documents continue to differ—and this is what fascinates us—is in their references to culturally-specific realms of life, particularly religious ones. (We suspect, but cannot prove at this point in our investigation, an increase, and an increasing divergence, in the religious content of constitutions. We guess this occurs especially as colonial history recedes into the past for the world's newer nations, and they reassert their own religiocultural identities.) In Thailand, to return to our initial example, the group drawn from the secular elite referred to above produced a document rife with religious references and content. (And in Thailand at least, such an outcome occurs rather frequently: the 1978 constitution was the nation's thirteenth, more than any other country has promulgated in a similar time span.) Even Heng Samrin, when he presented neighboring Kampuchea's draft constitution to the National Assembly, did not fail to locate his occupied country in an extra- or perhaps supra-societal frame of reference. Along with denouncing "French colonialists, . . . U.S. aggressors [and] . . . the genocidal Pol Pot-Ieng Sary-Khieu Samphan regime, lackeys of the Chinese expansionists," he sought to place the nation in the stream of international socialist history (1981). Thus religion of one sort or another emerges as a potent particularizing force, even in the constitutions of the world's nations.

In spite of the strong orientation to U.S. and European models and the sometimes dominant role of European or European-trained lawyers, we find rather striking divergences from those models among Islamic cases. Their autochthonous nature is clear whether the colonial past was English, French, Italian or none at all. And among Islamic cases we doubt that anyone would confuse the religious aspects of the constitutions of Iran, Indonesia or Turkey with any other; we suspect, indeed, that someone acquainted with the specificity of religious expression in these countries, presented with merely the relevant passages from these documents with the name of the state excised, would exclaim instantaneously, "This must be from Iran, or Indonesia, or Turkey."

But what does this religion content mean? To answer this question it is useful to consider first what constitutional references to religion do not mean.

Making Sense of Constitutional References to Religion

Most obviously, ideological documents such as constitutions, despite their binding legalistic tone, are undependable guides to political action. One should not expect one-to-one, or even remotely close to complete, correspondences between constitutional assertions and political behavior. Nor could even the most cynical observer make a credible claim that constitutional assertions represent the direct opposite of political behavior. Constitution-gazing is a perilously inaccurate way of discovering, much less predicting, a nation's politics. Does anyone, for instance, doubt Amnesty International's documentary evidence of human rights violations in Iran, Turkey and elsewhere? And yet the Constitution of the Islamic Republic of Iran, unlike that of its predecessor in the *ancien régime* with whose nefarious practices the new republic apparently shares much, states explicitly, "Any form of torture for the purpose of extracting confessions or gaining information is forbidden" (Article 38). And Article 14 of the avowedly secular Turkish constitution of 1961 guarantees, without qualification, that "no individual shall be subjected to ill-treatment or torture."

By now, in fact, practically every one of the world's nations proclaims an explicit commitment to guaranteeing fundamental human rights. These commitments, found in national constitutions (as well as in international agreements), are a recent phenomenon and not a carryover from the past; rather, the twentieth century embodies a virtual global movement, in principle, toward the delineation of an inviolable private niche within which individuals possess inalienable rights, and against which the state can make few if any claims. Despite all this, as is well known, most nations violate even their own list of rights. What Stanley Hoffman (1983), Irving Louis Horowitz (1978), and others have noted, regarding the international agreements which nations have signed, is also true for their constitutions: the gap between constitutional word and political deed has become a chasm. Even the constitutional statements themselves frequently teem with qualifying clauses, so that in many cases the guarantee of rights is far from absolute.

It is clear that constitutions fail to cast much direct, illumining light on actual political behavior. Although that complicates the interpretation of constitutional documents, it is no argument to dismiss them as devoid of significance. They mean something, but what?

One thing constitutions do is identify pretty clearly matters which are public issues of concern to a society, at least to its elites. Thus the actual incidence of torturous practices in Iran and Turkey may be unknown; that the issue of torture is important, both domestically and internationally, for those two countries is indisputable, judging from claims their national constitutions make about the matter. The same holds true, for example, for the problem of societal corruption. Countries that fail to mention the issue in their national constitutions may yet have a corruption problem; those that do mention it asssuredly do. Although no one would claim that religion constitutes a problem analogous to that of corruption or torture, we may apply similar reasoning to many cases in which constitutional references to religion appear. Sometimes religion is too potentially divisive an issue for the framers of constitutions to write about it. Religiously divided Lebanon—the constitution of which (1926, as amended to 1960) is remarkably devoid of religious content—is a case in point. And Israel's lack of a constitution may be owed to extreme sensitivity over religious issues. For some small number of religiously homogeneous societies, the religious content of constitutions is uncontroversial. In the constitution of Yemen, we suspect, the official declaration of Islam as state religion (without, incidentally, even including freedom of religion among the general rights listed) would be taken for granted, though no less significant for the lack of heat which such a declaration generates.

In most cases in which religious concerns are mentioned, however, it is clear that religion is a pressing issue for the society. Moreover, the specific content of religious references in national constitutions demarcates areas which are problematic in the relation between religious life and political order. Those references chart the ways in which religion enters into political conflict, and sometimes the ways in which political actors seek to adjudicate and control religiously based conflict. Thus, when the constitution of Czechoslovakia grants everyone "the right to profess any religious faith or to be without religious conviction, and to practice his religious beliefs insofar as this does not contravene the law," the qualification in that article identifies a point of tension between religion and the state. (Besides or instead of invoking claims of law and order, other nations subject the freedom of religious practice or worship to qualification by balancing it against political or moral restrictions.) When the Pakistani constitution of 1962 decrees that "no law shall be repugnant to the teachings and requirements of Islam as set out in the Holy Quran and Sunnah," we are aware of having been presented a compromise over the Islamic character of the state. (In fact, the rigors of defining that character were responsible, in part, for successive constitutional crises.) When the framers of the Cyprus constitution in 1960 incorporate elaborate agreements to regulate the allocation of resources of all kinds among Turkish Muslims and the Greek Orthodox community, their perception of the fearful potential of intergroup conflict is underlined. The same holds true for Yugoslavia, the constitution of which (1963) makes punishable and explicitly prohibits as unconstitutional the incitement to "religious hatred or intolerance."

Besides summarizing and identifying what is problematic about relations between the central state apparatus and other strategic groups or institutions, constitutions are clearly "aspirational" in nature. Although constitutional references cannot be taken as descriptions of politically relevant behavior, their meaning is surely normative. The assignment of normative or aspirational meaning to constitutions assumes the interpretability of texts—they are more than tabula rasa upon which succeeding generations affix their own social and political concerns—and the possibility of assigning substantive and not merely procedural import to constitutions. In doing so we adopt a position which grants primacy to the constitution itself rather than to some other fount of authority such as the judiciary. We do not deny that the adoption of constitutional documents, or their subsequent amendment, culminates a political process of compromise among competing factions. But we also wish to account for the way constitutions not only codify current political agreements but also cant toward future ones. From the framers' point of view, there is little doubt that their creation is intended for future generations, as well as the present one, and sometimes even for posterity. Thus a constitution possesses educative significance for the future. From the standpoint of those unnamed future generations, the document they are left with is hard to ignore, whether it constitutes a valuable gift or an albatross, written by public-minded servants or by thieves.

Our view of constitutional meaning and significance regards text as the best indication of the ideal state of affairs which the framers have adumbrated through their provisions, while remaining cognizant that a full interpretation requires probing beyond language to historical context. This view, which affirms the possibility of interpreting texts with something approaching the meaning accorded them by their originators, permits our comparative analysis of the religious content of constitutions to proceed, even though a complete analysis of all individual national contexts is beyond our reach here. The viewpoint on constitutional meaning adopted here also draws attention to the two types of legitimacy claims that constitutions in general, supported by their religious references in particular, make. The first of these is oriented to the present and seeks to render legitimate the framers' depiction of what has already been achieved and their claim that something solid and fundamental in the way the society governs itself is already in place. The second is oriented toward the future, and aims to make legitimate their image of an ideal future society. One set of legitimacy claims is thus confirmatory, asserting the rightfulness of that which, purportedly, has already been acquired, and the second is programmatic, asserting the desirability of that which, avowedly, has yet to be achieved.

In these ways, constitutional documents are meaningful, as they literally help constitute a society. Edward Shils (1982) writes of "the constitution of society through the formation of an image of the society in the minds of its members." Although the author barely mentions them, constitutional documents supply that image, or at least one of several possible images. As those documents, through symbols, define the boundaries of legitimate political discourse, so do they symbolically delineate the legitimate contours of political society. In a real way, then, to promulgate a new constitution is to reconstitute a society, and perhaps to provide a new basis of legitimacy for it. Besides this legitimating, integrative function, however, it is also true that, on occasion, an extant constitution can serve as a powerful source of political delegitimation.

In sum, although one would be foolhardy in attempting to infer the actual operation of social institutions or their relations with one another from constitutions (since they vary so much in the extent and the ways in which they describe present action or constrain the future), one may well come to grasp something of the nature of images of an ideal social order.

Legitimacy

Concerns of a religious character have often played a significant, at times central, role in the capacity of states to present themselves as legitimate.

Although academic observers sometimes downplay the significance of legitimacy, working politicians rarely do. They know it is infinitely preferable to command assent not merely through coercion, rewards or even effective problem-solving, but through a sense they foster that subjects or citizens have a moral duty to comply. As we discussed previously, Max Weber proposed that in the modern world one particular form of legitimacy—the rational-legal—was becoming dominant, and the proliferation of written constitutions in the nineteenth and twentieth centuries is itself a sign of the degree to which this form of legitimation has flourished. A constitution, as we have shown, may signify different things to different people. Among those various meanings is the belief that a written document can to some degree restrain the behavior of political elites and also a belief that a written document must claim to embody a set of fundamental principles of government. Although some may question whether one or another meaning is present in a given case, on neither count do we see in constitutions anything but a bureaucratic form of the claim to moral authority.

Thus a constitution might seem the worst place to look for some indication that political life needs a justification from on high. After all, are not such documents almost quintessential assertions that we men and women in this time and place can write down the rules by which we expect to structure our society? And yet, given the central role which religious concerns have played in the legitimation (and delegitimation) of the political orders of the past, one must wonder whether, as an ultimate justification for the mandate to rule, the law of humankind can command the same intensity and reliability of assent as the law of God.

In fact, on the evidence of these documents, one must conclude that the makers of constitutions are often unwilling to let the deliberately enacted rules of human beings stand bare. The Constitution of Indonesia, for example, declares that:

> Thanks to the blessing of God Almighty, and impelled by the Noble desire to lead their own free national life, the People of Indonesia hereby declare their Independence.

The preamble goes on to assert that the republic shall be based upon:

> Belief in the One Supreme God, just and civilized Humanity, the unity of Indonesia, and democracy which is guided by the inner wisdom in the unanimity arising out of deliberation among representatives.

Thus the "deliberation among representatives" is but one of the bases for justice for the whole of the people of Indonesia. (The reader will note, incidentally, the distinctive syncretism for which Indonesia is often noted:

unlike many other Islamic instances, this God is not specifically Allah.) The explicit recognition of God as the source of constitution-making, while far from universal, is hardly confined to the Islamic (or even the non-Western) world, as a contemporary newspaper reader might mistakenly presume. The constitution of Colombia identifies God as the "supreme source of all authority," while God is identified as the "source of all reason and justice" in the constitution of Argentina, a country that in recent years has had less than its full share of either.

Nor are such statements limited to documents written before the secular twentieth century. The constitution of Ireland, which dates from 1937, is enacted "in the Name of the Most Holy Trinity, from Whom is all authority and to Whom, as our final end, all actions both of men and States must be referred." The Basic Law of the Federal Republic of Germany, originally decreed in 1949, is held to be the enactment of the German People "conscious of its responsibility before God and Men." And the Greek constitution of 1952 is "in the name of the Holy, Consubstantial and Indivisible Trinity."

Our examples so far, which invoke a higher authority as judge of human actions or as source of human capacities, have been taken from preambles. But this is only the most explicit way in which constitutions deny that people's desires to shape their political arrangements are self-justifying. When, for example, a document proclaims a state religion, some purpose of the state other than realizing the will of its citizens is implied. In some of these instances, the state has as one of its purposes a sacred responsibility, not merely to respond to the intentions of its citizens, but to insure that those intentions are in accord with ultimate values. Consider the constitution of Greece, whose very first article simultaneously establishes a religion, proclaims the freedom of other faiths, and places an absolute ban on all proselytism. Or consider the Norwegian constitution which requires in its second article that Norwegians professing the Evangelical-Lutheran faith bring up their children accordingly.

Even constitutions which contain neither an explicit statement framing the operations of constitution-making with an eye on eternity nor specific institutional mechanisms assuring the primacy of ultimate values over the works of man may nevertheless provide for at least a fleeting reminder of a transcendental authority. Many constitutions, for example, explicitly mandate a religious oath of office for the head of state or legislators or both. When the president and vice-president of Indonesia "swear before God" to "hold faithfully to the Constitution," the moral force of that constitution is held to rest on something other than the desire that human rules be obeyed. This invocation of God may not have the same explicitness as the first article of the French Constitutional Law of 1875 which required that "public prayers shall be addressed to God in all the churches and temples in order to call upon His help for the work of the assemblies" (Dareste 1883). Nevertheless, widespread reliance upon religious oaths is further evidence of the modern nation-state's quest for something other than bureaucratic legitimacy, and of the vital role of constitutional references to religion in pursuing that goal. (While there are constitutions which prescribe no oath or which prescribe a nonreligious oath or which propose options, the Turkish constitution is at an extreme in requiring legislators to swear commitment "to the principles of a democratic and secular republic.")

Although no statistical tabulations are displayed here, we may report that a very substantial proportion of constitutions contain some one of these forms of religious sanction for human political actions. The largest cluster of late twentieth-century cases that, at first glance, lack this character are those under communist governments, many of which, in a special elaboration of clauses on freedom of religious expression, specifically protect the freedom of antireligious expression. Nevertheless, even this group of constitutions tends to find an extrasocietal bedrock on which to ground present political arrangements. We are hardly the first to note that an abstract conception of the movement of history can for some purposes be invoked in place of the purposes of God. If one sees history as preeminently the product of the interplay of human wills, then the invocation of a history within which the framing of a constitution is embedded is not an invocation of an extrasocietal legitimacy principle; but if one writes of a great and immutable historical drama, the movement of history itself may acquire something of the flavor of the purposes of God working themselves out in human affairs. The Mongolian text situates itself within "the age-old struggle of the Mongolian people for liberation;" the Czech document is part of "creating the material and moral conditions for the transition of our society to communism;" the Polish refers to "the most glorious progressive traditions of the Polish nation." Whether or not history is strictly limited to human will or is the unfolding of something external to it is at least ambiguous in these texts.

In sum, if written constitutions are one of the supreme expressions of the sense that, in the modern world, rules written by men and women following proper procedures carry a moral authority, they also simultaneously point to the limits of such claims to legitimacy. Few constitutions present themselves as simply the embodiment of what those alive today or their representatives desire for themselves; however minimally, weakly, or ambiguously, most constitutions point to some larger basis for justification.

The theoretical significance of this aspect of contemporary political constitutions poses questions that we will broach but not attempt to answer. One line of argument in the debate among American sociologists on civil religion, most eloquently represented by Robert Bellah (Richey and Jones 1974:257), has taken the Durkheimian position that all politically organized social arrangements find some form of religious expression for such solidarity as they have. Hence it follows that even those states with the greatest claims to a break with traditional symbols or institutional carriers of religion will develop new organizational vehicles for assessing national history against some standard of ultimate values. This helps assure political life of a sacred or quasi-sacred aspect so that politics is not merely a matter of force and fraud. Others, of whom we may take Richard Fenn (1978:34-35) as an instance, have contended that such an invocation of religious symbols is indeed characteristic of modern political life, but that it is entirely inauthentic. Developing a rather obscure discussion of Max Weber (1968:3:959), Fenn has contended that it is precisely the abandonment of anything beyond technical criteria for decision making that spawns a proliferation of wholly fraudulent claims to higher purposes (which do not actually constrain anyone's behavior). We limit ourselves here to the observation that such claims are quite widespread among the political systems of the world today. Whether they are authentic or not is another matter; our opening remarks on constitutions would suggest that they are sometimes one, sometimes the other (which again serves to make our point that the full interpretation of similar constitutional statements demands an investigation of the individual national context).

The Demarcation of Institutional Authority

Robert Bellah's deservedly celebrated paper on religious evolution (1970) suggests the critical but problematic character of the relationship between the organized structures of civil and of religious authority. As religious doctrines become more intellectually elaborate and abstract, religious practice more complex, and religious institutions increasingly staffed by specialists, the political relationships between those with this-worldly and those with other-worldly responsibilities become quite complex. In what Bellah calls the epoch of "historic religion" there is a body of passionately embraced belief in a higher, better or more advanced state of affairs in terms of which the current social and political order of this world might be found wanting; there is a body of specialists in the interpretation and transmission of sacred knowledge or in the performance of sacred rituals whose approval of the personnel or policies of this-worldly government is not automatic. Max Weber attempted to chart the various organizational relationships that might at least provisionally resolve this tension (1968:1159-63). At one pole we have caeseropapism in which the religious authorities are structurally subordinated to the state; at the other pole, hierocracy, it is the state which is subordinate. Our constitutions reveal traces of earlier settlements of these tensions and projected new resolutions as well. In the contemporary era, this zone of tension has sometimes been complicated by the explicit struggle for a secular state: one specialized in specifically this-worldly concern from which religious considerations have been removed. Although we have argued above that many constitutions do not break totally with some religious basis for legitimation, the struggle for a state in some sense emancipated from religious responsibilities has been a central strand in state-making at least from the Italian theorists of *ragione di stato*. Our examinations of constitutions also suggest another route into a secularized conception of the state: not so much a struggle to develop a separate sphere for political action, as the negative project of avoiding hopeless civil conflict in the face of multiple and potentially competitive groups which identify themselves as religious communities.

The state may be assigned quite specific religious responsibilities. In this regard, few constitutions are more elaborate or more specific than the Burmese in which the state is enjoined to support the study of Pali and Sanskrit, restore relics of the Buddha, and provide special hospitals for the monastic orders in conformity with the rules of their discipline. In line with our earlier remarks on legitimacy, we see here—and in the general injunction to

> promote and maintain Buddhism for its welfare and advancement . . . honor the Tiratana, namely, the Buddha, Dhamma and Sangha [and] protect the said religion in its three aspects and the Tiratana from all dangers including insult and false representation.

—a rather specifically Buddhist conception of the proper role of the monarch now transferred to the modern impersonal state. The very clear sense of a religious role for governing authority, quite at variance with some conceptions of a fundamentally antipolitical Buddhism, has been magnificently developed by recent scholars (e.g., see B. Smith 1978) of Southeast Asia.

Laying out vague or specific religious obligations for state authorities, however, is but one of the ways in which the line between institutions is clarified—or blurred. A constitution may provide a specific institutional mechanism to insure that the political authorities do not stray from the proper path. The Kampuchean constitution (of 1947, as amended to 1964), for example, places "the heads of the religious sects" on the Crown Council. In its explicitness, the (pre-Khomeini) Iranian constitution represents the most developed version. It is the task of "five devout doctors of Islamic law and jurisprudence" to examine proposed legislative enactments "and reject any that contravene the holy principles of Islam." Thus the rejection of an entire regime by devout and learned doctors of Islamic jurisprudence is an extension of their constitutionally legitimated authority to hold the state to its moral responsibilities.

Since so much of political life revolves around the extraction and allocation of resources, we are not surprised to find that assertion or denial of state responsibilities for the financial life of religious institutions is often spelled out. The Burmese and Indian documents might be taken as polar types. The Burmese constitution specifies a minimum proportion of the budget that must be spent for religious purposes. It goes on to explain that it is not only Buddhism that is to be supported but Islam, Christianity, Hinduism and Animism. The constitution of India, on the contrary, announces that: "No person shall be compelled to pay any taxes, the proceeds of which are specifically appropriated in payment of expenses for the promotion or maintenance of any particular religion or religious denomination."

If religious responsibilities of the state may be asserted or denied, we find that the social, economic or political autonomy of religiously constituted bodies may likewise be asserted, denied or passed over in silence. Some documents are more or less secular by virtue of implicitly avoiding discussion or explicitly disavowing state involvement in religious affairs; others are more strenuously secular by actively prohibiting or delimiting various forms of religious activity in social life. The communist states tend to combine a formal respect for freedom of conscience with a denial of any legitimate political role for religiously constituted bodies. The Mexican constitution is probably the most elaborate and detailed in this regard, far more so than the communist cases:

> Ministers of denominations may never, in a public or private meeting constituting an assembly, or in acts of worship or religious propaganda, criticize the fundamental laws of the country or the authorities of the Government, specifically or generally.

This insistence on an apolitical role for religious institutions (in the Mexican case at least a clear legacy of the rather traumatic birth of a modern set of political institutions) is by no means confined to avowedly secular states; although the Burmese constitution enjoins the state to a quite elaborate set of rather specific religious responsibilities, it, too, delineates a political sphere from which religion is to be barred. Political activities, for example, are excluded from Burma's clause concerning freedom of religious practice.

If the drawing of boundaries beyond which religious institutions are not to pass is not a certain indication of a secular conception of the state, neither is secularity necessarily marked by state neutrality in the management of religious affairs. Some constitutions recognize the autonomy of internal governance of religious organization by silence. Others, like India, explicitly assert the right of self-governance and property ownership for religious organizations, yet other states, at least equally secular, envisage a quite different relation of church and state. Again, the Mexican case appears extreme:

> The representative of each church building, jointly with ten other residents of the vicinity, shall inform the municipal authorities immediately who is the person in charge of the church in question. Any change of ministry must be reported by the departing minister in person, accompanied by the new incumbent and ten other residents. The municipal authority, under penalty of removal from office and a fine of up to one thousand pesos for each violation, shall see that this provision is complied with; under the same penalty, he shall keep one registry book of church buildings and another of the representatives in charge. The municipal authority shall give notice to the Secretariat of Government, through the governor of the State, of every permit to open a new church building to the public, or of any changes among representatives in charge. Donations in the form of movable objects shall be kept in the interior of church buildings.

If, in short, some constitutions embody an implicit conception that the mere disavowal of an established religion suffices to keep Caesar disentangled from God, the Mexican, Turkish and several others see the emancipation of politics from religion only achievable by continual control. This has a distinct caeseropapist ring to it with a modern state born in the fires of social upheaval replacing the sacralized monarch. One wonders whether this is not a rather secular continuation of an earlier pattern of legitimate church-state relations in which the state had the upper hand. Although they may not be as forceful in their assertion of political controls as Turkey or Mexico, the Communist cases are intellectually in the debt— to make the weakest possible statement—of the revolutionary successor state of the Czar's empire. It would be hard to find a purer twentieth-century example of caeseropapism than the relationship of Russian Orthodoxy to the Czarist bureaucracy (Pipes 1974:221-45).

Let us note that the state supervision of religious institutions in the late twentieth century is not confined to these instances of rather hostile struggle for secularity. The countries of Lutheran Scandinavia, for example, provide for at least an overall regulation of the national established church. The Danish constitution, for example, declares that the Evangelical Lutheran Church shall be governed by statute and that "religious bodies dissenting from the Established Church" shall be governed by statute as well. The Norwegian constitution assigns the King (who must profess the official creed) responsibility for ecclesiastical appointments (who swear obedience to the Constitution and the monarch), for organizing public worship and for regulating the teaching of religion. (To touch base with our theme of the individuality of religious/political relationships: Sweden, Denmark, Norway, Iceland and Finland, while sharing some sense of state authority in church affairs, otherwise differ considerably.)

One frequent focus of state supervision is the relationship of the dominant national religious community to transnational structures of belief and organization. A century ago Catholic states' claims to appoint the hierarchy or Orthodox states' scrutiny of international communication were less scarce than at present—but Mexico still insists that Catholic clerics be Mexican nationals and Switzerland still maintains in its basic political document a ban on the Jesuits.

Although one usually conceives of state disengagement from religion as animated by state-makers, the assertion of state control might be confining enough to generate support for separation on the religious side. The legacy of centuries of state dominance of the Brazilian church is clearly seen in the 1824 constitution (Dareste 1883). Although Catholicism is established as a privileged state cult, the old power of Portuguese monarchs to nominate bishops, confer benefices and pass on the acceptability of Rome's pronouncements is assigned to the Emperor of Brazil. In such a framework it is understandable that a powerful movement for disestablishment arose inside the Brazilian church—although the studiously secular Republican constitution of 1891 (Dareste and Dareste 1891) was held to go way too far (Bruneau 1974).

A far less dramatic form of limiting religious authority is extremely widespread. While by the late twentieth century most constitutions uphold freedom of conscience, a very large number propose something short of absolute freedom of worship. One no longer finds anything like the clause in the Brazilian Constitution of 1824 (Dareste 1883) to the effect that non-Catholics were free to worship as they liked behind closed doors. But it is quite common for the almost obligatory acknowledgement of individual freedom of religious practice to be made subject to the requirements of law and order or of morality, thereby granting state authorities the right to delineate such limits.

Apart from specifications of whether and how political authorities may regulate religious practice and organization (or, less commonly, how religious authorities may claim political prerogatives), two particular settings are occasionally made the locus for attempting to draw the boundary of sacred and secular domains. A number of constitutions specify the location of the power to perform valid marriages, as in the Albanian insistence that only the state can perform a lawful marriage (although an already properly married couple may then have a second, religious celebration).

More varied, and sometimes written in a dramatic language that suggests intense conflict, are the provisions that allocate responsibility for education. The Mexican constitution is again an extreme of sorts:

> Education shall be maintained entirely apart from any religious doctrine and, based on the results of scientific progress, shall strive against ignorance and its effects, servitudes, fanaticisms, and prejudices.

It is to this end one presumes that religious bodies are barred from "institutions giving elementary, secondary and normal education and education for laborers or field workers." Pakistan, by way of contrast, permits all religious communities to maintain educational institutions. That state, indeed, goes well beyond this rather common measure when it insists that "the teaching of Holy Quran and Islamiat to the Muslims of Pakistan should be compulsory." Although states permit, encourage or enjoin religious education, there is at least one case where secular education is explicitly limited. In Iran's document we find that "the study and teaching of science, education and art are free except as prohibited by religious law."

Finally, let us note the religious specificity of the church/state dividing line. As Donald Smith (1966) observed, the points at issue in creating a differentiated state vary with the religious tradition. In the Theravada past, the relationship of the organized monastic orders to the monarch was a carefully staged dialogue constrained within obligations on both sides. We are not surprised that the modern Burmese bureaucracy continues the royal task of preserving the doctrine and providing for the monks. In Islam the central religious specialists are interpreters of God's law; we are not surprised at the frequency with which Islamic constitutions deal with the proper place of the Sharia courts.

Restricting ourselves to the Islamic cases, if we had to guess on the basis of the constitutions in force at the moment of the overthrow of a regime, in which Islamic country the old order might be most vigorously denounced for being hopelessly contrary to Islam and in which one, uniquely, for granting too much to the devout, would any reader of the constitutions of the Shah's Iran and pre-coup Turkey have any hesitation?

The Treatment of Religious Diversity

"Most societies in the world today are 'plural societies'" (Bell 1980:199); many are deeply divided, some by religion. Where religion (or nonreligion) is a significant marker of group identity, how does a constitution portray the religious situation to its own nation's citizens and to the world? All constitutions are fictive, providing images of a state of governance which the framers claim has been attained already along with those which refer to an idealized social order of the future. Without contending that such documents, standing alone, bear a primary burden for regulating intergroup conflict, our question is, what particular images of religious tolerance do constitutions transmit? Further, what solutions do they envisage to the problem of ensuring mutually tolerable relations among different religious groups?

If an uninformed observer were to emerge, like Rip van Winkle or an extraterrestrial being, seeking clues for the answers to these questions in the religious references found in texts of national constitutions, the first thing to be noticed would be the variety of answers given. At one extreme for a religiously divided society, Lebanon's constitution tends to skirt the matter and does not, constitutionally, identify religious diversity as a burning issue. Neither a pressing problem to be solved nor, indeed, a societal characteristic to be celebrated, religious complexity is denied explicit public recognition. "All Lebanese shall be equal before the law," says Article 7 unequivocally, admitting no distinctions, religious or otherwise; no mention is made of religious qualification for particular officeholders; the presidential oath of office makes a nonspecific reference to "Almighty God" and nowhere is Islam or Christianity mentioned specifically. Besides respecting the personal status and religious interests of the population, "to whatever religious sect they belong," and guaranteeing "no violation of the right of religious communities to have their own schools," the only exception to the pattern sketched above, whereby religious differences fail to be accorded explicit recognition, is a clearly provisional measure which decrees that "the sects shall be equitably represented in public employment and in the composition of the Ministry, provided such measures will not harm the general welfare of the state."

At the other extreme from Lebanon is the 1960 constitution of Cyprus which, almost in its entirety, is devoted to allocative issues between members of the Greek and Turkish communities. Because the qualifying criteria for community membership are in part religious, the elaborate constitutional provisions have much to do with religious differences between Muslim and Greek Orthodox citizens of the republic. Even national citizenship appears to include some supranational, including religious, loyalty. Thus, in Cyprus, "the authorities of the Republic and any public corporation or public utility body . . . shall have the right to fly on holidays together with the flag of the Republic both the Greek and the Turkish flags at the same time;" indeed, the Greek and the Turkish communities "shall have the right to celebrate respectively the Greek and the Turkish national holidays."

One could say that both the Lebanese and Cypriot documents are misleading, one in virtually ignoring a problem and the other in conveying an impression that its solution is well worked out and practical. Such an assertion would depend, however, upon what one thinks constitutional documents lead an observer to. Although not indicative of actual political behavior, the Lebanese Constitution (of 1926, amended to 1960) does direct attention to what framers thought, or wanted others to think, an ideal Lebanon would, or should, look like. Its provisions embody publicly, for purposes of internal and external legitimation, a set of claims about a present society and a set of images of a future society. When it comes to the constitution of Cyprus, we are particularly attuned to a set of claims, or perhaps just hopes shaped by political necessity, about an effective philosophy of intercommunal accommodation.

Lebanon's inattention to the problem of religious division is rather unique. Austria, where the cleavage is between religiosity and secularity rather than between one religious group and another, comes close to the Lebanese pole in its dearth of recognition for the problem. So does Belgium, where the religious dividing line is also between practicing Catholics and anticlericals, although the constitution zealously guards the rights of secular citizens by decreeing that "no person may be constrained to assist in any way in the acts and ceremonies of any form of worship, nor to observe its days of rest," that "the civil wedding must always precede the nuptial benediction, save in exceptional cases," and that "no extraordinary commissions or courts may be set up under any denomination whatsoever."

Most of the other cases of religiously divided societies lay grouped around the other pole, represented by the constitution of Cyprus. Constitutionally, the Netherlands attempts to show evenhandedness in its grappling with the problem of religious division by stipulating that "all religious communities shall be afforded equal protection," that "the professors of the several religions shall all enjoy the same civil and civic rights," and that "the stipends, pensions, and other revenues . . . received by the several religious denominations or by their ministers, shall remain assured to those denominations." But it is also made clear that "the King shall see that all religious communities keep within the limits of obedience to the laws of the State." Through much of the document, Switzerland's constitution appears to pay scant attention to the matter of regulating religiously based conflict. But the document is clear enough when it comes to banning the Jesuits and the possibility of extending that ban "to other religious orders whose activity is dangerous to the State or disturbs the peace between the various religious bodies."

In setting up a federation, the framers of the Nigerian constitution of 1963 took religious diversity into account mainly by proclaiming freedom of religion, "including freedom to change [one's] religion," and by attempting to reassure Nigerians that there would be no compulsion to participate in another religious group's instruction or ceremony. There is also the claim that, with certain exceptions, there will be no prerogative or restriction conferred on citizens owing solely to their "community, tribe, place of origin, religion or political opinion." In religiously divided Sri Lanka, very similar assurances are to be found. There is also explicit concern for regulating potential conflict by the "division of [a] Province into electoral districts" to represent different communities of interest, "whether racial, religious or otherwise." India's voluminous constitution pays considerable attention to nondiscrimination and equality of citizens. When it comes to mentioning communities, the main concern expressed is not religious conflict per se, but rather "the advancement of any socially and educationally backward classes of citizens or for the Scheduled Castes and the Scheduled Tribes." And although religious tensions are not a prime concern expressed, the framers are careful to reserve regulatory power to the state in cases where "economic, financial, political or other secular activity which may be associated with religious practice" is regarded as too divisive. In Malaysia, Islam is the religion of the Federation, and the special position and rights of Malay-Muslims vis-à-vis other groups is acknowledged constitutionally. The relations among religious groups are clearly asymmetrical; for instance, "every person has the right to profess and practice his religion and . . . to propagate it," but "state law may control or restrict the propagation of any religious doctrine or belief among persons professing the Muslim religion." Thus, although Muslims are free to conduct missionary work among non-Muslims, state laws may—and do—curtail proselytizing among Muslims or even propagating certain Islamic beliefs among them.

These constitutional texts, besides evincing varying degrees of recognition for problems associated with religious cleavage and diversity, and putting forth varying claims as to their treatment, also suggest divergent images of an ideal future society. In Malaysia, for instance, the model espoused is one of assimilation. The intercommunal formula which is viewed constitutionally as legitimate seeks not the eradication of religious differences but their resolution along lines which (some) Muslims set. In Cyprus, on the other hand, the image proffered is a pluralist one in which the best that can be hoped for is peaceful competition among the religious communities. The same might be said for the Dutch constitution. Lebanon's constitution propagates an image of an ideal future in which the nation's diverse religious interests would merge into a single, and wholly fictional, "Lebanese" identity. In a number of other cases, of course, which we have not treated as instances of religiously divided societies, an image of the future depicts the subsidence of a dominant religion—in Mexico—or even of religion in general—some of the Marxist-Leninist states.

Concluding Remarks

It should be clear that constitutional invocations of religion exist, even flourish, in the modern world. In part these invocations serve to suggest some bedrock upon which political order rests that is beyond the authority of the framers to negotiate. Although the treatment of religious affairs varies a good deal, the national documents of which they are a part have become increasingly similar in many other respects. There is a gap between trends in the generalized content of constitutions on the one hand and their religious particularities on the other.

Such a gap suggests the importance of religious questions to governing elites. They try to appropriate religion, through the constitutions that both constrain and empower them, for political legitimation. The framers of constitutions tend to grant the activities of religious believers, although not necessarily the activities of religious organizations, some degree of leeway. Thus, claiming some degree of religious freedom is regarded as necessary for practically all the images of a "good" social order adumbrated through constitutional provisions. This appears to be the case whether or not the framers have any intention whatsoever of working toward the realization of those normative ideals, or would even be desirous of their realization.

But the theme which our investigation uncovers is not just one of freedom, nor a tale of religious exemption from political control. Through careful qualifications and outright restrictions, constitutional references to religion identify points of tension between political and religious authority. Although religious leaders are by no means always the losers in their struggle for autonomy if not power, the constitutions we have read contain numerous attempts to demarcate authority between civil and religious institutions. And, as we have shown, in plural societies those documents are more often than not full of attempts to control the competition for resources among religiously defined communities.

Whatever the complexities in interpreting them, these references to religion in national constitutions make sense of distinctions among groups or classes of nation-states. Although an economic mapping of the world may be dominated by a single global system, with individual nations taking their positions within it, the world religious map, through national constitutions, looks increasingly particularistic, with much variation between and within civilizational clusters identified by religious labels.

We have not attempted an exhaustive mapping of the world's nation-states into these clusters. But, as a fairly rough approximation, among the interesting and readily identifiable groupings we may locate an Islamic pattern, a Latin-Catholic one, a Buddhist group, a non-Islamic African one, a rather loose European-Christian cluster (with a fairly distinctive

Scandinavian Lutheran subcluster), and a communist grouping as well. Each of these classes has a modal form which is rather readily distinguishable from the others. Within these clusters there is also considerable variation. Turkey, Iran and Indonesia are strikingly unique among the Muslim nations and Malaysia has some subtly distinctive features; the Asian communist cases differ in their discussion of religion from the European ones and the Soviet Union's document is not identical to the eastern European countries it dominates; Mexico's constitution could not be confused with any other from Latin America; and the texts from western Europe turn out to be so diverse that we hesitate to speak of a western European pattern at all.

If the existence of a written constitution and much of its content as well may be read as an assertion to the effect that here is a nation-state like all others, the religious elements of these documents tend to tell us among which class of others to situate that nation-state; and sometimes we may read in effect, as well, the assertion that here is a nation-state unlike all others.

Bibliography

Arosemena, J. 1870. *Constituciones Políticas de la América Meridional*. Le Havre: Lemale.

_____. 1888. *Estudios Constitucionales sobre los Gobiernos de la América Latina*. 2 vols. Paris: Roger and Chernoviz.

Barber, S.A. 1984. *On What the Constitution Means*. Baltimore: Johns Hopkins University Press.

Bell, D. 1980. *The Winding Passage*. New York: Basic Books.

Bellah, R.N. 1970. "Religious Evolution." Pp. 211-44 in S.N. Eisenstadt, ed., *Readings in Social Evolution and Development*. Oxford: Pergamon.

Boli-Bennett, J.E. 1976. *The Expansion of Nation-States, 1870-1970*. Ann Arbor: University Microfilms.

Bruneau, T.C. 1974. *The Political Transformation of the Brazilian Catholic Church*. Cambridge: Cambridge University Press.

Dareste, F.R. 1883. *Les Constitutions Modernes*. 1st ed., 2 vols. Paris: Challamel.

Dareste, F.R. and P. Dareste. 1891. *Les Constitutions Modernes*. 2nd ed. 2 vols. Paris: Challamel.

Duchacek, I.D. 1973a. *Rights and Liberties in the World Today*. Santa Barbara: ABC-Clio.

_____. 1973b. *Power Maps: Comparative Politics of Constitutions*. Santa Barbara: ABC-Clio.

Fenn, R.K. "Toward a Theory of Secularization." *Society for the Scientific Study of Religion Monograph Series* 1 (1978).

Heng Samrin. "Documentation: President Heng Samrin Presents the Draft Constitution to the National Assembly." *Contemporary Southeast Asia* 3 (1981):177-78.

Hoffman, S. "Reaching for the Most Difficult: Human Rights as a Foreign Policy Goal." *Daedalus* 112 (1983):19-49.

Horowitz, I.L. 1978. "Foreword—On Human Rights and Social Obligations." Pp. vii-xii in *Human Rights and World Order*. A. Aziz Said, ed., New Brunswick, N.J.: Transaction Books.

Peaslee, A.J. 1965-1970. *Constitutions of Nations*. 4 vols. Rev. 3rd ed. Dorothy Peaslee Xydis, ed. The Hague: Martinus Nijhoff.

Pipes, R. 1974. *Russia Under the Old Regime*. New York: Scribner's.

Richey, R.E., and Donald G. Jones, eds. 1974. *American Civil Religion*. New York: Harper and Row.

Shils, E. 1982. *The Constitution of Society*. Chicago: University of Chicago Press.

Smith, B.L., ed. 1978. *Religion and Legitimation of Power in Thailand, Laos and Burma*. Chambersburg, PA: ANIMA.

Smith, D.E., ed. 1966. "Emerging Patterns of Religion and Politics." Pp. 21-48 in *South Asian Politics and Religion*. Princeton: Princeton University Press.

Tongdhamachart, K. "Thailand's 1978 Constitution and Its Implications." *Contemporary Southeast Asia* 1 (1979):125-40.

Weber, M. 1968. *Economy and Society*. 3 vols. New York: Bedminster Press.

Wolf-Phillips, L. 1972. *Comparative Constitutions*. London: Macmillan.

14

Symbiosis of Religious and Political Authorities in Islam

Hamid Dabashi

Know that you can have three sorts of relations with princes, governors, and oppressors. The first and worst is that you visit them, the second and the better is that they visit you, and the third and surest that you stay far from them, so that neither you see them nor they see you.

—Abū Ḥāmid Muḥammad al-Ghazzālī,
Muslim theologian
of the twelfth century.

In these times politics is everything.

—Soren Kierkegaard

Introduction

Extending the problem of church-state relations into an Islamic context necessitates some preliminary conceptual clarifications. *Church* is a christian institution. Our modern understanding of *state,* whether as a political expression of the ruling class, or as the legitimate monopoly of physical force, is deeply rooted in Post-Reformation European political experience. In their specific cultural setting and social significance, the tension and the debate over the church-state relationship are uniquely Western phenomena, already present in the ambivalent dialectic of "render therefore unto Caesar the things which be Caesar's and unto God the things which be God's" (Luke 21:25). Overloaded with Western cultural history, these two concepts cannot easily be translated into Islamic terminologies. Mosque is not church. *Dawlah* is not state. Only with the specific Durkheimian stip-

I am grateful to Professor Harold Bershady of the University of Pennsylvania and Dr. Thomas Robbins for their critical reading of an earlier version of this article.

183

ulation of *church* as the generic concept for *moral community, priest* for *the custodians of the sacred law,* and *state* for *political community* can we use these concepts in an Islamic context. To circumvent the hermeneutic problems of conceptual transliteration—a justifiable bypass given the limited objective of this article—we should simply consider the substance of these two institutions and concentrate on the symbiosis of religious and political authority in Islam.

On the theological level, the command-obedience nexus that constitutes the Islamic definition of authority is not demarcated by conceptual categories of religion and politics. Life as a physical reality is an expression of divine will and authority (*qudrah*). This metaphysical truth of Islam understood, there is no validity in separating the matters of piety from those of polity. They are both divinely ordained. Having stated the most characteristic signifier of Islam as a revealed faith, it must immediately be added that significant modifications have affected the translation of this signifier, i.e., Islam's metaphysical self-understanding, to the actual constitution of Muslim societies. Although both religious and political authorities are legitimated Islamically, my major proposition in this essay is that they have invariably constituted two independent social institutions, and that each interacted with the other. Indeed they could not have interacted were they not separate, and it is some of the variety of their interactions that I shall examine here.

From the establishment of the Muslim community (ummah) in mid-seventh century to the present time, Islamic societies have experienced structural tension in the various combinations of religion and politics. This experience is not monolithic: the diversity of its historical expressions is intensified by the geographical expansions of Islamic societies. Yet the single most important factor stitching all these particular expressions together is the *Qur'an* and its stipulation that the divine authority was transmitted to Allah's last messenger (khātim al-nabiyyin), Muhammad. The dynamics along with the tempo and flow of the relationships between religious and political authority were influenced by many factors: the pre-Islamic cultural milieu of both Arabs and the people they later conquered; the gradual development of Islamic theology (kalām); and significant historical events such as the Mongol invasion of the thirteenth century. But the power of religious symbolism over Muslims was always reinvigorated by a persistent reference back to the originating days of Islam. There and then Muhammad *rasūl Allah* established a new paradigm of authority that has held sway over Muslims to the present age. From their earliest expressions to their modern transfigurations into new ideological slogans, Islamic symbolics command the obedience of both Muslims and post-Muslims. To understand the symbiosis of religious and political authority in Islam, we have to go back to the originating book of Muslims, the *Qur'an*, to the divine authority of Allah, to the charismatic authority of Muhammad, and then to the historical-theological expressions—the progeny, two-fold source—of this dichotomy. That should lead us to a theoretical perspective on the dynamic relations between religious and political authority.

The nature and organization of authority—both religious and political—in Muslim societies are essentially determined by theological perspectives, and considerably modified by the vicissitudes of different cultural settings, social structures, historical episodes, and geographical expansions. These modifications are too extensive and too elaborate to be dealt with in a brief essay. They do not, however, alter the metaphysical and social constitution of authority in any significant way. We shall limit our analysis to the foundations of religious and political authority in Islam. The theoretical perspectives expressed here must be considered against the specific cases of various Islamic societies.

Allah: The Supreme Metaphysical Authority

Any understanding of authority in Islam must begin with the omnipotent sovereignty of Allah as stated in the *Qur'an*, the sacred book of Muslims:

> Say (O Muhammad): O mankind! Lo! I am the messenger of Allah to you all—(the messenger of) Him unto whom belongeth the sovereignty of the heavens and the earth. There is no God save Him. He quickens and He giveth death. So believe in Allah and His messenger, the prophet. . . , who believeth in Allah and His words, and follow him that haply ye may be led aright. (Qur'an VII:158).

Belief in the absolute authority of Allah is not a matter of personal piety on the part of Muslims. It is the most important metaphysical truth that permeates every aspect of Islamic social structure and Muslim personal character. Islamic culture, society, and character all evolve out of a fundamental belief in the validity of Allah's omnipotence. The Islamic community (ummah), according to Muslim self-understanding, is a particular manifestation of the divine will. The omnipotent Allah presides over this community. The whole texture of social relationships is framed within this metaphysical truth. As for the domains of His authority, "God's is the kingdom of the heavens and the earth . . ." (Qur'an XLVIII:14); and "Unto Him belongeth whatsoever is in the heavens and whatsoever is in the earth" (Qur'an II:255). The extent of His authority is boundless: "Allah is able to do all things" (Qur'an II:284). There is an absolute monotheism in Islam:

"Allah! There is no God save Him, the Alive, the Eternal" (Qur'an III:2).
He is the sole source of all authorities.

The extension of Allah's absolute authority into Islamic social life has
many manifestations. The formation of the Islamic community itself is an
expression of divine will: "And so (O Muhammad) We have revealed to you
an Arabic Qur'an that you may warn Mecca, Mother of Cities, and those
who dwell about her . . ." (Qur'an XLII:7). This is emphasized by the
conscious recognition of Muslims: "Our Lord! And make us submissive
unto thee and of our seed a nation submissive unto thee . . ." (Qur'an
II:128). Every member of this community pledges obedience to Allah on
the day of creation, when God asks the children of Adam: "Am I not your
Lord?" And they answered: "Yea, verily. We testify" (Qur'an VII:172). Man
is responsible for this testimony until the day of judgement: ". . . Those
who buy the life of the world at the price of the Hereafter, their punishment
will not be lightened, neither will they have support" (Qur'an II:86).
Within this span of time, in order to be judged favorably on the Day of
Resurrection (Yaum al-Qiyāmah), the Muslims have to regulate their lives,
both private and public, according to the specific mandates of Allah. They
have to believe in His oneness, His justice, the prophets He has sent, and in
the Day of Judgment. This system of belief is translated into ritual and
practical commands of praying, fasting, paying alms, making a pilgrimage
to Mecca, and if need be, fighting in His way and for the glory of God.
Every aspect of life—social, psychological, political, economic, artistic,
etc.,—is coordinated and regulated into an organically interrelated totality.
In man's relation to God—and only to God—there is nothing secular in
Islam; everything is sacred. Nothing political; everything is religious.
Things are either forbidden (harām) or permitted (halāl), with some os-
cillations in between—mubāḥ or makrūh. Everything falls within the command-obedience nexus connecting Allah and the Muslim community (see,
e.g., Williams 1971:133-87).

Muhammad: The Supreme Charismatic Authority

The mediator of Allah's omnipotent authority on earth is his messenger,
Muhammad, the seal of all previous prophets (khātim al-nabiyyin). Obedience is due to Allah through His delegate: "O You who believe, obey
God, and obey the Messenger, and those in authority among you" (Qur'an
IV:59). Muhammad's authority is charismatic par excellence, "the authority of the extraordinary and personal gift of grace (charisma)" (Weber
1946:79). His authority is extraordinary, since he establishes its interdic-
tory motifs against those of the traditional, pre-Islamic Arab society. He
reorganizes Arab social life on the basis of a new paradigm—predicated on

Islamic doctrines. Whatever is derived from the old order is assimilated into the new organism. His authority is personal: as a messenger of Allah he does not occupy any status formerly known to and recognized by Arabs; he is not a member of a family with exclusive right to leadership, nor does he have a position previously established and legitimated within that cultural order. His is an authority based on "the absolutely personal devotion and personal confidence in revelation, heroism, or other qualities of leadership" (Weber 1946:79). The Qur'an was the constant source of Muhammad's legitimacy throughout his prophetic career from 611 A.D. to 632 A.D. The verses of the Qur'an were not revealed all at once, but piece by piece in the course of those twenty-one years. The revelation of the Qur'anic verses to Muhammad along with his political victories over his Medinese and Meccan adversaries were the source and proof of his legitimacy.

In the emerging Muslim community of the early seventh century, Muhammad was the sole authority in all spheres. He was the supreme religious leader, the mediator between his followers and Allah. He led public prayers, and directed the pilgrimage to Mecca. He also commanded the political allegiance of his followers. The military expeditions of Badr (624 A.D.), and Uhud (625 A.D.) against the Meccan opposition, as well as the defense of Medina in the siege of Khandaq (627 A.D.) were all personally led by Muhammad. Not only did he provide religious, political, and military leadership, but Muhammad acted as the chief judge and administrator of his community. The omnipotence of Allah was translated into the comprehensive authority of Muhammad. There are many Qur'anic references that meticulously circumscribe the range and depth of authority of the doctrines established by Muhammad's mission in the Islamic community. Everything from specific punishments against adultery, to almsgiving, the rules of arbitration, cleanliness, contracts, marriage and divorce, trade, usury, war and fighting, wills and bequests, etc., fall under the jurisdiction of Qur'an, i.e., the physical embodiment of Allah/Muhammad's authority over the Islamic community (Qur'an' IV:15f.; II:190; IV:35; II:222; II:282f; II:226f; II:198; II:275f; II:190f; II:180f.). A complete merging of public and private life subjected all Muslims and Islamic society to the religious/political authority of Allah/Muhammad (see Watt 1961; Watt 1968).

Both the nascent Islamic community of Muhammad's time and all subsequent Islamic societies have been doctrinally based on this seminal understanding of the indissoluble fact of religious/political authority. The social organizations of these societies were structured on an interpretation of Muhammad's charismatic authority and its aftermath. Whatever measure of stability the patterns of social relationships achieved in post-

Muhammadan periods was directly based on this dual conception of religious/political authority. The complicated systems of social roles, norms, and shared meanings that defined and constituted the different Islamic societies legitimated themselves through, and lent support to, the validity of this symbiosis of religion and politics. This was the major theme on which all Islamic societies established their particular variations. From this time forward, the transpositional nature of both religious and political authorities, of one shifting into the other, animated the structural organization of all Islamic societies. Within these organizations, however, two separate institutions gradually developed that claimed exclusive jurisdiction over either religious or political spheres of life. How these institutions established and legitimated themselves is directly related to the problem of succession to Muhammad's charismatic authority which the Muslim community faced and finally resolved. In the diverse and ensuing resolutions, however, there is a practical shift away from the doctrinal position of Islam on matters of religion and politics to its social structure. While social institutions, particularly the religious and the political, are legitimated Islamically, as separate realities they establish independent nexuses of command and obedience.

Institutionalization of Allah/Muhammad's Authority

A charismatic movement, as Weber points out, is a transitional period in the social history of a community. Its antiinstitutional nature disrupts the full function of a traditional social setting. Yet in superseding the existing order, the charismatic movement establishes at the most fundamental level the paradigmatic structure of a new cultural order.

The paradigmatic origin of this new Islamic order is embodied, first, in the Qur'an as the supreme sacred text of Muslims—believed to be the very word of God; and, second, in *hadith,* the words and deeds of Muhammad—which were considered to have established an exemplary model for all Muslims. These were the two sources from which the community of followers gradually laid the structural foundation of the new cultural order. This order unfolded, developed, was transformed and yet retained its essential identity in all of its interactions with other objective social forces in the course of Islamic history. The particular directions in which this unfolding led were related to the mode of authority established in different segments of the Islamic community. This segmentation was essentially centered on the problem of post-Muhammadan legitimate authority.

Muhammad's charisma was legitimated by the source of all authorities in Islam: Allah. During his mission as the prophet of Allah (610-632 A.D.), Muhammad commanded the obedience of an ever-expanding community.

His authority, reflecting Allah's, was widespread and multidimensional. Upon his death no single figure was able to possess the same authority. In less than thirty years after his death, the Muslim community was doctrinally, and to a certain extent physically, divided into three distinct groups. Each distinction was based on specific solutions to the question of authority—its nature and organization—after Muhammad. The segmentation of the Islamic community was not only based on but gave expression to different readings of post-Muhammadan authority, to how religious and political dimensions of command-obedience were to be corelated and coordinated. These formed subparadigmatic patterns that were extended into the rest of Islamic history.

The three formulations of post-Muhammadan authority developed as follows: the majority of Muslims, later known as Sunnites, conceded to the caliphate (vicegerency) of Abū Bakr. Abū Bakr was a member of Muhammad's tribe, the Quraysh, and was selected by a council of the Muslim elders. The office of the caliphate was primarily a political institution. The caliph was the supreme political authority. He was not considered the inheritor of Muhammad's religious authority. As Allah's last messenger, Muhammad was believed not to be succeeded by a figure of similar religious/political authority. The caliphate, however, held some religious significance, it gained legitimacy through a doctrinal legacy: Islam.

A small minority of Muslims, later called the Shiites, believed that Muhammad's cousin and son-in-law Ali should have succeeded him. They maintained that leadership of the Islamic community must remain in Muhammad's household (ahl al-bayt). Since he was not survived by a son, his successor ought to have been his closest male descendant—Ali. In later Shiite doctrines, Ali became the first occupant of the position of *Imàmah* (leadership). Imams, in this specific Shiite sense, were believed to be divinely ordained to lead the Islamic community after Muhammad's death. Although lower in rank than Muhammad, Imams command the same charismatic and multidimensional authority. They are perceived as both the religious and the political leaders of their community.

From the initial supporters of Ali emerged a group of disillusioned Muslims who were later know as the Kharijites (those who seceded from Ali). As their doctrinal position developed, the Kharijites came to believe that the leadership of the Islamic community was neither the prerogative of the Quraysh tribe nor that of the prophet's household. They maintained that anybody—"even an Abyssinian slave"—could become the supreme authority of the *Ummah*. Their leader's authority, however, was severely curtailed by relentless moral scrutiny. The Kharijites did not consider their political leader as having religious authority. He was merely a first among the equals. Although they did not flourish to the same degree as the other two branches of Islam, the Kharijites did establish a particular pattern of authority with lasting effects on the rest of Islamic history (see Watt 1973).

We shall now examine each case in more detail. The theological and historical developments of these Islamic subgroups express the three paradigmatic patterns of authority in general and the religious/political dichotomy in particular. Within these structural patterns of authority, Islamic social life was organized. Each of the three provided the framework of moral integration that Simmel deemed indispensable to any relation of command and obedience. An examination of the three structures regulating and coordinating the religious and the political aspects of the Muslim life shall lead us to the very heart of Islam as a living organism. It is there that a subjective understanding of the relation between religion and politics can be achieved.

Sunnite-Islam: Segmentation/Institutionalization of Charismatic Authority

One of the most important characteristics of the Sunnite-Islam is the segmentation of Muhammad's charisma into distinct institutions of authority. In the course of Islamic history, a variety of institutions developed within the Sunnite branch, the most important of which were the caliphate (political authority) and the *ulama'* (the religious authority). The formation of these distinct institutions was a long process. As they emerged from Muhammad's charisma—which obviously held them both together—they were barely distinguishable from each other. Yet as they gradually evolved, religious (ulama') and political (caliphate) institutions became two distinct authorities—both legitimated by one source: Allah/Muhammad.

The period between the death of Muhammad (632 A.D.) and the establishment of the Umayyad dynasty (661 A.D.) is known among both Muslims and the Islamicists as the time of the "four rightly-guided caliphs" (khulafa' al-rāshidiyn). These four caliphs were Abū Bakr (632-634 A.D.), Umar (634-644 A.D.), Uthmān (644-656 A.D.), and Ali (656-661 A.D.). In this period, still so heavily under the charismatic weight of Muhammad, it is very difficult, indeed impossible, to distinguish between religious and political authority. The position of caliphate at this early stage carried both political and religious connotations. The title of caliph (khalīfah) was first used by Abū Bakr. It was the abbreviated form of *khalīfah rasūl Allah* (the vicegerant of the messenger of Allah). After Abū Bakr, Umar had intended to use the full title of *khalīfah khalīfah rasūl Allah* (the vicegerant of vicegerant of the messenger of Allah). Impractical as this proved to be, the generic title of *khalīfah rasūl Allah* was subsequently used by all other rightly guided caliphs after Abū Bakr.

Abū Bakr exercised both kinds of authority: political and religious. He was a close companion of the prophet and subsequently possessed what may be called a derivative charisma. On the one hand, he led the Muslims' public prayers, and on the other, he led the campaigns against the resurgent tribes intending to break away from the Muslim community. Moreover, during Abū Bakr's time, under his leadership, the northward movements of the Muslims toward the Byzantine territories began. Abū Bakr was one of the chief authorities on the sacred text—the Qur'an; and there is no indication that a separate group of religious authorities were forming in this period. Umar more or less falls within the same pattern. As another close companion of Muhammad, he possessed both political and religious authority. During his reign, however, there arose the first indications of a separate group of religious authorities, *qāḍīs* (religious judges) being formed (see Williams 1971:141). But as they were believed to have been appointed by Umar himself, they did not possess autonomous authority. Uthman carried the same tradition of religious/political authority. He demonstrated his political authority in a successful continuation of Umar's military campaigns into the Sassanid Persia, the Byzantine Asia Minor, and the Berber North Africa. One example of his religious authority was evident in his redaction and expurgation of the definitive Qur'anic text. As a caliph, Ali had global authority similar to the kind exercised by the preceding three. He never secured, however, the obedience of the entire Islamic community, and the eruption of the First Civil War (fitna) during his reign led to the end of the four rightly-guided caliphs and the establishment of the Umayyad dynasty.

From the reign of the first Umayyad caliph, Muawiyah, onward (661 A.D.), the position of caliphate assumed an increasingly political nature. Religious authority was then exclusively claimed by the rising class of *Ulama*.' A full knowledge of the Qur'an, prophetic traditions, hermeneutical and exegetical interpretations of the sacred text in Arabic, and other gradually developing religious sciences (ulūm al-dīn), necessitated a devout class of scholars. In turn, this group claimed religious authority by virtue of their knowledge.

Although both the positions of caliphate and *Ulama*' were religious, i.e., legitimated through Islamic doctrines, they constituted two distinct social institutions. The existence of these two institutions, moreover, was subject to a wide range of interactions; from explicit complacency to open hostility.

The advent of the Abbasiyd Revolution and the establishment of the Abbasiyd dynasty (750 A.D.) gradually introduced another element into the texture of religious/political authority of Sunnite-Islam: the vizierate. Adopted with other bureaucratic apparatuses from the Sassanids, the position of the vizier bifurcated political authority in the Abbasiyd period. The caliph remained the supreme symbolic figure of political authority, but the vizier assumed all administrative and executive responsibilities. A change in the honorific title of the caliph in this period from *khalīfah rasūl Allah* (the vicegerant of the prophet of Allah) to *khalīfah Allah* (the vicegerant of Allah) indicates, among other things, the further influence of the Sassanid idea that kings were divinely ordained. As with the Sassanid khosrows, however, this change of title was not concurrent with actual appropriation of religious authority. Still, *ulama'* were to caliphs as magi were to khosrows: a priestly institution balancing the kingly.

No major change modified the religious authority in the Abbasiyd period, except for an expansion in the class of *Ulama'* to include the emerging *fugaha'* (the jurisconsults), and the solidified *gādis* (judges). In addition, the appearance of the Sufi orders gradually polarized what may be termed spiritual authority, as opposed to both the religious and the political. Here I distinguish between religious and spiritual authorities; the former refers to the formal and exoteric aspects of the religion, and the latter to the mystical and esoteric. Although Muslim mystics usually lacked political or religious authority, they constituted social forces with which the caliphs and the *Ulama'* had to reckon. This overriding structural configuration of authority commanded the allegiance of different groups of Muslims with particular religious or political orientation inside Sunnite-Islam.

At the height of the Abbasiyd period (750-1258 A.D.), the Sunnite architecture of religious/political authority was solidly established. Religious and political authorities were institutionalized separately, yet legitimated collectively. Formation of other institutions such as the Sufis or viziers further expanded the segmentation of Muhammad's charismatic authority. Within this structural pattern, continuous interplay existed between the religious and political authorities. Subject to external historical exigencies, these two institutions either intensified and expanded each other's constituency or slackened and limited it (see, e.g., Watt 1973:253-318).

Shiite-Islam: Perpetuation/Institutionalization of Charismatic Authority

Shiite-Islam is the most successful attempt of charismatic authority perpetuated in the post-Muhammadan period. The continuation of this charisma was first personified in the figure of Ali and subsequently transferred to other Shiite Imams. This charisma represents both religious and political authorities.

Although Ali commanded the devout obedience of no more than a small minority of early Muslims, he was posthumously transformed into a charismatic figure. As a result, he inherited almost all dimensions of Muhammad's authority except his messengership and the reception of divine revelations. According to the Islamic theology, Muhammad was the *seal of the prophets* (khātim al-nabiyyin). No messenger would be sent after him. The Shiite tradition, however, maintained that Ali was nominated by Muhammad to lead the Islamic community. This leadership was multi-dimensional, with no distinction in kinds of authority. The later Shiite theology legitimated the charismatic authority of Ali through the doctrine of *Imāmah*. This doctrine decreed that the leadership of the Muslim community was transferred after the death of Muhammad to the male members of his household. This transference, moreover, was divinely ordained. The first male member of the household was Muhammad's cousin and son-in-law, the husband of his only surviving child (Fatimah), Ali. After Ali, the *Imāmah* was transferred to his male descendants.

The justification offered for this doctrinal position was that the establishment of the *Ummah* was not a matter of human choice, but of divine will. The question of successor to Muhammad, inextricably related to the future of the Muslim community, could not have been left to Muslims themselves. A community divinely ordained needs to be led by authorities divinely selected.

The Shiites did not believe that Imams could receive revelations. However they are perceived as having the knowledge of the hidden meanings of the Qur'an (ta'wīl). This emphasized the charismatic nature of their authority. Moreover, their not receiving revelations (wahy) was compensated by their having divine inspiration (ilhām). Through the doctrines of *ilhām* and *ta'wīl*, Imams possessed what Weber called supernatural or superpersonal qualities. As such their authority was charismatic, obeyed with devotion by a small community of followers.

Except for Ali, none of the other Shiite Imams possessed actual political/religious authority over a segment of the Islamic community. They were always controlled by the Umayyad and Abbasiyd caliphs and sometimes even persecuted or killed. However, among their immediate disciples and followers, as well as in the emerging Shiite doctrines, they were considered to have both religious and political—charismatic—authority.

Within the general Islamic context, Shiite-Islam represents a structural pattern of authority according to which Muhammad's charismatic authority, encompassing both religious and political spheres, is handed down to Ali and other Imams. In the course of Islamic history, this pattern survived, despite the fact that none of the Shiite Imams after Ali ever ruled a part of the Islamic territories. Yet, such Shiite dynasties as the Fatimids in Egypt (909-1171 A.D.), and the Buwahids (945-1055 A.D.) and the Safavids (1502-1736 A.D.) in Persia did claim putative descent from Ali's family. In these cases the nature and organization of authority followed the Shiite pattern, and no clear distinction was made between the religious and political authorities. However, even in the Shiite dynasties, we still observe the coexistence of two separate institutions, one claiming political the other religious sovereignty. But the political position was much more precarious to hold than in the Sunnite societies, and it was always subject to religious recognition. The important fact is that in none of the Shiite dynasties did the *ulama'* actually rule. Nor did the kings or sultans claim religious authority. Even in the case of the Safavids who were established by a sufi order, an independent class of religious authority, more exoterically-minded than the sufis, claimed its own constituency.

The overall characteristic of the Shiite pattern of authority was a persistent attempt to perpetuate charisma—maintaining a close affinity between religious and political domains. Although separate institutions of authority emerged from this pattern, the political was always susceptible to chronic waves of delegitimation issuing from the religious. Given the anti-institutional and dynamic nature of charisma, a point repeatedly emphasized by Weber, whatever measure of stability religious and political orders had secured in the Shiite pattern of authority was always subject to charismatic revolts. These chronic revolts challenged both the legitimacy of political institutions and the validity of the official religious authorities (see, e.g., Watt 1973:38-62; Jafri 1979).

Kharijite-Islam: Dissemination of Charismatic Authority

The third structural pattern of authority that emerged from the post-Muhammadan problem of legitimacy was expressed in the Kharijite movement. Rejecting both the Sunnite aristocracy of the Quraysh tribe and the Shiite oligarchy of the prophet's household, the Kharijites launched a furious but futile movement for a mass democracy. Refusing to recognize the authority of the caliph, they challenged the claim that Muhammad's tribe had a prerogative right to political supremacy. They denied the Imams any obedience, questioning the argument that Muhammad's household had an exclusive right to religious/political authority. The supreme authority, they maintained, belonged to Allah and, as Muhammad was dead, to the Islamic community—the people. *Primus inter pares*, Kharijite leaders were granted only administrative authority—always subject to severe scrutiny from below. This *authority from below* did not resemble the constitutional democracies of modern times. It was also far from the reciprocal interaction between leader and led that Simmel observed in relations of authority.

Within the Kharijite pattern of communal life, no authority was recognized as institutionally established or doctrinally sanctified. Thus, the separation between religious and political domains scarcely presented itself as a dilemma. For Kharijites the supreme communal problem was moral righteousness, not institutional expressions of religious or political authority. The Kharijites pardoned no sin, however insignificant, from committing adultery to drinking wine. All transgressions were punishable by death—or what they called *istirād*. Some particular groups of the Kharijites, such as the Najdites who ruled autonomously over Bahrayn, Umman, Yemen and Hadramawt from 686 A.D. to 692 A.D., later diverged from this extreme position of the early Kharijites (the Azraqites). The Najdites distinguished between fundamental and non-fundamental sins. In making this religious distinction, they were able to secure a measure of political independence from the mainstream Kharijites.

Within the structural patterns of authority in Islam, the significance of the Kharijites lay more in their raising questions about authority than in their giving institutional answers. Fundamental questions were asked by the Kharijites, particularly by their intellectual core, the Waqifites of Baghdad. Who is a Muslim? What is a Muslim community? Who is a rightful leader of the Muslim community? These questions posed, the institutional authorities of both the Sunnites and the Shiites were forced to address them. Acting basically as a theological catalyst, the Kharijites intensified and expanded the emerging patterns of Islamic authority.

As to their own communal life regulated by some minimal structure of authority, the Kharijites represented an attempt towards mass democracy, with severe moral sensitivity inhibiting the formation of any institutional nexus of command and obedience. Not preserved in any enduring institution—caliphate, Imamate, or other, Muhammad's charismatic authority was disseminated in the Kharijite community.

Except for some small groups in North Africa, the Kharijites did not survive as a political community. Doctrinally, however, they did establish their own notion of mass democracy as a latent pattern of authority. This latent tendency burst into revolutionary movements throughout Islamic history (see Watt 1973:9-37).

The General Structure of Authority in Classical and Medieval Islam

Despite these variations in the structural pattern of authority in Islam, certain generalizations can be made that characterize the organization of the command-obedience nexus in classical and medieval Islamic societies. Muhammad's charismatic authority ultimately lent legitimacy to two separate social institutions: (1) political authority, personified in figures such as caliphs, sultans, shahs, viziers, and others; and (2) religious authority, personified in figures such as *ulama', fugaha',* and *gaḍīs*. This significant bifurcation characterized the majority of the Islamic communities. The Shiite variation was more precarious in its distinction between the religious and the political sectors. However, this group always remained a small minority in the larger Islamic community; and whenever they did in fact give territorial expression to their religious/political beliefs, a separation between the religious and the political elite was manifest. The Kharijite pattern of authority remained only as a marginal and latent paradigm that occasionally gave rise to revolutionary movements.

Within the mainstream Islamic community, the religious and political authorities established two separate spheres of communal life that in turn gave rise to what Simmel has called an intersection of social circles (die Kreuzung sozialer kreiser). The possibility of participating more actively in one or the other of these two institutions—to be more religiously or politically oriented—enabled Muslims to "experience an enrichment of their lives, a tension and a doubling of their vitality, which they could probably not attain otherwise" (Simmel 1955:133).

The social intersection that Simmel saw in both primitive and modern societies was present in the gradual formation of the Islamic social structure. Religious and political circles drew many subsidiary spheres into their orbits, including cultural, social, economic, professional, literary, and artistic spheres. Religious and political authority was thus diffused through the entire gamut of life; the structural patterns of authority that resulted were diverse but organic in nature. Individual Muslims could affiliate themselves with different combinations of many social groupings.

Following Simmel's theoretical lead, we can see in Muslim names the complex texture of classical and medieval Islamic social structure. A name consists of (1) a proper name (ism), (2) the father's name (kunya), and (3) the filiation or geneology (ibn-x or bint-y). A Muslim's name also includes an adjectival expression (nisba) indicating the town or tribe from which he/she comes; as well as a *laqab*, which is the distinguishing factor of the individual as a learned person or a distinguished scholar. Individuals also belonged to occupational groups. We often see the *laqab* as *al-khabbāz* (baker), *al-banna'* (bricklayer), or *al-bazzāz* (cloth merchant). Other group-affiliations relate the individual Muslim to the particular school of *shariah* (divine law) with which every Sunnite Muslim must identify: *Shafiites, Hanbalites, Malikites,* and *Hanafites.* There are ethnic and racial divisions, including Arabs, Persians, and Turks, that persist despite the Islamic universality. The existence of these and a host of other group identities expands the diversity of Islamic social structure and dissipates any tendency to centralization that exists among religious and political institutional authorities. The result is a pervasive permeation of authority throughout the Islamic social structure. This in turn prevents the atomization of individuals, as well as the formation of massive total states—theocratic or autocratic.

The widespread notion that Muslims' lives were totally controlled and minutely regulated by a totalitarian faith which did not distinguish between the private and public, sacred and secular, atemporal and temporal, and religious and political spheres of life does not actually correspond to the social experience of traditional Muslims. It is true that every aspect of life has an Islamic doctrine regulating it. Yet dispersion of these doctrines throughout the texture of Islamic social structure provides a channeling of Muhammad's charismatic authority into a host of derivative social organizations. These intermediary associations act as the buffer zones between individuals and the possibility of a total state.

This theoretical suggestion is in direct disagreement with the position held by many leading Islamicists including the eminent British historian Ann K.S. Lambton who flatly rejects the existence of any separation between religious and political authority in Islam: "Islam knows no distinction between state and church" (Lambton 1981:XV). Lambton even rejects Van Ess's assertion that the absence of this distinction is only true for the first two or two and a half Islamic centuries (Lambton 1981:XV). Similar views are held by Roy P. Mottahedeh who maintains that "Islam allowed little room for the compartmentalization or separation of life into sacred and secular spheres, and hence little room for the dichotomy of church and state that has been such a familiar part of the Western Christian experience" (Mottahedeh 1984:55; Mottahedeh 1980).

The notion that religious and political authorities are inseparable in Islam stems from a confusion of Islamic doctrinal position with its expression into Islamic social structure. Doctrinally, indeed temporal and atemporal matters all go under the sacred canopy. But while institutions of religious and political authorities are legitimated Islamically, they constitute two distinct nexuses of command and obedience. The very existence of these two institutions of authority, as a matter of historical reality, necessitates a variety of religion-state relationships, which in turn are predicated on the existence of these two distinct institutions of authority.

The theoretical perspective developed in this article is more in accord with those of Said Amir Arjomand (1984) and Ira M. Lapidus (1975). However, Amir Arjomand's position that "there is no inherent dogmatic connection between God and political authority in Islam" is a highly problematic proposition. The repeated Qur'anic expressions—"For God's is the kingdom of the heavens and of the earth" (III:189; IV:19-20; VII:157; and so on—leave no doubt that the sovereignty of Allah is heavenly but also earthbound. This expansion of Allah's authority to include the earth, however, is manifested in the basis of institutional legitimacy and not in the monolithic appropriation of religious/political authority by earthly organizations of command and obedience. Distinguishing two spheres of religious and political authority in Islam does not warrant a severence of the sole source of all authorities—Allah—from its diverse institutional expressions.

Institutional Problems of Authority in Islamic Modernity

The three structural patterns of authority that emerged in the post-Muhammadan period have survived the last fourteen centuries and have been instrumental in shaping the nature and organization of Islamic culture. Despite the fact that both religious and political institutions within these patterns are legitimated through a direct connection to Allah and Muhammad, as objectified in the Qur'an and the *hadīth*, they have constituted, particularly in the case of the Sunnite majority, two distinct spheres of dominance. The relationship between the two institutions has varied from time to time, and place to place. The balance between them gave Islamic social structure its cohesion and permanence, and provided Muslims with the possibility of at least dual group affiliations. There is scarcely a period in Islamic history when a complete alliance between the religious and the political authorities existed. Nor do we know of a period when either religious or political institutions has singularly dominated Muslim social life.

The advent of modernity, however, introduced new structural patterns of power—usually associated with a particular Western ideology. When Disraeli bailed out the bankrupt Khedive of Egypt, Ismael Pasha, and bought all his shares of the Suez Canal (1875)—a prelude to British rule in Egypt—Islamic societies had already been affected by the new wave of European colonialism in more than one way. Political subjugation was only one aspect—perhaps the most important—of a pervasive cultural hegemony that the modernized West was to exercise over the traditional East.

European political supremacy and cultural hegemony over the rest of the world was a byproduct of six centuries of moral and social transformations, from the religious and political struggles of the Later Middle Ages to the Renaissance, the Reformation, and the French Revolution. By mid-nineteenth century, European colonial powers dominated the mind and body of the Islamic world—from India to North Africa. This was the Europe of Jeremy Bentham—fiercely antitraditional, and deeply devoted to the pursuit of rational self-interest—a perhaps an unanticipated by-product of postenlightenment philosophical radicalism (Halevy 1972). It was a period in Europe when small *Gemeinschaften* yielded obediently to the encroachments of gigantic *Gesellschaften*. Europe became dominated by the rising, self-confident bourgeoisie, nullifying and displacing the dying, self-doubting aristocracy. It was a Europe chiefly shaped by Cartesian rationalism, laissez faire capitalism, and Benthem/Mill utilitarianism, a Europe fully awake after a long medieval quietude.

The Islamic world, whose last vestiges of glory had withered in the melancholic finale of the Ottoman-Safavid self-destruction, could hardly meet the Western onslaught. With the death of Suleiman the Magnificent in 1566, the Ottoman Empire—and with it Islamic political supremacy—began its downward movement. The defeat of the Turkish navy at Lepanto by the Spanish-Venetian fleet (1571) marked the beginning of the Turkish-Islamic downfall and the European resurgence. Politically defeated and spiritually demoralized, Islamic societies relapsed into the secure confinements of their medieval citadels—now mere shells that enclosed cultural and intellectual stagnation. When European colonial supremacy reached its zenith in mid-nineteenth century, Islamic societies fell into political servitude. Disproportionately inferior to European military might, Muslim societies responded to Western political and technological superiority with a peculiar combination of awe, resignation, admiration, *ressentement*, and a desperate urge to emulate and *modernize*. Reactions were diffused, unified only as common responses to the mighty West.

It is within the tension and the dialectic of this encounter—Western technological/social activity and Islamic political/moral passivity—that the Muslim fastidious adoption of European political ideologies should be understood. The initial responses were obviously confused and directed in an anxious search for identity—what does it mean to be a modern Muslim? The universal appeal of Jamāl al-Dīn al-Afghānī (1838-1897) and his Egyptian disciple Muhammad Abduh (1849-1905) stems partly from their commitment to providing a mobilizing answer to that common, pressing question. Asking the question already implies the weakened state of the questioner. Other attempts to deal with the problems of modernity inevitably assumed ideological postures of European origin. Nationalism was among the first to claim the allegiance of an increasing number of Arab, Persian, or Turkish Muslims. Rashīd Riḍa (1865-1935), Hasan al-Banna' (1906-1949), and Abu-l-Ala' Mawdūdī (1903-1979) were among the chief ideologues. Socialism closely followed, with Sayyid Qutb (1906-1966), Shaykh Mahmud Shaltut (1892-1963) and Khalifa Abd al-Ḥakīm (d. 1959) addressing the central problems of Islamic socialism (Hourani 1962; Enayat 1982; Donohue and Esposito 1982).

More serious than the wholesale adoption of European ideologies was the concealed transfiguration of them into an Islamic posture. To address and mobilize a significant proportion of Muslims still tradition bound, a particular mode of ideology developed that read specific political statements into the Islamic doctrinal terminology. Chief among these ideologues was Ali Sharī atī (1933-1977) who put upon himself the stupendous task of rewriting the entire Islamic history based on his post-Marxist, Existentialist, and Fanonist ideological amalgam (Dabashi 1983).

Concurrent with these ideological movements were more indigenous Islamic responses to European political and cultural hegemony. One of the most important was messianism. From the Mahdi movement in Sudan to the Bāb uprising in Persia, charismatic reactions to an increasingly hostile and disenchanting world assumed messianic and eschatological proportions. Another major form of indigenous Islamic reaction were the so-called puritanical movements, such as the Wahābis, that sought a total return to the perceived "Golden Age" of Muhammad's time.

The interplay between the European outlook and the diffused Islamic responses confronted Islamic structural patterns of authority with competing Western ideologies and their modalities of power. Whether nationalism and socialism bred constitutional movements or socialist parties, the immediate consequence was a juxtaposition of alternative patterns of authority against those inherent in Islam. Whatever institutional equilibrium existed—or did not exist—between religious and political authority was destabilized by the infusion of new modalities of power. Political parties, constitutions, Houses of Parliament, etc., were all institutions of power alien to an Islamic context. Yet, they were superimposed on traditional forms of religious and political authority still operative in Islamic societies. More often than not the consequence was an uneasy coexistence of diverse institutions of authority, either legitimated traditionally or legitimized ideologically. This in turn led to deeply polarized social structures. Thus, from the Iranian Constitutional Revolution of 1906 to the Islamic Revolution of 1979, we can observe how the infusion of one alien institution of authority, the Constitution, created enough tension for traditional religious authority to mobilize the force needed to expel the exogenous institutions of power. Despite the obvious cultural differences, the assassinations of President Sadat in Egypt and of Indira Ghandi in India both fall under the same category.

Moreover, to the degree that the Western ideological movements were able to launch revolutions and establish secular political regimes, the traditional Islamic social structures have been transformed into modern totalitarian states. With the rise of these states in modern Islamic societies, ideologically legitimized institutions of power extended the domains of their constituency into the private and public lives of their citizens. This was accomplished with a much deeper effect than that exercised by traditional antecedents. Within the traditional Islamic social structure, the possibility of multiple group affiliations provided individuals with a considerable measure of flexibility and maneuverability. The modern totalitarian states have stripped the Muslims from all possible cultural affiliations, identities, and thus institutional protections, leaving them isolated and atomized—sometimes mere citizens of a vast bureaucracy. This massive process of acculturation sometimes has been blurred by the ideological foundations of these total states assuming an Islamic garb.

Presently, existing relationships between religious and political authority in various Islamic societies largely depends on the particular mixture of traditional and rational/legal modalities of power concurrent in a given society. Today there is no Islamic society that is totally structured on traditional lines. Nor do we have a completely reconstituted Muslim state along modern Western parameters. Generally, religious authorities are subject to political institutions not traditionally legitimated, as in the case of Algeria and Morocco. Sometimes modern political institutions, such as the presidency in Egypt, is challenged by revolutionary religious movements outside the established (al-Azhar) institution. Occasionally, as in Syria, such revolutionary religious movements are severely suppressed by political authorities that have only recently been recognized. And so in every modern Islamic state the precarious tension between religious and political authorities provides either a measure of stability or a token of anarchy.

Concluding Remarks

Muhammad's charismatic movement in the early seventh century, and the attempts of the Islamic community to deal with the problem of legitimacy after him, provided Islamic culture with three significant structural patterns of authority. These paradigmatic modalities were instrumental in shaping the course of Islamic history, culture, and civilization. With varying degrees of success and stability, separate institutions of religious and political authority developed according to the three patterns. The two institutions were always separate, sometimes cooperative, often suspicious of each other, rarely heedless of each other's power, and never legitimated through anything but Islam.

Modern Islamic societies are at a revolutionary turning point. The universal truth, the *veritas*, of their traditional culture has begun losing its validity. There is no emerging order gathering enough legitimacy to assume conclusive supremacy. As a trajectory of commonly shared symbolics, the Islamic culture has lost its exclusive sway over modern Muslims. In their reconstitution of the present and future moral demands, Muslims of modernity are left with relics from their past they cannot do without, with new ideological doctrines demanding ever larger shares of their disobedience, and with a world ever fuller with paralyzing disenchantments. Modern political figures and institutions exercise power but want authority. Traditional figures and institutions of religious authority are increasingly losing their grip on the conscious obedience of modern Muslims—left only to command the frenzied fury of their suicidal triumphalism. Religious and political powers in modern Islam are equally unable to induce a measure of inner justification, so crucial to the notion of authority, as Weber observed. Instead they rely increasingly on external means (i.e., physical force). They remain separated however, by the two cultural paradigms that have begotten them and that they represent so vaguely, two paradigms best identified with their supreme symbolics: truth versus ideology.

Bibliography

Amir Arjomand, S. 1984. *The Shadow of God and The Hidden Imam: Religion, Political Order, and Societal Change in Shiite Iran from the Beginning to 1890.* Chicago: University of Chicago Press.

Dabashi, H. "Shariati's Islam: Revolutionary Uses of Faith in a Post-Traditional Society." *The Islamic Quarterly* 27 (Fourth Quarter 1983):203-22.

Donohue, J.J. and John L. Esposito, eds., 1982. *Islam in Transition: Muslim Perspectives.* Oxford: Oxford University Press.

Enayat, H. 1982. *Modern Islamic Political Thought.* Austin: University of Texas Press.

Halevy, E. 1972. *The Growth of Philosophic Radicalism.* Clifton: Augustus M. Kelley Publishers.

Hourani, A. 1962. *Arabic Thought in the Liberal Age: 1798-1939.* Cambridge: Cambridge University Press.

Jafri, S.H.M. 1979. *The Origins and Early Developments of Shia Islam.* New York: Longman.

Lambton, A.K.S. 1981. *State and Government in Medieval Islam.* Oxford: Oxford University Press.

Lapidus, I.M. "The Separation of State and Religion in the Development of Early Islamic Society." *IJMES* 6 (1975):363-85.

Mottahedeh, R. P. 1980. *Loyalty and Leadership in an Early Islamic Society.* Princeton: Princeton University Press.

_____. 1984. "The Foundation of State and Society." In Marjorie Kelley, ed., *Islam: The Religious and Political Life of a World Community.* New York: Praeger.

Pickthall, Marmaduke. 1976. *The Glorious Koran.* London: George Allen and Unwin.

Rahman, F. 1966. *Islam.* Chicago: University of Chicago Press.

Simmel, G. 1955. *Conflict and The Web of Group Affiliation.* Trans. Kurt H. Wolff and Reinhard Bendix. New York: The Free Press.

Watt, W. M. 1961. *Muhammad: Prophet and Statesman.* Oxford: Oxford University Press.

_____. 1968. *Islamic Political Thought.* Edinburgh: Edinburgh University Press.

_____. 1973. *The Formative Period of Islamic Thought.* Edinburgh: Edinburgh University Press.

Weber, M. 1946. *From Max Weber: Essays in Sociology.* H. H. Gerth and C. Wright Mills, eds. New York: Oxford University Press.

Williams, J.A., ed. 1971. *Themes of Islamic Civilization.* Berkeley: University of California Press.

15

Latin America and Liberation Theology

Roland Robertson

The fanning of the Spanish *conquistadores* across what became known as Latin America during the sixteenth century occurred within the historical context of two crucial circumstances: the occurrence of the splits within Christendom occasioned by the rise of Protestantism and the recent repulsion of Islam from the Iberian peninsula. In combination those circumstances gave something of a millennial cast to the conquering of the Latin American continent. The capture of Latin America was both a compensation for the loss of large portions of Europe north of the Mediterranean, as far as Catholics were concerned, and a continuation and further implementation of the spirit which had repelled the Moslems. In this first major wave of modern European imperialism, church and state went to the new lands in partnership, although an unequal one in the sense that from the beginning the Church in each conquered or staked-out territory was subordinate to the regal, colonial regime.

That this was indeed the earliest form of modern imperialism, and that it occurred during the century of the Protestant revolt against the Church in Europe, constitute the most important general considerations with respect to religion in Latin America and the latter's place in the modern world. That the colonization and the subjugation of the new continent took place so long ago had much to do with—although it is certainly not the only reason for—the fact that Latin American societies were the first newly independent societies of modern times (other than the United States, which inspired the leaders of Latin American independence movements). That Catholicism was introduced to Latin America in a basically medieval, pre-Reformational form (and in close, if unequal, alliance with precapitalist dominant classes) has had much to do with the relatively peripheral status of Latin America in relation to international Roman Catholicism.

In two closely related senses, Latin American Catholicism has been, until very recently, unique: (1) in its presence on a continent which enjoys a very ambiguous position in the modern world system, and (2) in its traditional manifestation of premodern theology and marginality in international Catholicism. That ambiguity (and from the Latin American's point of view, ambivalence) is further underlined by the selective susceptibility of Latin America to the impact of externally-generated, particularly European, culture. This is most acutely evidenced, as far as present interests are concerned, by the fact that the intimacy between the founding land-owning classes of Iberian Latin America and the Church was largely responsible for the heavy reliance upon European secularist ideas on the part of the leaders of the independence movements which began to grow in the wake of the French and American Revolutions at the end of the eighteenth century—a circumstance which, in turn, led to the consolidation of neo-medieval Catholic ideas in Latin America as a form of defense against the anti-Church leaders of the independence movements and, later, regimes.

In the 1950s and 1960s there developed a widespread international movement for independence in societies (mainly in Africa and Asia) which had, for the most part, been subject to Western imperialism long after the Iberian conquest of Latin America and a diffuse sense of revolutionism took hold of intellectual and youth elites in many parts of the world (notably in the revival and revamping of Marxist ideas). It was then the turn, so to speak, of Latin American Catholics to become greatly influenced by mainly European ideas and for the successors of the secular "liberals" of the nineteenth century to insulate themselves from external cultural influences. In this very recent phase it is again the "revolutionaries" who are more in touch with Europe.

Before beginning directly to trace the origins of liberation theology—both as a system of ideas and as a sociocultural movement—within the Latin American context, it is necessary to introduce another set of general considerations, which hinge to a large degree on what has already been said about Latin American history in relation to the rest of the world. It has frequently been observed in recent years that by around the end of the twentieth century Latin Americans will constitute about one-quarter of global Catholicism and that already Brazil is the largest Catholic country in the world. Bruneau's (1982:30) observation that the latter statistic hides as much as it reveals is just as applicable to the former (regardless of demographic trends). As far as Latin America as a whole is concerned, even though the baptismal rate is about 90 percent of the population, it is doubtful whether more than 30 percent of Latin Americans are subject to the "pervasive influence" of the Church (D'Antonio 1964), while only about 20 percent are active in the Church's formal activities on a regular basis. Moreover, many areas of Central and South America have not been in any meaningful sense evangelized (although in recent years Mormons, Protestant Pentacostalists and other Protestant groups have been particularly active in that regard), one of the major indicators of that situation being the fact that many rural areas are devoid of an official Church presence. Specifically in Brazil, it should be noted that in parts of the northeast there is only one priest to as many as 150,000 people, while—even more relevantly—in that country (and to a lesser degree in other Latin American societies) participation in and commitment to the doctrinal tenets of the Catholic Church are combined in many sections of the population with involvement in thaumaturgical cults. Moreover, in Brazil and many other parts of Latin America Catholicism has, so to say, floated on top of indigenous magicoreligious beliefs and practices, with the latter being the more resilient and profound layer of religious orientation.

Catholicism in Latin America has thus existed in Latin America for nearly two centuries between indigenous Indian religious systems, as well as spiritist thaumaturgical cults (some of them of African origin), on the one hand, and often militantly antireligious political and military elites, on the other. Moreover, as we have seen, it has largely existed in isolation from the general thrust of European Catholicism until quite recently. It has, moreover, had to confront two other, mainly twentieth century challenges: communism, Marxism, and socialism on the secular front; and Protestantism, most strongly in the form of Pentacostalism (until the recent surge of Mormonism) on the religious front. Nevertheless, largely because of its historic structural and diffuse cultural significance (if only as a target of hostile forces) the Catholic Church remains a formidable presence in Latin American societies.

In what follows the major concern will be with the growth since the 1960s of liberation theology both as part of Latin American Catholicism per se and as an important, if often exaggerated, ingredient of Latin American public life. It is not a simple matter to keep a sense or perspective in relation to the liberationist movement, since it is in large part via its claims and its programs for change that it has become well-known. The main danger of taking the numerous, but still largely similar, pronouncements of leading liberation theologians and their epigones at their face value is that prognosis gets mistaken for analysis. Unfortunately not merely political and religious activists but also social scientists, theologians and religious historians have been led into treating liberation theology as strictly analytic, or at least into eschewing interest in its analytical status or factual accuracy. This arises to some degree from the fact that not merely has liberation theology produced its own account of its origins but that in the process, and as part of its positive program, it has requisitioned "social science" (mainly in the form of Marxist or neo-Marxist theories).

Latin American Catholicism in Historical Perspective

To all intents and purposes, the individual Catholic churches were closely allied with the colonial regimes in South and Central America from the *conquistador* period of the sixteenth century up to the period during the nineteenth century, when liberal movements for independence succeeded in throwing off the shackles of formal domination throughout Latin America. That period of approximately three hundred years was characterized by fusion of church and state along the lines of the caesaropapist model of subjection of the church to state control and the use of the church for purposes of political legitimation and social control, even though the church in each society had, under regal domination, considerable influence in many walks of life. During most of that long period the church in virtually all Latin American countries was possessed by what Vallier (1970) called a monopolistic strategy, in the sense that it identified itself with the dominant political classes in the name of extending Christendom—a conception which was, however, very much less tied to the aspirations of international Catholicism per se than it was to specifically Iberian-colonial concerns.

The movements which swept Latin America during the nineteenth century in opposition to Spanish (or, as in the case of Brazil, Portuguese) colonial control were, in varying degrees, hostile to the church for two main reasons. First, the church was opposed—as it was by the French revolutionaries and their European successors—because of its identification with the *ancien regime* and the classes which sustained the latter. Second, the so-called liberals were greatly influenced by a series of European, Enlightenment-inspired philosophies and ideologies of a rationalist nature. Among the more significant of those were, in the earlier years of the century, utilitarianism (in its more collectivist form) and, later and more extensively, positivism of the kind associated with Auguste Comte. The general thrust of these developments was to heighten the presence of the strong, penetrative secular state, even though in various parts of Latin America the liberals were interested also in the promotion of capitalism. One of the major consequences of the installation of "liberal" regimes (not infrequently in the form of dictatorships) was that the church was thrust (with varying degrees of reluctance) even more clearly into the arms of the old dominant classes. Thus was consolidated the view, which has prevailed in Latin America until very recently, that Catholicism is essentially conservative and supportive of the forces of reaction.

Given the perceived sociocultural significance of religion in Latin America, the new political elites and dominant classes of nineteenth century did not, on the whole, seek to obliterate the church, but rather to reduce greatly

FIGURE 1
Types of Church Position in
Latin American Societies

		Degree to Which Church is Established	
		High	Low
Degree of Church Autonomy	Much	1	3
	Little	2	4

its capacity to impede reform. Nevertheless by the later years of the nineteenth century the church found itself in a more-or-less explicitly political role, allied frequently with conservative parties and factions. That circumstance derived partly from necessity (as a strategy of self-protection) and partly from choice (in the sense that the traditionalistic Catholicism of Latin America was even more hostile to modernity than the forms of Catholicism which prevailed in Europe at the end of the nineteenth century).

In spite of considerable similarity with respect to colonial history and great overlap in the political styles and programs of the nascent liberal parties and leaders there was in fact great variation with respect to the ways in which the church was treated by the new secular states. Following Vallier (1970:35) and Smith (1974) we can distinguish the major patterns of church position that became formalized during the period lasting from about 1850 through the 1920s, remembering that such arrangements were made mainly by liberal regimes (in the Latin American sense of *liberal*) and usually for the express purpose of speeding the process of secularization.

Even in those relatively few societies in which the church maintained a privileged position, it was less securely part of the social order than it had been prior to the onslaught of the liberals. In any case disestablishment was common. It occurred throughout Central America, as well as in Brazil, Ecuador, Chile, Uruguay, and other societies. Peru, Colombia, Venezuela, and Argentina were the most clear-cut cases of establishment. But in each of the main categories of formal establishment, on the one hand, and disestablishment (or separation), on the other, there was considerable variation.

The major variation in the latter respect was the extent to which the church was allowed to maintain control over its internal affairs (which, as we have seen, had been extensive in the colonial period in spite of the formal domination of the church by the colonial regimes). Within the category of cases in which formal separation of church and state occurred, we find great variation between, for example, Mexico—where the Constitution of 1917 heavily accentuated mid-nineteenth century laws that had severely circumscribed the Church's arena of legitimate activity—and Chile, where by the 1920s a separation had been achieved which allowed the Chilean Catholic Church (and other religious organizations) great freedom in the domain of religious belief and practice. Societies which approached the case of disestablishment with considerable autonomy for the church included Brazil and Uruguay. In the category of establishment, the variation between establishment with little church autonomy and considerable church autonomy is exampled by Argentina and Colombia respectively.

In any case, the later years of the nineteenth and the early years of the twentieth century witnessed something of an admission in the Catholic hierarchies of Latin America that the strategy of political alliance formation was not fruitful and so, to again invoke Vallier (1970), the churches, again to different degrees, adopted a missionary strategy, which centered upon insulating Catholics from their increasingly secular societal contexts and engaging in efforts to enlarge the numerical base and diffuse influence of the Catholic population. By the 1930s two prominent Catholic orientations had developed, namely fascism and neo-Thomism (Sanders 1974). While the former advocated—in the face of the perceived threat of communism and individualistic capitalism—an integral, organic type of nationalistic society, the latter attempted to maintain or promote democracy in the face of fascism and secular authoritarianism. Of the two conflicting orientations it was the second which became the most influential—indeed, probably critically so—in the emergence of modern trends within Latin American Catholicism; although, as Sanders (1974:283) has argued, the significance of Catholic fascism in Latin America should not be overlooked, in that it provided "something new and dynamic to a relatively unreflective and socially indifferent church." Both fascism and neo-Thomism were new developments of importance in the evolution of Latin American Catholicism in that they marked a shift in the direction of the church taking a positive interest in the shape of the societal order.

Thus was established, under the particular influence of neo-Thomist ideas, another stage in the history of the church in Latin America—one which Vallier (1970) described as the stage of the strategy of social development, involving a reentry into the political domain and the adumbration of programs for social reform. This is the stage which formed the immediate backdrop to the emergence of the liberationist movement. Of central significance in that regard has been the recognition of a relatively independent realm of political discourse and action, in reference to which theology and religious philosophy has to be developed. To put the matter a little differently, by the 1950s the church in Latin America—even though it was not unified across national boundaries—had come to a critical turning point in the degree to which it more-or-less fully recognized that there was a definite problem of the relationship between religion and politics. To be sure, the church had been embroiled in politics throughout its history in Latin America, but now the problem became that of developing an orientation which, in recognition of the prevailing differentiation of religion from politics, dealt directly with the issue of the relationship between those two domains of societal life.

During the modern period, four major orientations to the relationship between the political and the religious domains have been evident among Latin American Catholics (Levine 1981:304-12). The Christendom orientation—in continuity with the fascistic (or integralist) orientation of the 1930s and in historical reference to the Iberian-colonial period—has sought a reunification of the political and religious realms, and of church and state, in terms of an organic or corporatist image of a society dominated by Christian principles. The neo-Christendom orientation—which is continuous with neo-Thomism—"differs sharply in social content, seeking to reform the world and make it more just through an application of more modern and advanced Catholic social thought" (Levine 1981:305). The laity is granted considerable autonomy and it is they, rather than the clergy, who are supposed to be directly involved in politics. The modern neo-Christendom orientation developed mainly in terms of the advocacy and founding (under European influence) of Christian Democratic parties, notably in Chile and Venezuela. A major ingredient of the programs of the new Christian Democratic parties was the desire to pursue political policies between (in a sense, beyond) capitalism and communism. In a broader sense the political philosophy of those parties was in tune with the societal modernization theories which were prevalent in the social sciences and with the Alliance for Progress of the Kennedy years in the United States.

Levine (1981:305) maintains that for certain purposes Christendom and neo-Christendom can be lumped together, insofar as both, in spite of their being so dissimilar with respect to political-philosophical content, adhere to the view that society can and should be ordered on the basis of Christian principles. The two other major contemporary orientations—liberation theology and evangelical-pastoralism—share a rejection of the view that the world should, as Levine (1981) puts it, be reconquered. In his masterful analysis of Latin American Catholicism, Vallier (1970) maintained that by the late 1960s these two orientations, or strategies, were the most likely to prevail. For him the liberationist strategy contained significant echoes of the Christendom ideal—the only major difference being that whereas the latter was right wing and atavistic, embryonic liberationism was left wing and revolutionary. To the extent that one of the major features of the more political or ideological side of liberation theology has been its concern with praxis directed at the undoing of traditional cultural hegemony that is a plausible interpretation.

One of the most significant features of the liberationist movement has been its concern with the remaking of the world. Levine (1981) maintains (like many recent interpreters of liberation theology) that the emphasis upon remaking the world via the understanding of history, social content and contemporary circumstances should be clearly demarcated from the notion of reconquering the world. However, without denying for a moment that Christendomism and liberationism are radically at odds in terms of the content of their programs, the fact remains that both insist upon—at least in comparison with neo-Christendomism and evangelical-pastoralism, which Vallier (1970:76) called cultural-pastoralism—the unity of religion and politics. (Indeed, an assumption of Levine's analysis, in contrast to that of Vallier, is that in the modern world religion is *inexorably* synthesized with politics in the traditional sense.)

The evangelical-pastoral (or cultural-pastoral) orientation involves the view, in Vallier's (1970:76) words, that the church "assumes the role of spokesman for a higher moral order." In that perspective the layman is "able to live in a pluralistic, secular society as a Christian and a citizen simultaneously" (Vallier 1970:76). Thus the evangelical-pastoral orientation (which Vallier favored and which the Vatican has clearly promoted in opposition to liberation theology) shares with neo-Christendom the view that the religious and the political arenas should be regarded as relatively independent (but still interpenetrative). However, it has in common with liberationism the view that the world cannot be reconquered as opposed to remade.

Emphasizing that the second and fourth types have been in the ascendant for about the last twenty years in most Latin American societies, we may delineate the major types of Church strategy as in figure 2.

The Emergence of Liberation Theology

The modern Latin American idea of liberation theology was first expressed by the Peruvian Catholic theologian, Gustavo Gutiérrez in the mid-1960s—most fully in *A Theology of Liberation* (1973). However, a

FIGURE 2
Types of Church Strategy

Religion-Politics Image

Christianity-Society Image		Merge	Keep Separate
	Retake Society for Christianity	[1] Christendom	[3] Neo-Christendom
	Change Society for Christianity	[2] Liberation Theology	[4] Evangelical-Pastoral

nontheological work of the same period by the Brazilian educationist Paulo Freire—namely, *Pedagogy of the Oppressed* (1970)—was also of great importance in the crystallization of the liberation theology explicitly espoused by Gutiérrez. It is not an exaggeration to say that most of the major ideational attributes of liberation theology as a movement in Latin America (including the not insignificant Protestant wing of the latter) remain those originally espoused by Gutiérrez and Freire. However, the issue of the relationship between liberationist Christianity and Marxist thought has received sustained attention on the part of a few liberationists since the foundational statements of Gutiérrez.

Two major, general trends have developed over the years among liberation theologians, trends which have hinged considerably upon orientations to Freire's theme of *conscientization* (consciousness-raising with respect to the concrete circumstances in which individuals, particularly the oppressed, find themselves). The more conservative trend involves elaboration of the idea of liberation without explicitly relating it to the pedagogical and praxiological principles of conscientization. In other words, liberation theology remains in this perspective a matter of theological and historical reflection. At the opposite, radical end of the continuum one finds the position presented by the Uruguayan, Juan Luis Segundo in *The Liberation of Theology* (1976). Segundo's form of liberation theology envisages, in effect, the end of theology via the demythologizing processes of conscientization. Rather obviously, it is this strand of liberationism which has been particularly open to rapprochement with Marxism. Even though only a relatively small number of liberationist intellectuals have been publicly concerned with the minutiae of that issue, the fact remains that it is a vital strand as far as analysis of and prognosis with respect to liberation theology are concerned, for it suggests that religion may eventually be superseded by a realization of the Kingdom of God in terms of a conscienticized culture. (To that matter I will briefly return in connection with the Nicaraguan situation.)

Gutiérrez's earliest well-noted statement on the idea of a theology of liberation was presented in 1968 at a conference immediately preceding the Medellín Conference of Latin America Episcopacies (CELAM), which brought more than a semblance of unified action to Latin American Catholicism for the first time. (Of course, 1968 was a year of expression of rebellious and revolutionary sentiment in many parts of the globe.) The Medellín conference is well recognized as having constituted a critical turning point in Latin American Catholicism. It concluded that the Latin American continent was living in "a situation of sin." Class oppression, international imperialism, and institutional violence on the part of dominant classes were held responsible for the poverty and circumstance of exploitation of the lower classes and excluded. It was agreed that special efforts should be made to promote the education of the poor, and develop popular organizations, notably the base communities.

In spite of the expression of these ideas—stated mainly in three out of a total of sixteen sections—the final Medellín document was not in its overall textual sweep a greatly radical document. Penny Lernoux (1979:12) has noted that in spite of the "strong social criticism and prophetic commitment" in the sections on justice, peace and poverty, the document, even in its most critical passages, "failed to analyze the causes of 'institutionalized violence' or offer an alternative, still holding out for a 'third way' between communism and capitalism." However, "once committed to official paper . . . words take on a life of their own, and so it was with the Medellín Conclusions, certain phrases of which, such as *institutionalized violence,* were written into the Magna Carta of a socially activist Church."

The Medellín conference took place at a time of considerable flux in Latin American Catholicism and in Latin America generally. The Vatican Council had met earlier in the decade (1962-1965) and had had considerable impact with respect to its emphasis upon the idea of the Church as a "Pilgrim People of God," its acknowledgment of historical change, its concern with the human dimension of religious doctrine and practice, its underwriting of the need for more lay involvement in the running of the church, its plea for evangelization and its promotion of sensitivity to local cultural circumstances. Meanwhile there had occurred a sharp swing in the mid-1960s to political authoritarianism (even neototalitarianism) in many parts of Latin America, much of it in the name of the doctrine of national security. Thus, at the very same time that the Latin American church was being thoroughly exposed to democratic and humanitarian ideas and becoming more unified under the inspiration of Vatican II (for it was at the Council meetings that leaders of Latin American churches had their first major opportunity to share their experiences), Latin American polities were experiencing a substantial shift in the opposite direction.

In the immediate background of these two critical—and, perhaps, mutually reinforcing developments—stood the occurrence of the Cuban Revolution of the late 1950s and the ensuing crystallization of sharp attitudes toward the Revolution, the United States, and the relationship between Latin America and the rest of the world. One of the major cleavages which began to develop within the church in this ideologized climate was that between those who were deeply interested in the growing and international dialogue between Christianity and Marxism and those who sought, in contrast, to resist Marxism and communism through the promotion of the idea of Christian Democracy, which—as has been mentioned previously—involved rejection of both capitalism and extreme communism. The coming to power of the Christian Democrats in Chile and the ensuing political events in that country played a crucial role in the development of the liberationist movement.

The founding of the Christians for Socialism movement in the late 1960s was partly inspired by Camilio Torres, a Colombian revolutionary who left the priesthood protesting that it was possible to be both a Christian and a revolutionary, and died in 1966 while fighting with the Colombian Army of Liberation. The movement became politically significant in Chile during the years of the Marxist Allende government. In the early 1970s about one in eight of Chilean priests supported Christians for Socialism, many members of which supported Castro's call for a strategic alliance between Marxists and Christian revolutionaries. It should also be said that, as was the case with a number of Latin American societies, Chile experienced a large inflow of European priests in that period. The latter played a very important part in the attempt to incorporate Marxist ideas into Latin American Catholicism.

The Christians for Socialism movement was but one—although almost certainly the most important—of a number of radical religious movements which grew in Latin America in the late 1960s and early 1970s. One of the major reasons for that development was the disillusionment which had been occasioned by the failure of Christian Democracy (or neo-Christendom) to repel the surge of authoritarianism and oppression across Latin America. In the case of the Christians for Socialism movement itself—but less so in other parallel movements—there was a strong tendency to oppose the official Catholic leadership, as well as a tilting toward the idea that religion is an aspect of alienation and therefore religious needs may well disappear with the overcoming of alienation in a postcapitalist society. The general ideas advanced by Christians for Socialism (which was not a solely Chilean movement), the Movement for Third World Priests in Argentina, and the National Office of Social Information in Peru concerning poverty, injustice and suffering were close to those developed in more circumscribed, theological mode by liberation theologians. Indeed, prominent liberation theologians—including Gutiérrez—went to Chile in the early 1970s to advise Christians for Socialism.

Events in Chile in the early 1970s have had a great impact on the recent development of liberation theology and reactions to it. From the broadly liberationist standpoint the alleged failure of Christian Democracy, followed by the collapse of the Allende government (partly, as the left sees it, because the latter was ultimately opposed by many in the higher reaches of the church), should lead to the conclusion that radical liberationism is the true path. From the points of view of many others, the Allende years were marked by splits within the church which were largely produced by the Christian revolutionaries themselves, which show the dangers of the church being closely allied with those who seek to inject Marxism into Catholicism.

Through the 1970s liberation theology became increasingly conspicuous, not least because the idea took hold in many quarters—notably in the United States—that the Christian base communities which had sprung up in virtually all Latin American societies were manifestations of liberation theology itself. By the end of the decade this conception was given heightened expression in reference to the part played by leaders of and participants in base communities in the Nicaraguan revolution. The general impression has been conveyed in many quarters that the base community is liberation theology in action and that it has been largely inspired by liberationist ideas. That, however, is by no means the case. It can be safely said that while, indeed, some base communities stress direct use of the Bible, working for and with the poor, empowerment of the laity, and development of the idea that the Catholic church is the church of the people, others are much more concerned with strictly religious matters. In fact base communities range, at one extreme, from being settings in which religion takes a very secondary place (if it has a place at all) to concern for political, economic and social issues to, at the other extreme, settings in which mainly middle class individuals engage in spiritual exercises. Moreover, in some areas—notably, Brazil—base communities developed well before liberationist ideas began to make their mark, mainly as an alternative to traditional parish structures and in order to meet the shortage of priests.

Controversy about the more political of the base communities was part of the drawing of battle lines as the third CELAM was anticipated in the late 1970s. In spite of strenuous efforts to do so on the part of conservative Catholics, the meeting at Puebla in Mexico in 1979 did not condemn liberation theology. Nor did it condemn any form of the base community. To a considerable degree, liberationists interpreted Puebla as a partial victory, in the sense that they withstood the opposition of the CELAM secretariat, conservative European Church officials and the Vatican itself. In a sociological sense, it might be concluded that the great debate about the agenda of liberation theology and the kind of base community for which it stood institutionalized the problem of liberation theology in the Latin American Church.

Liberation Theology in the 1980s

The general thrust of liberation theology may be summarized thus (Robertson 1986):

1. The traditional doctrinal focus upon inner spirituality and personal sin has prevented realization of the ideas that sin can and, indeed, should be regarded as a structural property of society and that salvation can and should be considered in collective and historical terms. This perspective is closely related to the claim that whereas the dominant theological method has been ahistorical and apolitical, the Bible should be read with emphasis precisely on historicity and the inevitable conjunction of politics and religion. Thus Moses and the Promised Land and Jesus and the Kingdom of God are the exemplary Biblical themes. In sum, theology should be existentialist rather than essentialist; homocentric rather than theocentric; inductive rather than deductive; biblical and circumstantial rather than scholastic and eternalistic.
2. Latin America's circumstance of widespread poverty and inequality, as well as its religious condition, result from a long history of imperialistic or neocolonialistic subjection, beginning with Spain and Portugal in the sixteenth century, continuing with other European countries (notably Britain) in the nineteenth century and culminating with the United States in the twentieth century. More specifically, the present Latin American condition is a consequence of the operation of a world system of economic and political exploitation. (For some liberation theologians Latin America has a privileged role to play in releasing the Third World from bondage.)
3. Vatican II, in effect, validated the idea of a church of and for the people—a greater concern with the material condition of humanity (more specifically, the poor, marginal and excluded). According to Gutiérrez, traditional theology begins with the problem of the nonbeliever, whereas liberationism begins with "the man who is not a man." The-

ology should be geared to the establishment of a terrestrial Kingdom of God.

In essence, these are the liberationist ideas which have been increasingly adumbrated within Latin America. (They have, moreover, had considerable positive impact on other continents, including North America.) It should be noted that the summary does not as such include specifically Marxist ideas. That is very deliberate, since in spite of much of the comment upon and critique of liberation theology Marxism does not constitute a core component of the strictly theological dimension of liberation theology. The modal attitude toward Marxism among liberation theologians—at least in their public comments and writings—is that Marxism provides a necessary methodological supplement to theology and, as I noted previously, relatively few liberation theologians have explicitly incorporated Marxist ideas into the mainstream of their writings. Nevertheless, the line between maintaining that Marxism is required in order to understand how, for example, injustice has been historically sustained and how it may be eradicated, on the one hand, and *conceiving of religion itself as a strictly historical phenomenon,* on the other, is thin.

In the 1980s much of the interest in liberation theology has centered upon its role in Sandinistan Nicaragua. Indeed many—from different judgmental standpoints—have come to regard Nicaragua as something of a test case for liberation theology. Not unlike the situation in Chile in the early 1970s, Nicaragua has experienced since the revolution of 1979 an early validation of a leftward leap on the part of the church hierarchy, followed—after "a honeymoon period"—by a split within the church with respect to the policies and activities of a revolutionary regime. Leading church officials have become increasingly disenchanted with the Sandinistan leadership, while—on all the available evidence—the church leadership has been regarded less and less positively by the Sandinistan regime. As part of that development there has emerged, largely under the aegis of the Sandinistas, a "popular" or "parallel" church, one which is supportive of the revolution.

The complexity of this circumstance (which derives in part from the fact that, as in Chile but as was not the case in Cuba, the church has in recent history been relatively free) is considerable. In spite of the fact that base communities had played a significant role in generating support for the Sandinistan revolution, there are signs (Christian 1985:203-34) that from quite early on some of the more powerful Sandinistas advocated a basically antireligious policy—one which would involve using popular religious sentiment to strengthen support for the revolution but which would in the long run promote the demise of religion. We have seen that there is a strand of liberation theology itself which points in the latter direction, a strand which overlaps with the idea that the major point of theology and religion is to realize concretely the Kingdom of God.

In such a circumstance what counts as being antireligious, or even anti-church, becomes difficult to discern. There are aspects of liberationist thought which would *encourage* an antireligious policy—in the conventional sense of antireligious—on the part of a revolutionary state. For the revolutionary effort can be regarded as directed at the consummation of the promise of religion. In that regard it is possible to have it both ways. In effect, religion can be opposed in the name of religion. That makes comparison between the Nicaraguan circumstance and others in which a revolutionary regime faces a significant church and/or religious presence particularly interesting (Greil and Kowalewski 1985). For the Nicaraguan case may be (thus far) unique in that it is, in principle, possible for it to garner legitimacy from religious sources with respect to its own policies aiming at the demise of religion. Let it be clearly understood that I am not arguing that the Sandinistan policy has been or will become emphatically antireligious. I am simply underlining the complexity and the sociologically intriguing nature of the situation, an additional dimension of which concerns the fact that the international liberation movement, particularly as it relates to liberationism in the United States, is playing a crucial role with respect to the Nicaraguan situation.

Undoubtedly liberation theology is destined to play a very significant role not only in Latin America but in the Catholic Church as a whole—the seriousness of the latter situation being underlined by the attempt on the part of the Vatican in 1985 to modify the impact of Vatican II.

Bibliography

Berryman, Phillip. 1984. *The Religious Roots of Rebellion: Christians in Central American Revolutions.* Maryknoll, N.Y.: Orbis Books.

Bruneau, Thomas C. 1982. *The Church in Brazil.* Austin: University of Texas Press.

———. 1979. "Basic Christian Communities in Latin America: Their Nature and Significance (especially in Brazil)." Pp. 225-37 in Daniel H. Levine, ed., *Churches and Politics in Latin America.* Beverly Hills: Sage Publications.

Cabal, Hugo Latorre. 1978. *The Revolution of the Latin American Church.* Trans. Frances K. Hendricks and Beatrice Berler. Norman, OK: University of Oklahoma Press.

Christian, Shirley. 1985. *Nicaragua: Revolution in the Family.* New York: Random House.

Cleary, Edward L. 1985. *Crisis, Change, and the Church in Latin America.* Maryknoll, N.Y.: Orbis Books.

D'Antonio, William V. 1964. "Democracy and Religion in Latin America." Pp. 241-65 in William V. D'Antonio and Fredrick B. Pike, eds., *Religion, Revolu-*

tion, and Reform: New Forces for Change in Latin America. New York: Praeger.

Dussel, Enrique. 1976. *History and the Theology of Liberation.* Trans. by John Drury. Maryknoll, N.Y.: Orbis Books.

Eagleson, John and Scharper, Philip, eds. 1979. *Puebla and Beyond.* Trans. John Drury. Maryknoll, N.Y.: Orbis Books.

Freire, Paulo. 1970. *Pedagogy of the Oppressed.* Trans. Myra Bergman Ramos. New York: Seabury Press.

Greil, Arthur L. and David Kowalewski. "Church-State Relations in Russia and Nicaragua: Early Revolutionary Years." Unpublished paper, 1985.

Gutiérrez, Gustavo. 1973. *Theology of Liberation.* Trans. Sister Caridad Inda and John Eagleson. Maryknoll, N.Y.: Orbis Books.

Kirk, J. Andrew. 1979. *Liberation Theology: An Evangelical View from the Third World.* Atlanta: John Knox.

Lernoux, Penny. 1979. "The Long Path to Puebla." Pp. 3-27 in John Eagleson and Philip Scharper, eds., *Puebla and Beyond.* Maryknoll, N.Y.: Orbis Books.

Levine, Daniel H. 1981. *Religion and Politics in Latin America: The Catholic Church in Venezuela and Colombia.* Princeton: Princeton University Press.

Levine, Daniel H., ed. 1979. *Churches and Politics in Latin America.* Beverly Hills: Sage Publications.

Mahan, Brian and Richesin, L. Dale, eds. 1981. *The Challenge of Liberation Theology.* Maryknoll, N.Y.: Orbis Books.

Neely, Alan. "Liberation Theology in Latin America: Antecedents and Autochthony." *Missiology: An International Review* VI (1978): 343-69.

Norman, Edward. 1981. *Christianity in the Southern Hemisphere.* Oxford: Clarendon Press.

———. 1979. *Christianity and the World Order.* Oxford: Oxford University Press.

Randall, Margaret. 1983. *Christians in the Nicaraguan Revolution.* Trans. Mariana Valverde. Vancouver: New Star Books.

Robertson, Roland. 1986. "Liberation Theology in Latin America: Sociological Problems of Interpretation and Explanation." In Jeffrey Hadden and Anton Shupe, eds., *Prophetic Religion and Politics.* New York: Paragon Books.

Sanders, Thomas G. 1974. "The New Latin American Catholicism." Pp. 282-302 in Donald E. Smith., ed., *Religion and Political Modernization.* New Haven and London: Yale University Press.

Segundo, Juan Luis. 1976. *The Liberation of Theology.* Trans. John Drury. Maryknoll, N.Y.: Orbis Books.

Smith, Brian H. 1982. *The Church and Politics in Chile.* Princeton: Princeton University Press.

Smith, Donald E. 1974. "Patterns of Secularization in Latin America." Pp. 116-31 in Donald E. Smith., ed., *Religion and Political Modernization.* New Haven and London: Yale University Press.

Torres, Sergio and Eagleson, John, eds. 1981. *The Challenge of Basic Christian Communities.* Maryknoll, N.Y.: Orbis Books.

———. 1976. *Theology in the Americas.* Maryknoll, N.Y.: Orbis Books.

Vallier, Ivan. 1970. *Catholicism, Social Control, and Modernization in Latin America.* Englewood Cliffs, N.J.: Prentice-Hall.

Walzer, Michael. 1985. *Exodus and Revolution.* New York: Basic Books.

16

Civil Religion Versus State Power in Poland

Ewa Morawska

Since the appearance in 1967 of Robert Bellah's essay on civil religion, the meaning and significance of this concept have become increasingly obscure. In an interpretation of the historical case of Poland, I would like to shift the discussion of civil religion from the focus on western countries and emerging nation-states.

Thrice partitioned between 1772 and 1795 by Russia, Prussia, and Austria, Poland as a political entity disappeared from the map of Europe for six generations. In 1918, it briefly regained sovereignty, only to lose it again twenty years later under the German and Soviet occupations. In 1945, Poland found itself with the rest of eastern Europe under Soviet domination. The fall of the ancient Polish Commonwealth from political grandeur came as a shock to its citizens, and was to reverberate in the national consciousness for generations. After 1795 the prepartition image of the Polish nation-state became inadequate. The republic of nobles enjoying their "golden freedoms" had been based on the principle of government by consent and a political covenant with the elected monarch. One generation after the last partition, drawing upon current European philosophical, religious, and literary trends, there developed in Poland a powerful new national-religious ideology.

In western Europe, the revolutionary Springtime of the Nations in 1848 marked the end of Romanticism in literature, philosophy, and politics. The second half of the century witnessed the triumph of realism and practical pursuits. By 1880, via political maneuvers and diplomatic alliances, most national movements in Europe had already achieved their goals. The cause of Poland—opposed to the vital interests of expansive, powerful neighbors—remained an exception. Confronted with alien states determined to keep the country partitioned, root out local institutions, and denationalize Polish culture, the Poles had at their disposal neither the legal rights nor peaceful means to assert their demands. They searched for answers to

221

questions of the meaning and purpose of their collective and individual existence in the romantic national poetry, philosophy, and religion.[1]

The language and symbolism of Romanticism became the basic, shared code of cultural communication for the majority of Poles. With legal and state institutions dismantled and replaced by imposed alien authority, Poland became for its "invisible citizens" an idea—a memory of the past and an aspiration for the future. Deprived of political reality, it became the reality of spirit and imagination, the second Israel that revitalized the ancient Judaic version of mystical nationalism. The words "If I forget Thee, oh Jerusalem" echoed in the Polish national anthem (created a few years after the last partition): "Poland is not yet lost . . . as long as we live" (Talmon 1960). Nearly every generation launched another unsuccessful struggle to reestablish the Polish sovereign state.

The Polish romantic faith is a civil religion, constituted and reconstituted through sustained conflict between the obstinately renascent civil society and imposed alien rule. This proposition could be generalized to include the historical experience of other eastern European nations (with the exception of Russia and possibly Hungary). It specifies a different set of crisis conditions for the emergence of civil religion than those suggested by Markoff and Regan (1982) in "The Rise and Fall of Civil Religion: Comparative Perspectives." Asking why civil religions emerge at certain historical junctures, Markoff and Regan relate them to the crises engendered by the emergent states' assaults on their citizens' particularistic political identities. In Poland, the emergence of a new civil religion in the nineteenth century and its stubborn persistence into the 1980s has been the nation's response to the fundamental crisis resulting from the loss of political sovereignty. Its major function has been not to legitimate, but to delegitimate this state of affairs by rallying Polish society around a counterview of a past and future free, independent Poland.

Specialists define civil religion as a set of religiopolitical symbols and rituals regarding a nation's history and destiny. They address issues of political ethos and legitimacy that are not fused with either state or church but differentiated from both.[2] The separation of postpartition Polish civil religion from the state is self-evident. Statelessness, or alien-stateness, has been the condition of Poland for most of its modern history. The opposition between the ideals of citizenship and the state became characteristic of the Polish national-religious ideology. After partition, good citizenship for patriotic Poles became synonymous with dissidence and protest against the established political order. With the exception of national insurrections, open defiance of the authorities was a prerogative of a small minority of dissidents. Civil opposition was asserted privately in the widely shared moral consensus that defined Poland's political status as hostile to its national interests and accorded respect and admiration to the heroic national avant-garde.

The relationship between Polish civil religion and the Catholic Church has been more complex and ambivalent. Throughout the nineteenth century the Vatican lent open support to the existing political order in Europe. Its attitude toward national movements was indifferent, if not negative. The situation of the local Polish Catholic Church vis-à-vis the partitioning powers was less difficult in Austria, where, in spite of restrictive laws, it enjoyed relative security. In both Czarist Russia and Bismarckian Germany, church-state relations were much more precarious. In all three partitions the Polish Catholic Church was confronted with a similar dilemma. Open defiance of the authorities would have resulted in swift reprisals and further limitations on the performance of its essential, extrapolitical functions. Refusal to lend support to Poland's national cause would have meant the betrayal of the moral values upheld by the majority of Poles. Restrained on all sides, the Polish Catholic Church tried to steer a middle course. While it neither generated nor controlled nor even openly endorsed romantic civil religion, tradition as well as political circumstance turned the church into its sponsor and "carrier." With freedom of organizations severely curtailed, education and publications controlled, and the Polish language banned from public usage (it was reinstituted in the Austrian part after 1869), religious practices provided the only peaceful occasion for Poles to publicly relive and reassert their national community and its social bonds.

Created in its classical version by poets and philosophers in the first third of the last century, the Polish romantic creed represents a peculiar, original blend of several European intellectual trends, modified and adjusted to fit the particular Polish situation. The creed combines the German philosophical idealism of Fichte and Schelling, the conservative Romanticism of Müller and Baader; Herderian historicism; French revolutionary ideals; the Christian socialism of Michelet, Fourier, St. Simon, and Leroux; and the politicized messianic Catholicism of Lemmenais, Ballanche, de Maistre, and Vico. The Polish romantic faith establishes a relationship between God and the individual through a chain of mediating fusions that occur horizontally in time and space, and vertically between the deity and individuals in the nation, humanity and history. This realizes a dialectic of universal and global versus particular and national purposes, and of societal versus individual ones. The main tenets of the Polish romantic faith in its ideal form can be summarized as follows.

First, God reveals Himself in universal history that unfolds through the repetition of the Christian course of sacrifice and redemption. Second, Poland, through her defeat and innocent suffering under tyranny, has been selected as the primary agent of God in universal history; as a collective body it renews and replicates the Passion, death and resurrection of Christ. This is expressed by Kazimierz Brodziński (1832): "Hail O Christ, Thou Lord of men!/Poland, in Thy footsteps treading/Like Thee suffers, at Thy bidding/Like Thee, too, shall rise again!" Polish Romantic mysticism has an innerworldly orientation: fulfilling the providential design of history, Poland's cosuffering with Christ, her "crucifixion" and "descent into the tomb," will bring the defeat of her oppressors and her resurrection as a politically sovereign and socially just nation of equal citizens. Her sacrifice will result in the Christian kingdom on earth and the realization of universal charity, freedom, and justice among spiritually transformed mankind.

Imbued with such transcendent purpose, Poland becomes a commanding divine force—a moral ideal and obligation, at the same time universal and national.

> *No more are you a land for me*
> *A place—or home—or custom*
> *Or the defunct state*
> *Or a phantom*
> *But the Faith!*
> *The Law!*

wrote Zygmunt Krasiński (1843). In the Polish Romantic creed, *citizenship* ceases to function as it did in the prepartition Commonwealth, as a covenant—a retractable and modifiable arrangement between the individual and the nation-state. It becomes a notion of an absolute, total, and indivisible divine idea/Poland and her universal mission. This view is embedded in a highly moralistic, dualistic perception of history as the scene of combatant collective forces: the ethical—embodied in the innocently suffering (Poland)—and the unethical—represented by the oppressors (partitioners)—between which there must be no accommodation and no acceptance of partial solutions.

The divine scheme in the purposeful unfolding of universal history in which Poland, cosuffering with Christ, plays a leading role, presupposes that individual self-realization is dependent upon the unfolding of the collective pattern. The concept of *freedom* in the prepartition republic of nobles referred to the personal liberties and civil rights that were to protect citizens against the despotic attempts of the monarch and the government. It now connotes the collective freedom of a nation to be reestablished after the defeat of its oppressor-partitioner(s). In the Polish romantic creed, the present yoke and martyrdom of Poland and, through it, the fulfillment of its universal liberationist calling, require that the individual become totally absorbed into and identified with the nation. The private and public spheres are to be fused and inseparable, individual autonomy given up to the collective national identity.

Radical deindividuation as the highest moral commandment and civil virtue of a patriotic Pole, finds forceful expression in Adam Mickiewicz's *Forefathers' Eve* (1832), the most important romantic classic of the epoch: "I am one with my Nation/My name is a Million/Because for Millions I love and I suffer." There is a specifically Polish conversion, replicated in all major romantic works: the hero abandons his private identity and individualistic pursuits and interests. He assumes an ethically superior attitude of ascetic collectivism—a selfless and absolute service to the national idea. To fulfill God's plans and by the same token, Poland's fate, the offering—as in the poem by Juliusz Stowacki (1840)—must be complete: "Woe to him/ Who offers to his country only half of his soul/And another keeps for his happiness." The transformation in *Forefathers' Eve* of Gustaw—"lover of a woman," a romantic individualist preoccupied with his private emotional affairs and spiritual turmoils—into Konrad—"lover of the Country," a romantic ascetic collectivist always on patriotic duty—is the main symbolic figure in the Polish romantic ideology. It assumes two equivalent forms: Tyreteian—activist, conspirator and insurrectionist—symbolized in the image of *héro luttant*/Polish nation in armed confrontation with the oppressors; and Sacrificial, represented by *héro funèbre*/Poland suffering and overcome, accepting the Cross.

For most of the nineteenth century, the lengthy mystical improvisations of poets and the dense philosophical treatises containing the Polish romantic creed were banned by the partitioners. They were scarcely known to the Polish public. The ideas were replicated for everyday use in endless popularized imitations, in legends of heroes and martyrs, and in emotional images and representations of crucial themes. Constant repetition of the symbols on innumerable ritual occasions made the national Romantic faith personally and intensely familiar to generations of Poles.

Home, church, and informal social gatherings were the main institutional carriers of popular civil religion in partitioned Poland. In the nineteenth century, a patriotic pattern of home decoration developed in all three partitioned areas. On the walls, there usually hung popular lithographs representing scenes from the nation's battles and portraits of national heroes or relatives memorialized in the glorious moment of giving their lives for Poland. There was usually a piano on which, in the afternoons and during holidays, patriotic melodies were played, mindful of Poland's past glories and present fate. There were often a few half-hidden works by the nationally acclaimed—and banned—dissident poets. Families gathered regularly with friends and neighbors for patriotic singing and the reading aloud of patriotic tales. Generations of Polish women taught their children kindergarten verses which commanded them to imitate patriots, such as Thaddeus Kościuszko and Prince Józef Poniatowski, who "lived for their Country and died for her Glory."

Catholic practices served as a powerful vehicle for the popularization of the national creed. The Romantic ideal, representing the Polish nation as a cosufferer with Christ, sharing his Passion, facilitated the fusion of religious rituals with civil national celebrations. Every Sunday, in churches in all three partitions, Mass ended with the singing of *Boże Coś Polskę*, a patriotic hymn composed by Alojzy Feliński in 1816:

> *o God, who through the ages*
> *Has girded Poland with power and fame*
> *Whose shield hath kept Her in Thy care*
> *From evils that would cause her harm*
> *Before Thy alters, we bring our entreaty*
> *Restore, o Lord, our free country.*

Every Easter, the traditional celebration of the death and resurrection of Christ provided an occasion for the commemoration of Poland's "crucifixion" and her "descent into the tomb," and for public prayers for her redemption. Every Christmas, in churches around the country, crèches displayed the main themes of the national romantic faith: the Polish eagle (the ancient national symbol) wearing a crown of thorns; Kościuszko, Poniatowski, and the insurrectionists from successive uprisings; blood, chains, and patriotic duty; heroic death; and trust in God.

The Virgin Mary figured prominently in the nineteenth century popular rituals of the romantic faith. Since the seventeenth century, her cult had become one of national devotion. In 1656, King John Casimir declared the Virgin the Queen of Poland in thanksgiving for her protection in the defense of the Jasna Góra Monastery. For the next hundred years, the Virgin Mary was the patroness of the avenging wars that Poland led with her neighbors. After the partition, she became the Dolorosa, the Sufferer, equated with Poland under the Cross. During the nineteenth century, the image of Poland as the Virgin Mother suffering at Calvary was replicated in innumerable popular poems and paintings. She was also seen as a comforter of the crucified nation. To her, Mother of Christ and Protectoress of Poland, went daily prayers during the special patriotic Marian litanies, rosaries, adorations, chaplets, and pilgrimages for which Poles gathered in all seasons.

Just as the national and political condition of Polish society at the closing of the nineteenth century differed from that of western Europe, so did its civil religion. By sanctifying history and elevating Poland as innocent martyr to the role of Christ's collective cosufferer in bringing earthly redemption to mankind, the Polish romantic faith responded to the needs of Poles who rejected the subjugation of their country as inhumane and immoral. They desperately searched for the meaning of their humiliating experience. In the transformation of politically annihilated Poland into an ideal and a commanding moral community, the romantic faith made possible the survival of Polish society. Dispossessed by the partitioners of its public civil institutions—the natural "carriers" of societal bonds—it was now bound together by the collective memory of the past and the hope for the future. By deprivatizing the individual and assigning the highest moral value to the collectivist ascetic conversion, the Polish romantic faith erected a strong ethical-religious dam against the disintegration of society and the social and political disorientation of its members. Absent were the routine civil rituals through which the citizens of a sovereign nation-state could daily reconfirm their allegiance. The moralistic counterposing of the satanic (oppressive partitioning states) and angelic (suffering Poland) forces in history served to sustain moral commitment to the divine national cause and resistance to evil, oppressive rule.

The twenty-year period of Poland's political independence between the two world wars was apparently too short and turbulent to significantly alter the Polish civil religion inherited from the partition era. Reestablished after World War II under the imposed protectorate of the Soviet Union as part of a communist empire, Poland has again been managed in accordance with foreign interests and alien ideology. The majority of Poles see Poland's postwar condition as the continuation of her historical subjection to foreign domination. The perception by Polish civil society of the party controlled, atheistic communistic regime as an alien imposition perpetuates and reasserts traditional alienation from the state. In the eyes of a great many Poles, several attempts since 1956 to achieve emancipation from a totalistic, atheistic state and from an alien power, represent the continuation of earlier efforts beginning in the eighteenth century.

Many nineteenth century elements of the old Polish civil religion have retained their meaning and vitality as ideological rallying points of Polish civil society. The home, informal social gatherings and various unofficial political and cultural activities, remain the important carriers of Polish civil religion. Paradoxically, so are state-controlled educational and cultural programs. In trying to enmesh itself into national history and be perceived as its legitimate heir, the Polish communist regime caters to the widespread historical interests of Polish society. The classical works of the nineteenth-century Polish romantic writers figure prominently, for example, in the standard school programs in Polish literature and history, in many publications, in theaters, and radio and television programs. Most of the state's attempts at self-legitimization have been counterproductive. The old symbols and images of the defiant nation resisting the partitioners in the nineteenth century are perceived by Poles as masks for problems and attitudes of present-day Polish society, saddled again with imposed political authority.

Under communist rule the Polish Catholic Church, through its parishes and rituals, continues to function as the traditional carrier of Polish civil religion. With its position and principles strengthened over the years by confrontation with the Marxist totalistic state, the Polish Catholic Church has become the major public spokesman for Polish civil society. Traditionally it keeps to the middle ground, avoiding open support for radical dissident activities in order not to provoke the reprisals of hostile local authorities or of Soviet intervention. A public opinion poll conducted unofficially in Poland by a French agency shortly before John Paul II's visit in the summer of 1983 revealed that over sixty percent of respondents perceived the Polish Catholic Church and/or the Pope as "the best representatives of the interests of Polish society" (another twenty-four percent pointed to Solidarity and 3 percent to the communist party and the government).[3]

Generated and sustained by subjugation to an alien ideology and political order, carried in institutions traditionally opposed to the state, the contemporary civil religion in Poland is not simply a replica of the nineteenth-century romantic faith. It is a familiar but transformed and changing symbolic code, a framework in which the old themes and patterns coexist with new and renovated elements.

During the sixteen months of the Solidarity movement's legal existence, the traditional themes of Polish civil religion were conveyed more openly and forcefully than ever since Poland has been under communist rule. The idea of national death and resurrection was pronounced in the huge crosses, decorated with the Polish national colors and Solidarity's emblems. These were erected in Poznań, Gdańsk, and Gdynia to commemorate the victims of the "People's Republic." Despite the protests of party officials, similar images representing Poland as the follower of Christ's Passion were replicated in other Polish cities, during the workers' strikes and mass demonstrations, in the union's regional and local headquarters, in churches, and even in state-controlled schools. Even more ubiquitous is the symbol of the Virgin Mary, the Patroness of Poland. It has been strongly promoted by the Catholic Church, particularly by the late Cardinal Stefan Wyszyński and the former Archbishop of Kraków, Pope John Paul II—both devoted Marian mystics. Millions of Poles have participated in church-sponsored solemn vows offering the whole nation to the Mother of God "in the bondage of love." The symbolism of these acts clearly echoes the historical idea of *Polonia Revivificanda* and Romantic Messianism. By a collective offering to the Virgin Mary, the suffering nation wishes to secure in her hands the preservation of its national identity and civil rights. These are threatened by the imposed totalistic, atheistic order. The participants also wish to contribute to the universal freedom of the church and all humanity.

Forty years of confrontations with a totalistic political order and an atheistic ideology have sustained and reinforced the moralistic dualistic world view contained in the Polish civil religion. What the Poles perceive as the global project of Soviet Marxism-Leninism universalizes the image of polarized combatant forces—moral/human/God-loving versus immoral/inhuman/Godless—beyond the boundaries of Poland and eastern Europe to the whole world. By opposing the atheistic community order, defined as aggressive evil incarnated, the Polish nation collectively serves threatened humanity as the *antemurale* of Christianity and freedom. Necessitated by the ongoing conflict with similarly Manichean but inimical ideology and politics, these perceptions reinforce the confrontational, all-or-nothing tendencies of the Polish world view.

The civil religion of present-day Polish society continues to define freedom as the collective freedom of the nation. In the romantic tradition it fuses the private and public attitudes and behavior of the individual and assigns the highest moral value to a collectivist virtue rendered through sacrificial service in the cause of national salvation. (Bitter defeats have diminished the appeal of the insurrectionist model of a patriotic hero.) The communist totalistic state threatens not only national identity and the integrity of the social bonds of a subjugated society, but also the individual and his or her rights. Parallel to the traditional collectivist orientation focusing on national salvation, Polish civil religion today contains a moral commandment of individual freedom related to political democracy. It has drawn from three major sources: the old native tradition of civil liberties in the prepartition Polish Commonwealth, the philosophical and political foundations of modern liberal democracies in the West, and contemporary Christian teachings. Perceived in the West as staunchly conservative, Polish Catholicism has changed significantly since the beginning of the century. From the pulpits as well as in the publications and activities of organized groups of lay Catholic intelligentsia, the church espouses and teaches Christian social doctrine, Catholic humanism, and personalism. These stress the sanctity of the human persons in their inalienable rights, the dignity of work and social justice, the freedom of individual conscience, civil liberties, and the right to the truth and participation in government (Malia 1983). The two orientations, collectivist and individualist, are each related to a different civil sphere threatened by the imposed political order. They coexist in the Polish civil religion, rather than being systematically reconciled and incorporated in one embracing interpretation in public debates or in scholarly works.

Without their civil religion, the Poles as a nation-society might not have survived the partitions. There might be no Poland today. The strengths of this national creed have also been its weaknesses. Created with a perfectionist impulse to serve simultaneously God and man, universal and particular purposes, society and the individual, Polish civil religion has been cleaved and punctured by unresolved tensions and contradictions. In each successive generation, these have been lamented, ridiculed, taunted, and derided by some of the Polish romantics and, with the greatest passion, by a vocal minority of antiromantic rebels, blasphemers, and jesters. These are the rationalists, positivists, modernists, and liberals.

One trap that Polish civil religion has slipped into again and again since its inception has been the particularization of universal Christian concerns. In high romantic theodicy, Poland takes on the Cross, joining God in His Passion. In its contemporary version, Poland suffers under it with Mary, the Patroness. Through sacrifice and love, the nation—the particular and concrete—serves the divine, transcendent, and universal purpose, the redemption of mankind. The banners of Polish insurrectionists in the nineteenth century carried the slogan "For Your Freedom and Ours"; in the national solemn vows taken in Częstochowa Monastery in 1966, the Poles offered themselves to Mary "for the Freedom of the Universal Church and Humanity." The sustained historical condition of alien oppression and the need to constantly defend "what is ours" against the unrelenting attempts of hostile "others," has unavoidably pushed Polish society toward the antinomic experience of the categories of particular and universal. That same historical circumstance has put the Christian ideal of universal love and charity in conflict with values calling for the resentful distance from and the loathing of the oppressors.

The situation of continuing subjugation and struggle and the need to keep Polish society morally integrated to endure confrontation, has pushed toward the polarization of humanity into opposite segments: we/innocent sufferers and others/evil oppressors. Today, this dichotomy runs within Polish society, between the minority representatives of state power and the rest of the nation. Exclusively appropriated by only part of humanity, the cosuffering with God, the goodness, and ultimately God himself, tend to become particularized. Their universal Christian dimension is radically shortened or totally disappears. Since 1978, the greatly admired Polish Pope has counteracted this tendency. His message, heard in most Polish homes, reextends the horizon of Polish civil religion to universal applicability.

Hiding within the trap of particularization there inheres another, deeper trap: the idolatrous deification of Poland and, by implication, of the individual Pole fused and identified with it through the romantic collectivist conversion. In the high civil-religion creed, Poland cosuffers with God, fulfilling His will to redeem herself and humanity. This idea has also been represented in the image of the Virgin Mary as Poland—humble and acquiescing under the Cross, offering herself to God. The repeated vows offering the Polish nation and each of its members to Mary "in the bondage of love" are to uphold this fundamental dependence. The situation in which suffering Poland, conquered by the oppressors, needs the committed devotion of all her "children," has made it difficult to sustain this true Christian relation of service linking individual, nation, and God. Imperceptibly, Christ becomes the Polish eagle in a crown of thorns; the Cross becomes persecuted Solidarity; the defeated nation becomes the sanctified object of adoration; God the Redeemer becomes Poland itself. This tendency toward the sacralization of the world by Polish civil religion leads to what Stanistaw Brzozowski (1910), one of the most passionate antiromantic critics writing at the beginning of the century, called the *Polish Oberammergau:* Poland and her national-political freedom become religion and are idolized as a sacred reliquary. Not for the infinite and unattainable God, but for Poland and her national-political cause one now lives and offers one's services, redeeming and gaining redemption. God/Mary/Poland become fused in one. Martyred Christ/Poland is seen on the Cross, and, under it, the Dolorosa/Poland is watching her own Passion and Death.

Notes

1. In my discussion of nineteenth-century Poland the term *Polish society* refers to the gentry class and those in the urban stratum who identified as Poles. The peasantry did not become nationally conscious until later in the century.
2. See Coleman (1970) and Hammond (1980).
3. *Paris-Match,* (24 June 1983). The poll was taken May/June 1983. See also *Nowy Dziennik,* New York (8-9 October 1983):2.

Bibliography

Bellah, Robert. "Civil Religion in America." *Daedalus* 96 (Winter 1967):1-21.
Brodziński, Kazimierz. "Na Dzień Zmartwychwsatania Pańskiego r. 1831." *Poezja* (Wroctaw) (1959):239-40. (Quoted by J. Rose, *Poland.* London, 1939, p. 38.)
Brzozowski, Stanistaw. 1910. "Polskie Oberammergau." Ch. 7 in *Legenda Mtodej Polski.* Lwow.
Coleman, John A. "Civil Religion." *Sociological Analysis* 31 (1970):67-77.
Davies, Norman. 1982. *God's Playground: A History of Poland.* New York: Columbia University Press.
Feliński, Alojzy. 1974. "Hymn na Rocznicę Ogtoszenia Królestwa Polskiego z Woli Naczelnego Wodza Wojsku Polskiemu do Spiewu Podany." Pp. 254-55 in A. Jastrzebski and A. Podsiad, eds., *Z Głębokości. . . . Antologia Polskiej*

Modlitwy Poetyckiej. Warszawa. Quoted by N. Davies, *God's Playground: A History of Poland.* New York: Columbia University Press, 1982, II, p. 19.

Hammond, Phillip. 1980. "The Conditions for Civil Religion: A Comparison of the United States and Mexico." Pp. 43-85 in Robert Bellah and Phillip Hammond, eds., *Varieties of Civil Religion.* San Francisco: University of California Press.

Krasiński, Zygmunt. "Przedświt." *Dzieta Literackie* (Warszawa) I, 187 (1973):pp. 1004-07.

Malia, Martin. "Poland's Eternal Return." *New York Review of Books* 30 (September 1983):20-28.

Markoff, John and Daniel Regan. "The Rise and Fall of Civil Religion: Comparative Perspectives." *Sociological Analysis* 42 (1982):333-58.

Mickiewicz, Adam. "Dziady." Part III, *Utwory Dramatyczne* (Warszawa) II, Scene 2 (1955):pp. 259-60.

Stowacki, Juliusz. "Beniowski." *Dzieta* (Wroctaw) III, Song 2 (1959):pp. 721-22.

Talmon, J. L. 1960. *Political Messianism: The Romantic Phase.* New York: Irvington.

———. 1981. *The Myth of the Nation and the Vision of Revolution: The Origins of Ideological Polarization in the Twentieth Century.* Berkeley: University of California Press.

Walicki, Andrzej. 1981. *Philosophy and Romantic Nationalism: The Case of Poland.* Oxford: Oxford University Press.

17

Religion, State and Civil Society: Nation-Building in Australia

Bryan S. Turner

The Secularization Problem

Classical sociology of religion was based upon the assumption that religion would disappear with the development of an urban industrial capitalist culture. This assumption about the inevitable demise of Christianity was an essential assumption of early Marxism which treated religion as an epiphenomenal problem, where religion functioned as a mystification of real class interests. In the German tradition which followed from Nietzsche there was also a commitment to the assumption that God is dead and that the modern world is characterized by a chaos of values which renders absolute commitment problematic. This Nietzsche tradition found its primary expression in Max Weber's speeches on science and politics as vocations (Turner 1983). This perspective on secularity was also prominent in Georg Simmel's views on the tragedy of culture. In the psychoanalytic tradition of Freud, the presence of Nietzsche's argument is quite clear although disguised in the Freudian orthodoxy, since Freud argues that modern culture is characterized by the collapse of a systematic moral tradition uniting the superego with cultural constraints. In the modern Freudian legacy this problem was expressed primarily by Philip Rieff in *The Triumph of the Therapeutic* (1966). It was primarily within the Durkheim tradition in sociology that a crucial ambiguity was expressed with respect to the functions of religion in a postreligious era since it was Durkheim who argued that any viable social system had to be grounded in a set of powerful beliefs, symbols and practices.

While Durkheim, in *The Division of Labour in Society* had argued via the distinction between mechanical and organic solidarity, that contemporary societies would discover social solidarity in the reciprocity between individuals involved in exchange, a somewhat different account appeared in *The Elementary Forms of the Religious Life* where Durkheim began to outline a theory of civil religions. This notion of the significance of nationalism in civil religions was further elaborated in Durkheim's wartime pamphlets (*Who Wanted the War?* and *Germany Above All*) where Durkheim spoke confidently of new sources of shared values and national commitment. Durkheim's views on the importance of national symbolism in the establishment of a national unity have proved influential, despite their somewhat sketchy treatment in Durkheim's final political sociology.

The secularization thesis has become increasingly problematic as a major plank of modern sociology of religion. The arguments for and against secularization are now well established (Robertson 1970, 1978). Behind the secularization debate there was the more fundamental problem of defining religion itself, but on almost any definition of religion contemporary industrial societies could not be described as significantly secular. The original secularization debate tended to confuse the issue of de-Christianization with the secularization of religion as such. In an attempt to overcome this limitation a number of sociologists proposed alternative classifications of invisible religion and common religion. The trend of modern sociology of religion is toward a more comparative and historical perspective on religion which attempts to conceptualize more adequately the emerging relationship between national ideologies, the political process of citizenship and the presence of religion as a moral basis for political participation. The sociology of religion has, therefore, tended to develop in association with theories of nationalism (Gellner 1983), the political sociology of anti-colonialism (Turner 1984) and with the whole problem of nation-building in Third World social systems. Although Weber had been specifically concerned with the relationship between politics and religion, there is now a more fundamental awareness of the continuity of religious belief and symbolism at the substructure of contemporary national political systems. This necessary relationship between religious roots and secular politics is especially evident in modern Israel (Turner 1984), in Islamic revivalism and in Buddhist politics. The analysis of politics and religion consequently provides one of the theoretically more progressive features of contemporary sociology of religion and at the same time lays the basis for an extended critique of the secularization thesis. Although these studies are well under way with respect to Middle Eastern Islam, Christian revivalism and nationalist movements in the Pacific, the study of religion and politics in the white colonial settlers societies of the old Commonwealth is somewhat underdeveloped.

The white colonial settler societies of the British Empire (Australia, Canada, New Zealand and Rhodesia) shared a number of features in common since their political and civic culture was based upon an assumption about the supremacy of Protestantism and especially the predominance of the Church of England. These societies were established by the suppression or destruction of local aboriginal populations as a consequence of forceful white colonization. They were also characterized by the emergence of pastoral agrarian capitalism where economic and political power resided in large-scale latifundia, where industrialization was weak and protracted. The establishment of an Anglo-Saxon Protestant supremacy was never fully achieved because migration from the European Protestant bases was never sufficient to supply an adequate population. These colonial societies had, therefore, to come to terms with various forms of multiculturalism and ethnic diversity either through the "melting pot" or the "mosaic" model (Palmer 1975). Irish settlement in Australia and French settlement in Canada created a significant division between Protestants and Catholics which further fragmented the splintered social system of these peripheral colonial societies (Coward and Kawamura 1978; Lacey and Poole 1979). Colonial settler societies, under conditions of ethnic diversity, face enormous problems in terms of nation-building and the creation of a national identity in a situation where the primary institutions of civil society are underdeveloped. Religion in this context has an important role to play in the development of a national-moral basis for the political system but the religious institutions of these societies are often weak and therefore religion has to be sponsored by the state in order to fulfill these moral functions within civil society. The problem is to create a sense of national citizenship in a context where the ethnic community provides the basis for personal identity and social security. The strength of these ethnic communities stands in opposition to the growth of a national political culture based upon some notion of universal citizenship rather than on the specific and peculiar characteristics of ethnicity. The growth of a national state in these societies tends to emphasize a common religiosity over and against the divisions of culture and ethnicity (Martin 1981). The creation of cultural nationalism requires some basic features of language, religion and culture in order to establish a common denominator (Gellner 1964). In the white colonial societies of recent history there is, as it were, an abundance of such cultural features which could be deployed as the basis of a national culture. In this context, the state and the development of a modern system of broadcasting are indispensable features for the spread of a universalistic culture grounded in some traditional religious culture.

The Formation of National Identity

Contemporary interpretations of the state have emphasized the cohesive functions of the state in contemporary capitalist societies where there is considerable economic, political and cultural division within the social system. Marxist theorists of the state, notably Althusser, have argued that religion, the family and the educational system perform ideological functions in society in order to integrate citizens within the political process. Although these theories are a considerable improvement on previous Marxist formulations of the state, they often adhere to a dominant ideology thesis which is highly problematic as an explanation of the character of modern political cultures (Abercrombie, Hill and Turner 1980). Contemporary Marxist theory typically overstates the cohesive capacity of the state ideology and underestimates the roll of contradictory processes within modern political systems. The paradox of the modern state is that, in attempting to establish some form of cultural unity, it inevitably also promotes various forms of disunity. We need to see contemporary democratic political systems as caught in a contradictory process between the political system and the economic base. Modern societies in general are characterized by a contradiction between class and citizenship.

In this paper, my argument is that, in multicultural societies of peripheral colonial development, publicly owned broadcasting is one of the main arms of the state in the creation of a sense of national unity and national identity. We should assume that in these societies the institutions of civil society are weak and underdeveloped, forcing the state to intervene to sponsor and develop such institutions as an essential feature of the development of the citizenship. Publicly owned broadcasting is seen to have a role in the maintenance and continuity of the family and religious institutions where the church and the family are regarded as crucial in the establishment of a national moral system. Morality is the ultimate bedrock of the modern state where the state requires some form of moral legitimacy from this moral structure. The state seeks a social anchorage via the church and the family in a moral system which is the basis of communal unity (alongside the law and the educational system). Following Habermas (1976), it can be argued that the search for stability and unity through the political processes related to the state is somewhat counteracted by the divisive and negative effects which flow from the economic system under forms of private property. For example, commercial broadcasting is thought to lower public standards of morality, to threaten the unity of the family, and to undermine religion by providing alternative life styles, especially for the younger generation. The marketplace generates inequalities of income which are somewhat incompatible with the norms of the political system based upon a democratic polity; commercialization and the dominance of commodities are thought to destabilize the family. The entry of women into the labor force and changes in the nature of education and employment are associated with the decline of the nuclear family and the

FIGURE 1
The Location of Religion in
Australian Life

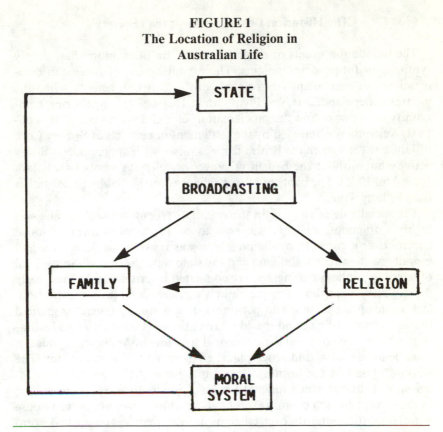

transformation of the modern household. In this context, the state is thought to be relatively neutral from the economic system so that there is an institutional separation of politics and economics. The state intervenes in the social system to buttress the family and the church in the interests of national unity but the state also depends upon the free market to generate an economic surplus as the basis of public taxation. The state is thus forced to support the private sector in the interests of economic growth while also seeking to regulate the social system and to compensate for the negative consequences of commercialization on public standards, especially moral standards. The state is caught in a set of contradictory forces where the interests of capital and the interests of public unity are often contradictory. The state is consequently caught in a balancing act which can never be fully resolved. To understand contemporary religious developments, we need to see religious institutions and practices in the context of these macropolitical and economic developments.

The Historical Context of Australian Society

The foundation events of modern nations are often more than simply symbolic of future developments. The establishment of American colonization was permanently associated with a Christian activity when the pilgrim fathers landed at New Plymouth in 1620 celebrating the new community with prayer and the proclamation of a church covenant. By contrast, Australia was founded by the settlement of convicts at Sydney Cove in January, 1788 when the British flag was raised with appropriate military activity but without the benefit of prayer or religious symbolism (Clark 1963; Mol 1985). The baptism of Australia was celebrated by liquor rather than by holy wine.

The social role of religion in the colonial settlements of Australia was highly ambiguous. Religion was seen to be an essential form of social control over a convict population which was regarded as dangerous and morally contaminated. Religion and the state were thus united in the goal of securing public order in a society populated by criminals. In these early days of settlement, however, the church was very weak as an institution, lacking adequate finance and personnel. It was simply taken for granted that the Church of England would become the dominant religious institution in the new colony, but the traditional structure of Anglicanism was not suitable in the social and geographical environment of a new colony. The working class and the farming community were often untouched by religious institutions which suffered a crisis of funding and adequate staffing in the late nineteenth century. The Anglican church was unable to impose a monopolistic authority over religious activity and was compelled eventually to exist in a tripartite religious system made up by evangelical nonconformists, Irish Roman Catholics and establishment Anglicanism.

Although the churches were institutionally weak and often unable to enforce their view on matters relating to alcoholism and public behavior, the churches were nevertheless seen as the main buttress for the family and the enforcement of Christian standards. This social control of the church was seen to be particularly important in sexual relations. Given the widespread existence of drunkenness, prostitution, and gambling, there was strong support, at least in principle, from the political system for chaplains and clergy to work alongside school teachers and wives in the civilizing of society. Women came to have a paradoxical social location, becoming either prostitutes or God's police (Summers 1975). In the early days of colonial development it was Caroline Chisholm who, as a great social reformer, had defined wives as God's police arguing that it was these virtuous women who would stabilize the colony. In Australia this strong conservative alliance between the state, the family, and religion has continued into the contemporary period, becoming inevitably a focus of feminist critique.

The significant feature of this situation was the dominance of the state in the development of Australia as a modern society. The origins of state intervention in Australia are diverse and complex but one feature of so-called colonial socialism was the direct action by government to attract foreign resources of capital and labor through public borrowing abroad and large-scale programs of assisted migration to the colony (Butlin, Barnard and Pincus 1982). The Australian state was, of course, also the penal arm of Britain and the state was necessary in order to control convict settlement and later to stimulate the development of private land-ownership and the expansion of a free-wage labor force. It can also be argued that the state became prominent precisely because of the weakness of the institutions of civil society.

The Mass Media and Religion

In the twentieth century, public debate in Australia over the development of broadcasting and communications has persistently been addressed to the problem of providing adequate spiritual and moral education for the community as the foundation of the social system. For example, the joint committee on wireless broadcasting (the Gibson Committee of 1942) argued that public broadcasting had an important part to play in protecting cultural values from commercial stations and in promoting the moral development of a young nation through the development of educational programs and religious broadcasting. The committee noted that "legislation cannot of course change immoral mentality in an individual, but it can prevent that individual from using facilities for the propagation of national degeneracy" (Gibson Committee Report 1942:65). The committee argued that

> Australia (was) a Christian nation and that Christian teaching, both in its spiritual and moral aspects, is of great importance to national morale and national development . . . and that lack of co-operation in this regard . . . seems wholly unjustifiable by an organization to which the government of a Christian country has granted a type of monopoly (Gibson Committee Report 1942:61).

The state, nevertheless, was still committed to a free market in broadcasting and did not attempt to ban advertising on Sundays. Commercial broadcasters were required under statutory obligation (Section 103 of the Broadcasting and Television Act 1942) to broadcast religious programs.

Australia is probably the only country where a law exists compelling commercial stations to broadcast religious material but these religious programs are normally confined to periods in the week when hardly any of the general public would be listening or watching their television services. While the state is committed to the development of a religious moral system in Australia, it is also dedicated to the principle of free market competition. There is a recognized ambiguity between the promotion of high moral standards through a public service and the possibility that morals will become degenerate as a consequence of a free market economy in the information system.

A number of other reports on broadcasting also draw attention to the role of the state via the churches in supporting the family and Christian morality. In the postwar period there was considerable public anxiety over the spread of popular music, especially jazz, which was seen as "an erotic manifestation of pure sense-life. Its most characteristic forms are those which carry this eroticism to an extreme which, to anyone with the good of the community at heart, is frankly frightening. It was born, reared, and revelled in in the company of moll-houses, barrel houses, gin and drugs" (Parliamentary Standing Committee on Broadcasting, Eleventh Report 1946: 7).

This "jungle music" was a direct threat to the moral fiber of the nation and the protection of a Christian democracy depended heavily on the moral upbringing of the younger generation. A secular education system was not in itself sufficient to ensure the development of an enlightened and moral population and there had to be the provision of a moral system of instruction in religious values via the media. The reports on broadcasting in the postwar period also recognized that Australian society was undergoing a profound process of Americanization, partly because American programs were cheap to buy and the production of local material was expensive and in short supply (White 1983). The development of a sound moral system was thus closely associated with the development of national identity through the sponsorship of Australian film and television programs. The profit motive, commercialization and the input of American mass standards were overtly seen as a threat to a Christian moral code which was essential for the development of national pride (Parliamentary Standing Committee on Broadcasting, Eleventh Report 1946:9). This anxiety for the state of the nation focused considerably on sexual matters since the stability of family life was seen to be threatened by these developments. The ninth report on sexuality and broadcasting in 1946 quoted with approval the statement of King George V that "the greatness of the nation rests on the sweet clean life of the family" and also gave support to a report by religious leaders in 1943 that "family life should be protected against disintegrating influences such as prevalence of divorce, trafficking contraceptives and all subversive teaching directed to any of these ends" (Parliamentary Standing Committee on Broadcasting, Ninth Report 1946:4). The Committee was, however, caught in a dilemma, since it concluded that too much public discussion of venereal disease and promiscuity could have the opposite effect of moral instruction by encouraging greater promiscuity.

Although these early reports were clearly committed to religious broadcasting for the sake of national unity, they nevertheless faced the problem of denominational diversity and religious differences within the community. It attempted to resolve this problem in terms of the numerical strength of the various denominations as revealed by the Commonwealth Census, while also paying due regard to the claims of minority groups irrespective of their particular denominational strength. The Report of the Royal Commission on Television in 1954 addressed a similar range of problems. The report recommended that commercial stations should provide religious broadcasting alongside the provision of a Christian message by the Australian Broadcasting Commission (A.B.C.). The conclusion of the Royal Commission on Television was that

> the presentation in suitable form of religious services and other religious matter is one of the important obligations of television stations to the public, to be discharged in co-operation with the churches and other religious bodies (Royal Commission on Television 1954:192-93).

The Committee also recommended that the mixture of private and public provision of television programs should be encouraged and that in practice the role of the public sector would be to counteract the low standards often associated with commercial stations.

The traditional role of the A.B.C. as a nation-building agency was reaffirmed by the Dix Committee on national broadcasting in the 1980s (Report by the Committee of Review of the A.B.C., 1981), when it was asserted that the A.B.C. was to see itself as "the principal vehicle for the generation of a sense of national unity" (Dix Committee Vol. 2:84). While serving a national purpose, the A.B.C. also had to provide adequate coverage for minority and special interest groups. In this respect, religious broadcasting is somewhat problematic since, although the church provides a moral basis for society, the church also reflects the extreme ethnic and cultural diversity of the Australian cultural system. The report noted that while Australia is often described as secular, the 1976 Commonwealth Census found that approximately 79 percent of the Australian population described itself as Christian. It also noted an important increase in the

Muslim population and argued that on the basis of equity it would be necessary to include some Islamic material in public broadcasting. The A.B.C., in responding to this diversity, has adopted a definition of religion which is distinctively Durkheimian whereby religion is "any set of practices and/or ideas which one believes will lead to liberation or fulfillment of one's being" (Dix Committee Report Vol. 2, chapter ll:261).

With the increasing recruitment of migrants from South-East Asia, there will be an increase in the Islamic and Buddhist community in Australia and one would expect this diversity to be reflected in religious broadcasting. This contrast between a national unity and democratic egalitarianism operates at a number of levels—with respect to ethnic minorities, regional variations, minority interest groups, and religious pluralism. The underlying community is fractured by cultural and religious differences and the role of the state is both to articulate these divisions via democratic processes and to express some form of Australian national identity where nation-state formation is underdeveloped. The role of the state is consequently to create a moral community rather than simply to express it.

The Australian Religious System

We can divide the Australian religious system into two sectors: the formal institutionalized churches and the subcultural traditions of the civil religion. In terms of formal adherence the majority of Australians regard themselves as Christian and the number of Christians in absolute terms has increased from 1947 to the 1980s. However, as a percentage of the total population, the number of persons identifying in the Census figures as Christians has declined from 88 percent in 1947 to 76.4 percent in 1981. The Anglican population has declined significantly from 39 percent to 26 percent during this period and similar losses have been experienced by the main nonconformist denominations. The Catholic Church has remained relatively stable at about 26 percent of the total population, having benefited from southern Mediterranean migration in the postwar period. There has been a similar increase in the representation of the Orthodox Churches from 0.2 percent in 1947 to 3 percent in 1981, as a consequence of Greek migration. For both Greek and Italian migrants the church has played an important role in consolidating the migrant community as a separate social group (Thompson 1980). There has also been a marginal increase in the Lutheran population from 0.9 percent to 1.4 percent as a result of German migration. The non-Christian population of Muslims, Jews and Buddhists has increased from 0.5 percent to 1.4 percent with the most significant increase being a consequence of Muslim migration. Finally, there has been a significant increase in the number of people defining themselves as having no religion from 0.3 percent to 10.8 percent in 1981. While these figures suggest a relatively high identification with the Christian churches, the statistics on church attendance, participation in prayer and Bible reading suggest relatively low rates of active religious involvement. For example, Gallup polls show that between 1950 and 1981 only 22 percent of Australians said that they had been to church within the last week. Similarly, research from the diocese of Melbourne found that of those indicating an Anglican preference, only 10.9 percent were communicants in 1951 and 16.9 percent were communicants in 1981. About half of the total population rarely or never attends church (Black and Glasner 1983).

There are a number of peculiarities to the institutionalized religious system in Australia. First, the Australian tradition has never generated a substantial theological position and has no real intellectual tradition within the churches. In Australia, the universities have never contributed significantly to the study of religious thought or religious systems and indeed some universities, such as Melbourne, Hobart and Adelaide, have explicitly excluded divinity as an academic discipline. There have been no great theological colleges in Australia and until recent times the churches were forced to import rather than train their own theologians. There is a failure to develop a self-sufficient theological tradition and this is associated with the fact that religion in Australia is highly derivative especially of the European tradition. The religions of the new consciousness have also been imported and the Australian religious tradition has adopted nothing from the Aboriginal "dreaming" tradition of religious mysticism. Since there is no indigenous national religious tradition, there is a sense in which the Australian church is largely sectarian, being divided along every conceivable denominational distinction. It is difficult for this system to sustain the notion of the parish since religious life is essentially organized around the denominational congregation. This denominational rivalry provided some of the background for the long dispute over state aid for church schools which reinforced the division between Catholic and Protestant in the recent political history of Australia. This division was particularly bitter during the conscription disputes of World War I when there was a general distrust for the political loyalty of the Irish Catholic population. The character of Australian religion can be summarized in the following way:

> Precisely by emphasizing their derivativeness, the churches have provided symbols of familiar security in a strange, unsettling environment, and by underpinning a vague liberal-humanism the churches have provided a stable value-system within which personal and political questions can be discussed without serious clash between church and the state . . . . Yet while Chris-

tianity has served this conservative role in these ways, it has made no clear doctrinal contribution to the sense of national identity of the kind we've noted in America (Campbell 1977:182).

The institutionalized churches have not provided a central plank of a civil religious tradition partly because the churches are relatively weak in the cultural system and partly because denominational and cultural differences have not yet been liquidated within a melting pot. Indeed, the recent emphasis in multiculturalism and the negative view of assimilation may well contribute to the continuity of this diverse religious and cultural tradition. The national sense of identity in Australia is thus relatively weak and the state, while supporting the churches, has not been able to draw upon a central religious tradition as the cornerstone of national identity. The state has attempted to use the mass media (especially the state-owned A.B.C.) to foster a sense of Australian identity via these public institutions.

Within the contemporary sociology of religion, it is more common for sociologists to turn to the notion of an invisible religion or covert civic religious tradition as the basis of national culture. Although the institutionalized churches have been relatively insignificant in contributing to the sense of national identity, there are certain common cultural elements which assume the character of a subcultural religious tradition uniting the diverse cultures together.

If we accept Clifford Geertz's (1966) definition of religion as "a system of symbols which acts to establish powerful persuasive and long lasting moods and motivations in men," then the most significant feature of Australian religion is organized around the tragedy of war, the sacrifice of Australian manpower and the celebration of military virtues. One of the central features of the Australian religious culture is the so-called Anzac myth (Mol 1985). Although Anzac Day celebrations specifically remember the disaster of Gallipoli, the Anzac tradition also embodies many of the central virtues or values of male culture, namely "mateship" and a popular egalitarianism which is hostile to formal bureaucracy and hierarchy. The elaborate war memorials which are a universal feature of rural Australian townships represent the architectural reminder of these essentially male concerns with comradeship, ruggedness and sacrifice. The male clubs organized by the Return Servicemen's League are the chapels of this tradition in Australia which now embraces the survivors of the two World Wars and Korea and Vietnam. The Anzac Day celebrations are thus an essential feature of the Australian civil religious tradition (Glasner 1983). The other dimensions of the civil religion are closely connected to the Anzac mythology, namely the predominance of violent sport in Australian culture which again expresses the virtues of comradeship and strength within a masculine environment. Australian-rules football embodies the folk commitment to popular "mateship" but it also expresses a transcendence against the routines of everyday life and evokes extreme forms of commitment and fervor among the general population. The other features of the civil religion are bound up with the romantic commitment to the bush and a religious involvement in the notion of wilderness as a transformative experience, despite the fact that by the 1970s some 85 percent of the population of Australia was concentrated in metropolitan and urban areas. For some social groups, the "outback" represents a spiritual arena which is lacking in the urban landscape (Campbell 1977).

Although it is possible to develop an argument in favor of the cohesive significance of a civil religious tradition in Australia organized around war and sport, the peculiarity of this tradition is that it is in fact highly divisive within the society. While some writers have noted the importance of sport as a nation-building activity within Australia, more recently a number of writers have suggested that, precisely because Australian football emphasizes maleness and legitimates violence, it excludes and precludes women from this civil religious tradition. Australian sport typically puts men at the center of the cultural picture and demotes women from the culture of mateship. The crisis which surrounded the male tradition in New Zealand as a consequence of the 1981 Springbok tour would be another illustration of this capacity of ritual to promote division as much as unity. The same divisive problem surrounds Anzac Day celebrations and other military rituals since they typically exclude German, Turkish and Asian migrants to Australian society, and Anzac celebrations have also given rise to a separation between the white and the Aboriginal population. Finally, the environmentalist lobby in defense of the wilderness and the bush has also reinforced a division between the left- and right-wing of Australian politics, where the free-market principle of liberal politics is clearly incompatible with a conservationist view of wilderness. The problem is that the civil religion expresses and maintains a series of cultural divisions within the society rather than offering a social cement which will generate a coherent Australian identity.

The State and the Household

The argument of this paper has been that the state supports religion through education and broadcasting on the assumption that religion is a necessary support of the family, where the family is seen to be indispensable for the continuity of the state and the establishment of a viable morality. While the support of the state for religion is relatively obvious, the place of religion in Australian society is less than central and the church is relatively weak in national affairs. Although religion has not been a central aspect of Australian national identity, the churches have received strong support from the Liberal Party and the Catholic dominated Democratic Labor Party since both parties have regarded religion as the main bastion against communist influence and the main prop for the family. The political parties have appealed to religious authority in the campaign against homosexuality, divorce and abortion; the recent public outcry against Acquired Immune Deficiency Syndrome (A.I.D.S.) has been one strong illustration of the alliance between conservative politics and conservative Christianity, especially in Queensland. The maintenance of the family under the authoritative umbrella of religion is associated with the argument that women's liberation is ultimately incompatible with the continuity of family morality and thus one role for religion is the regulation of sexuality (Turner 1983).

Although the state has an interest in social unity, it is characteristically faced by highly divisive institutions and cultures within civil society. One paradox is that, while the conservative political parties support religious institutions on behalf of family unity, these parties are also in favor of free market principles, but the free market has been unable to deliver an adequate religious broadcasting service. The state has thus intervened via the A.B.C. in the provision of a religious message. One further paradox is that in many respects it is the economic system which has contributed to the decline of the nuclear family, partly as a consequence of increased female participation in the work force. By providing the legislation to make divorce possible, the state contributes to the dissolution of the nuclear family. However, the state is also active in supporting the household via various benefits and taxation schemes. The traditional nuclear family in Australia, as in other modern industrial societies, has undergone rapid transformation in the postwar period. In Australia, where there has been traditionally an imbalance in the sex ratio resulting in a relatively low rate of marriage, in the 1980s 30 percent of all households were defined as single households (that is, the never-married, de facto marriages, widowed, divorced and separated). Between 1968 and 1981 the number of one parent families doubled and by 1981 almost 13 percent of families with children were one parent families (Burns, Bottomley and Jools 1983). In this situation the state functions as a surrogate breadwinner and head of household where female single parents cannot enter the market place. Government pensions were the main source of income for 57 percent of one-parent income units by the late 1970s and 83 percent of these families were headed by women. The state intervenes systematically in the household in an attempt to maintain these primary relations in the interests of a future generation of citizens whose commitment and loyalty to the society can be more or less guaranteed.

In a political culture where national identity and nation-building are underdeveloped, the family and the church function as an aspect of state policy where the state seeks to secure a moral basis for political action. The state employs the educational and broadcasting systems to support religion in the interests of family life while intervening through welfare and social policy to maintain the household as an institution for the socialization of children. The state is caught in a paradox since the support of these institutions is often at the cost of a free capitalist market and the tax base for these family and religious qualities normally implies some interference in the profitability of the private sector. This account can be seen as a version of Habermas's *Legitimation Crisis*, since the state experiences a scarcity of legitimations from civil society where the traditional institutions of the community have been somewhat eroded by social change. The weakness of the Australian state is further intensified as a consequence of a federal political structure where an identity with Queensland may well outweigh an identification with Australia as a whole. Given the extreme geographical dispersion of the population, this lack of central integration is evident at the local level.

Conclusion

In a variety of different political systems, religion has survived the onslaught of capitalism and secularization by providing the moral basis for nationalist movements and anticolonial struggles. Islamic fundamentalism is one example but religion has played an important part in subnational movements for regional autonomy within the advanced industrial societies (Turner 1981). Religion functions to provide a moral coherence for nationalist development and nation-building by merging with a variety of secular and national rituals and symbols. These forms of nation-building are often associated with policies for the conservation of the family and religion as the essential ingredient of a national moral culture.

In the Australian case, religious sentiments have been closely associated with wartime crisis, especially around the mythology of Anzac. The Japanese threat and the bombing of Darwin were crucial events in the development of a modern Australian consciousness which has a distinctively religious dimension. Institutionalized religion is, however, somewhat weakly developed in the Australian context. Although the majority of the population identifies formally with Christianity, the level of practice and organizational commitment is relatively low. More importantly, most of the institutions of national unity are also paradoxically highly divisive. The general culture is an unresolved amalgam of English traditions with a strong component of Americanized cultural values diversified by a significant migrant tradition from the southern Mediterranean. The ethnic churches, while providing a strong system of community solidarity, do not lend themselves at present to a melting pot situation which would contribute to a form of national integration. The strength of ethnic churches in creating intrasocial solidarity prevents these churches from contributing to intersocial integration (Turner 1977). The state lacks strong moral buttresses in the civil society, especially of a familial and ecclesiastical character. In this situation, while the state has an extensive administrative intervention in the society as a whole, the capacity for nation-building is seriously undermined by the absence of common institutional locations for the whole population within the civil society.

While colonial Australia inherited the church-state relations which had been developed in the English context, the traditional English compromise between politics and religion could not be maintained in the Australian colony where Anglicans, Catholics, Presbyterians and other nonconformists were mixed together in a migrant society. The colonial administration recognized that public order would be best served by fostering the religious authority of Catholic chaplains over their Irish congregations. Furthermore, there was a growing need for education in the colonies which could be best served by supporting the major denominations. Indeed, as early as 1828 it became clear that the privileged position of an established Anglican church could not be maintained in the colonial situation. The Church Act 1836 recognized the formal equality of the four main churches (Anglican, Catholic, Presbyterian and Methodist) in providing equal subsidies for the building of churches and ministers' houses and excluded smaller religious groups such as the Jews. State aid for religion in New South Wales was withdrawn on an equal basis by the Grants for Public Worship Prohibition Act 1862. But state aid for denominational schools lasted slightly longer than state provision for religion generally, partly because this issue was politically more complex. However, in 1866 in New South Wales the decision was made to terminate denominational schools, replacing them with state schools.

As the colonies moved progressively toward self-government, various forms of legislation were passed to bring about political autonomy but few of these constitutional acts refer specifically to the church-state relationship. There is no clear or precise principle of separation between religion and politics in terms of the constitutional legislation for the different states. In general, the states have been reluctant to intervene in religious affairs but in certain exceptional cases such as the suppression of Scientology, Australian governments have intervened forcefully in the control of religious behavior. Another illustration would be the enforcement of health regulations on Muslim practices for slaughtering and the regulation of assembly of the Hare Krishna. The separation of church and state is also transgressed in situations where religion is seen to have a positive benefit for the state or community. State aid to denominational schools would be one illustration of this breach in the political/religious divide.

The Commonwealth Constitution Section 116 reflects the formal separation of the state from religion by noting that

> the Commonwealth shall not make any law for establishing any religion, or for imposing any religious observance, or for prohibiting the free exercise of any religion, and no religious test shall be required as a qualification for any office or public trust under the Commonwealth.

In many respects, the Australian constitution involves a transcription from the First Amendment to the Constitution of the United States. This legislation has been tested in a number of interesting cases, particularly with respect to the Jehovah's Witnesses and Scientology where the state upheld the importance of communal values over those of individual freedom of choice and consciousness. Jehovah's Witnesses were subject to significant control by the state of South Australia on the grounds that their institution was incompatible with the defense of the Commonwealth.

A variety of legal cases which have tested Section 116 have shown that, in practice, the constitution does not guarantee in any significant way freedom of religious belief, but it does show that the state is prepared to intervene in religious affairs when it appears beneficial to some wider community activity such as the preservation of morality and social harmony. The history of church-state legislation is a further example of the argument of this paper, namely that in practice there is a strong relationship between religion and politics in Australia where the state depends upon religion as a buttress in the maintenance of the family life, values related to normal sexuality and a general moral system. There is a functional relationship between state, religion and family but this functional relationship is periodically disrupted by market or more generally socioeconomic forces.

Any general theory of secularization is consequently difficult to maintain since the character of religion and religious institutions is determined by quite specific conditions in different social formations over time. The sociohistorical conditions of Australia are, in many respects, quite unique and the role of religion in a society in transition from a convict settlement to a liberal democracy is unlike the history of religion in more settled communities. In Australia as elsewhere, religion is an important feature of nation-building and national identity but it has been argued in the case of Australia that a national identity is underdeveloped and that Australia is still characterized by extreme cultural and ethnic diversity. Whether a common civil religious tradition can weld these various forces into a social unity is still highly questionable and problematic.

Bibliography

Abercrombie, N., S. Hill and Turner, B.S. 1980. *The Dominant Ideology Thesis.* London: Allen and Unwin.

Black, A. and Glasner, P., eds. 1983. *Practice and Belief, Studies in the Sociology of Australian Religion.* Sydney: Allen and Unwin.

Burns, A., G. Bottomley and Jools, P., eds. 1983. *The Family in the Modern World.* Sydney: Allen and Unwin.

Butlin, N.G., A. Barnard and Pincus, J.J. 1982. *Government and Capitalism.* Sydney: Allen and Unwin.

Campbell, R. "The Character of Australian Religion." *Meanjin* 36 (1977):178-88.

Clark, M. 1963. *A Short History of Australia.* New York: Mentor Books.

Coward, H. and Kawamura, L. eds. 1978. *Religion and Ethnicity.* Waterloo, Ontario: Wilfrid Laurier University Press.

Geertz, C. 1966. "Religion as a Cultural System." Pp. 1-46 in Michael Banton, ed., *Anthropological Approaches to the Study of Religion.* Tavistock Publications Ltd.

Gellner, E. 1983. *Nations and Nationalism.* Oxford: Basil Blackwell.

_____. 1964. *Thought and Change.* London: Weidenfeld and Nicholson.

Glasner, P. 1983. "The Study of Australian Folk Religion: Some Theoretical and Practical Problems." Pp. 167-80 in A. Black and P. Glasner, eds., *Practice and Belief, Studies in the Sociology of Australian Religion.* Sydney: Allen and Unwin.

Habermas, J. 1976. *Legitimation Crisis.* London: Heinemann.

Lacey, P.R. de and Poole, N.E. 1979. *Mosaic or Melting Pot, Cultural Evolution in Australia.* Sydney: Harcourt Brace Jovanovich.

Martin, J. 1981. *The Ethnic Dimension.* Sydney: Allen and Unwin.

Mol, H. 1985. *The Faith of Australians.* Sydney: Allen and Unwin.

Palmer, H., ed. 1975. *Immigration and the Rise of Multiculturalism.* Toronto: Copp Clark Publishing.

Rieff, P. 1966. *The Triumph of the Therapeutic.* London: Chatto and Windus.

Robertson, R. 1978. *Meaning and Change.* New York: New York University Press.

_____. 1970. *The Sociological Interpretation of Religion.* New York: Schocken.

Summers, A. 1975. *Damned Whores and God's Police, The Colonisation of Women in Australia.* Ringwood: Penguin.

Thompson, S.L. 1980. *Australia Through Italian Eyes.* Melbourne: Oxford University Press.

Turner, B.S. 1984. *Capitalism and Class in the Middle East.* London: Heinemann.

_____. 1983. *Religion and Social Theory, A Materialist Perspective.* London: Heinemann.

_____. "Marginal Politics, Cultural Identities and the Clergy in Australia." *International Journal of Sociology and Social Policy* 1 (1981):89-133.

_____. "Class Solidarity and System Integration." *Sociological Analysis* 38, (1977):345-58.

White, R. "A Backwater Awash: The Australian Experience of Americanisation." *Theory, Culture and Society* 1 (1983):108-22.

Reports

Eleventh Report of the Parliamentary Standing Committee on Broadcasting, Canberra, 12 March 1946.

Ninth Report of the Parliamentary Standing Committee on Broadcasting, Canberra, 11 March 1946.

Report of the Committee of Review of the Australian Broadcasting Commission (Dix Report), 2 vols., Sydney, May 1981.

Report of the Joint Committee on Wireless Broadcasting (Gibson Committee), March 1942.

Report of the Royal Commission on Television, Canberra, 1954.

18

State, Religion and Law In Ireland

John Fulton

The entire island of Ireland is about 300 miles long and 150 miles wide. The small statelet of Northern Ireland, which is part of the United Kingdom, is only about 100 miles in any direction and has a million and a half inhabitants. The Republic of Ireland, having had a stable population of about three million for over half a century, has increased to three and a half million over the past decade or so. Over half its population is under 25 years of age.

Representatives of the one million Protestant Loyalists of Northern Ireland put forward two main reasons that they refuse to join up with Catholic Nationalists in one all-Ireland state. First, they claim to be British and to be part of that nation's democratic and cultural heritage. Second, they argue that a united Ireland independent from Britain would be opposed to that identity and dominated by an alien culture and religion, that is by Gaelic traditions and the Roman Catholic Church. They argue that the Southern Irish state is now—and a united Ireland would be in the future—a Catholic state, and no amount of evidence to the contrary can persuade them otherwise: evidence such as the absence of clergy in the apparatus of the state, the fact that the church is financed out of voluntary contributions, that the state has no role in the appointment of bishops, and that the juridical processes of church and state are kept totally separate.

Why then do Protestant Loyalists continue with their deeply held belief? Why do they fear the curtailment of their "protestant" liberties in a united Ireland? Surely if they examined the present state of affairs south of the border and took the trouble to stay there a while (the majority only travel south if there are convenient services to Britain), they would find their fears totally unfounded.

The author is indebted to J.H. Whyte (1980) for much of the factual material in the first part of this essay.

Ay, so to speak, there's the rub, for Northern Protestant fears have a firm foundation in social reality. The Southern Irish state may indeed be secular in its state apparatus. But it is deeply imbued with a Roman Catholic ethos which, historically, has penetrated into the affairs of state with all too alarming frequency. There is evidence to argue that the Protestant Loyalists have genuine reason to fear. That evidence can be seen in brushes between church and state in which the church has had its way. But there have been relatively few such encounters. Rather, it is in the constitutional fabric of the state and in its supportive consensus that the power of Roman Catholicism in the Irish Republic is most apparent.

The Irish Constitution

The first constitution of 1922 recognized *the Irish Free State* (Southern Ireland) as having dominion status in the British Empire with the monarch as head of state. The prime reason for bringing in a new constitution in 1937 was to assert Irish independence to the full in both these matters by leaving the Empire and providing a president to replace the monarchy. The first constitution, approved by Britain, was considered a model of libertarian democracy. One has to judge the second one by its content. The preamble to the articles proclaims

> In the Name of the Most Holy Trinity
> We, the people of Eire,
> Humbly acknowledging all our obligations
> to our Divine Lord, Jesus Christ, Who
> sustained our fathers through centuries of trial,
> Gratefully remembering their heroic and
> unremitting struggle to regain the rightful
> independence of our Nation
> Do hereby adopt, enact, and give to ourselves
> this Constitution.

One is left in little doubt as to what the "spirit of the laws" (Montesquieu 1848) of this Irish state was to be: a *religious* spirit—in which case, a misfortune for the then 1,000 (now 10,000) of the population in the Southern state who professed no religion. But it was also an explicitly *Christian* spirit—unfortunate therefore for the 4,000 Jews and for the very small but increasing numbers of Hindus, Buddhists, Muslims and Taoists.

The preamble was reinforced by article 44, paragraph 1:

> The state acknowledges that the homage of public worship is due to Almighty God. It shall hold His Name in reverence and shall respect and honour religion.

Clearly there was already an impact made by Roman Catholic teaching of the day. The spirit of papal statements throughout the nineteenth and early twentieth centuries was that it was the duty of the state to oppose freedom of conscience in matters of religion (Gregory XVI in the encyclical *Mirari Vos* 1832; the *Syllabus of Errors,* error no. 15) and freedom of worship (*Syllabus,* error no. 78), and to celebrate openly the worship of God "in that way which he has shown to be his will," namely Roman Catholicism (Leo XIII, 1903:111-12). Of course, in a sense the new Irish constitution was going against part of the spirit of this approach. For paragraph 3 of the same article *recognized* the main Protestant churches then existing in Ireland. However, this was a fairly necessary compromise: paragraph 2 had already conferred on the Roman Catholic Church a special position in the state, on the grounds that that church was "the guardian of the Faith professed by the great majority of its citizens. The "majority" is an important concept in both British and Irish politics which will be discussed further on. What matters for the moment is to examine the contention that the Roman Catholic Church only had this special position *because of* this matter of fact. It is true that the constitution was explicit in recognizing important personal rights: equality before the law, the nonrecognition of nobility privileges, defense of person and property, liberty, no detention without trial, freedom of speech and assembly (cf. Article 40). Yet the articles which followed appear to qualify certain of these rights in a typically Roman Catholic way and in the terms of the papal teaching of the day. Consider article 41:

> The State recognizes the Family as the natural primary and fundamental unit group of Society and as a moral institution possessing inalienable and imprescriptible rights, antecedent and superior to all positive law.

Compare this with Pius XI's teaching, six years earlier on the same subject: ". . . the very fountainhead from which the State draws its life, namely, wedlock and the family" (Piux XI 1930:63) and with the dispositions of the *Code of Canon Law* which had come into effect in 1917:

> The marriage of baptized persons is governed not only by divine law but also by church law. The civil power only has competence in matters regarding the effects of such marriages (Canon 1016).

The dispositions of the Irish constitution were clearly designed to accommodate such a position in full. For the implications of such a position were spelled out in paragraphs 2 and 3 of article 41, which pledged the state to protect marriage and the family and forbade divorce. Thus were echoed again the themes of the indissolubility of both Christian and non-Christian

marriage and of the state's obligation to reinforce that indissolubility (cf.
Leo XIII, 1903:68, 77, 78; Pius XI, 1930:4, 16; Canon Law 1917:1013).
   Article 42 recognized

> that the primary and natural educator of the child is the Family.

Compare this with Canon Law:

> The primary purpose of marriage is the procreation and education of chil-
> dren (Canon Law 1917:1013, par. 1).

Article 42 went on to give an almost supplementary right to the state in
providing for a child's education by acknowledging the right of parents to
school their children in their own home should they wish it. The article as a
whole seems strangely lopsided in favor of family control. But then historically and in terms of Roman Catholic doctrine, the problem had already
been sorted out. As the Irish nation had moved toward independence in the
first decades of the century, Catholic politicians and bishops had agreed on
the boundaries of their proper spheres of sacred and profane; the schools
were to be under the control of the church with supplementary financial
aid coming from the state (cf. Miller 1973:268-92). The article now left the
way open for the full expression of the teaching of Pius XI that, though the
family had "priority of nature and therefore of rights over civil society,"
education belonged

> preeminently to the Church, by reason of a double title in the supernatural
> order, conferred exclusively upon her by God Himself; absolutely superior
> therefore to any other title in the natural order (Pius XI 1929:5-6).

The double title consisted of the church's mission to teach under infallible
guidance and her "supernatural motherhood" by which the church "edu-
cates souls in the divine life of grace" (Pius XI 1929:7).
   More was to follow. As if to repeat the church's social teaching against
communism that "every man has by nature the right to possess property as
his own" (Leo XIII, 1903:210), article 43 announced that

> The state acknowledges that man, in virtue of his rational being, has the
> natural right, antecedent to positive law, to the private ownership of external
> goods.

Not only did Roman Catholic social teaching directly enter into the
definition of rights, wrongs and obligations within this nation-state, but it
was also to affect one aspect of the structure of government. The Senate

was to have 60 members: eleven were to be directly appointed by the Prime Minister (Taoiseach) and 49 by election. Six of the latter were to be elected by the two Irish universities. But the remaining 43 were to be elected by local and national politicians on a *vocational* basis: that is, they had to be elected to five panels for which they would qualify by having the requisite vocational expertise—administrative, cultural-educational, labor, industrial and commercial, and agricultural. A somewhat unusual system one might think: but not if one read the papal encyclical *Quadragesimo Anno.* It sought to overcome conflict within capitalist societies by encouraging Christian leaders to reconsider Leo XIII's suggestion of introducing industrial associations. These were to be intermediary between capital and labor and based precisely upon types of vocational expertise in a way similar to medieval guilds (cf. Leo XIII, 1903:240-47; Pius XI, 1931:32-34).

The way the various aspects of current Roman Catholic social teaching was presented in the Irish constitution can hardly be taken as fulfillment of the need to reflect the opinions of the majority of the Republic's population. The confessional articles of the constitution were largely the work of the constitution's architect, the then Prime Minister Eamon de Valera, who dominated Irish politics for four decades. He certainly felt that the culture of the state should reflect the fact that it was 93 percent Roman Catholic. But how was that to be reconciled with the claim of article II of the constitution to be the legitimate means of government for the entire island, which included over one million Protestants? Was their culture not to be considered at all in the constitution? One is faced here with the blind spot of traditional Irish nationalism. For instance, in the case of "Dev," as de Valera was affectionately known, the Irish nation was essentially Catholic. In his St. Patrick's Day address to the United States broadcast in 1935, he stated:

> Since the coming of St. Patrick, fifteen hundred years ago, Ireland has been a Christian and a Catholic nation. All the ruthless attempts made down through the centuries to force her from this allegiance have not shaken her faith. She remains a Catholic nation.

Clearly the practical attitude here, like the preamble to the constitution cited above, excluded the 22 percent of the population of the island which were Protestant and left Protestant Loyalists in no ambiguity as to their place in any future order of affairs. If Ireland was a Catholic nation, then its law and government would be correspondingly so regardless of the disposition of church-state relationships, theocratic or secular.

But there is also a second likely reason, and it is implicit in the presence of the papal-oriented articles of the constitution themselves. Pius XI had made it clear in 1930, subsequent to the success of the Vatican-Italian Concordate of 1929, that good sons of the church with political power were to look to the church itself for guidance in the statesmanship:

> Governments can assist the Church greatly in the execution of its important office if, in laying down their ordinances, they take account of what is pre-scribed by divine and ecclesiastical law, and if penalties were fixed for offend-ers . . . As Leo XIII has already so clearly set forth: . . . The dignity of the State will be enhanced, and with religion as its guide, there will never be a rule that is not just (Pius XI, 1930:64).

In fact, de Valera studied what Irish theologians had to say on the rela-tionships between church and state and submitted drafts of articles 41 to 44 to some well known figures among them (cf. Longford and O'Neill 1970:295-96; Whyte 1980:379, taken from T. O'Neill and P. O'Fiannachta, *De Valera*). Several of the theologians either were or were to become Irish bishops. They had been trained either at Maynooth or Rome or both, where they had become familiar with the treatises on *Ius Publicum* (church and state relations) of the time. These were heavily biased toward the view that there were two perfect societies, church and state, both supreme in their own orders, with the church supreme in spiritual and moral matters (cf. Pius XI's *Syllabus of Errors* in Freemantle 1956:145-46, 152; Leo XIII, 1903:114; Pius XI, 1930:65; for typical treatise approaches cf. Van Noort 1960:235-41; Bender 1960). Of course, it was for the church to decide what constituted a spiritual or moral matter.

There is, in all likelihood, a third reason for this pursuit of a public morality which mirrored Roman Catholic teaching. The issue of heeding the church was not simply one of seeking a mediator of divine guidance on matters of Christian conscience. For the Roman Catholic social teaching of the day laid down certain things as of *natural law* which, therefore, anyone who was reasonable and honest would be able to recognize. The device of the church's moral experts and authoritative clerics was thus pertinent to the entire population of the world, let alone that of Ireland. The church was acting on behalf of all and had a prime obligation to push for a public morality which matched its perception of the natural law lest the very fabric of society be torn asunder and its members cast on the road of moral decline.

In fairness to de Valera, it must be said that he opposed any attempt to incorporate the church into the apparatus of state and in this was going against the form of relationship preferred by the popes of the day. In fact, the secular approach was a longstanding practice in Ireland and had grown up over the centuries of British rule. The Irish, including the majority of bishops, saw no reason to upset long established routines in this respect.

But that did not mean that the ethos of a Catholic state would be in any way diminished.

The Supportive Consensus and the Power behind the Constitution

What should now be readily apparent is that the political leadership of the country professed their nationalism in the same way as they professed their Roman Catholicism, that in terms of their lifeworld experience, their nationalism and their Catholicism converged. Even those who may have wished things otherwise had to accept the social nature of the Southern Irish state. The Irish Labor Party was forced to amend its own draft constitution in 1939 to defend itself against criticism of taking a stance opposed to papal teaching. It excised from the statement of its political goals the phrases "a Workers' Republic" and "public ownership" of the sources of wealth, as they had been seen by some members to counter papal opposition to a class-war interpretation of society. Members of the Irish National Teachers' Organization who were affiliated to the Labor Party and who had sought guarantees on the catholicity of party doctrine, were informed by their executive:

> The new draft is in accord with that suggested by the Committee of Experts to whom the question was originally submitted by the Hierarchy [Irish Bishops]. The Executive believe that it is due to their action and efforts that these desirable changes have been made, and their action in the matter has received the express commendation of the general body of Bishops (as reported by Whyte 1980:84).

However, the power which the Roman Catholic bishops wielded in the Irish state was much more apparent in matters which touched upon the role of the state in its relationship to the family and to matters of public morality, particularly those which bore on family life. It began to emerge— as was the spirit of the constitution in any case—that the state was being viewed by the Hierarchy as having a subordinate function. Roman Catholic social teaching of the day stressed, against totalitarian tendencies, that what primary institutions and intermediate association could do for the good of individuals and groups should not be supplanted by the state, but should rather be encouraged and directly aided by the state. This was the principle of subsidiarity which formed the mainstay of the church's social teaching at the time. Both before and after the 1937 constitution, the state "aided" public morality and the family by the fairly heavy censorship of books, magazines, newspapers and films (Censorship of Films Act 1923, Censorship of Publications Act 1929); by banning the making, importation or distribution of contraceptives and the distribution of any literature informing of such matters. The prohibition of divorce was and is so strict that couples who have been granted a nullity degree by Roman Catholic canonical tribunals have found that they may still not be recognized as unmarried by the state.

But two cases indicating the political power of religion are particularly notable. The first was the inordinate delay on the part of the Irish Parliament in legislating adoption. Moves to bring in legislation before parliament were continually being delayed by ministers over a four-year period from 1947 to 1951. When both the Ministers for Justice, General McEoin, and the Attorney General, Mr. Charles Casey made it clear that they considered the legislation inopportune, pressure for an explanation eventually brought forward a response from Mr. Casey. He argued that article 42 of the constitution claimed the primary right of care to belong to the natural parents (an interpretation later overruled by the Supreme Court); in addition, one could not permit non-Catholic parents to adopt children whose eternal salvation might be endangered (cf. Whyte 1980:192-93). It later became clear that the relevant ministers had consulted the Archbishop of Dublin before delivering their judgment on the matter.

The second case, and one which marked the high point of direct episcopal intervention into legislative matters, was the controversy surrounding the mother and child scheme. The controversy occurred at the same time as the one over adoption, coming to a conclusion in 1951. A piece of welfare legislation was designed to provide free assistance for mothers in childbirth and for the subsequent care of the newly born. The scheme was eventually dropped by the government under direct and secret opposition from the bishops. The Minister for Health, Dr. Noel Browne, even went to visit the bishops to plead the case. It was Dr. Browne who eventually blew the whistle by publishing his correspondence on the matter in the newspapers. The grounds for opposition by the bishops were predictable. They feared the extension of the state into the sphere of the family and felt that solutions at the prestate level had to be found (the classic source for this controversy is Whyte 1980:197-302).

After the public embarrassment of the mother and child controversy, the bishops appear to have dropped this particular technique of political influence and have since continually sought to distance themselves from direct relationships with the government of the day. It could be said that such a strategy was in any case unnecessary. The Catholic-Nationalist bloc, North or South, had an allegiance to the church unparalleled in the Western world. Even as late as 1979, over 90 percent of the Catholic population of the island attended Sunday mass, with one third of them regular communicants. Prior to the exodus from the convents in the late 1960s, there was hardly a family without one or two members in the religious life or priesthood, and even after the exodus the numbers of priests remained at the level of the 1940s. The entire panoply of a new form of Catholic hegemony had been painstakingly created over a period of some 150 years and was most effective. There was a high degree of status conferred on priests in the local community. They had a fair degree of influence in local matters, from overseeing courtship rituals of couples at dances and on walks, to deep involvement in the formation and running of local associations such as Gaelic sports or farmer groups. The church controlled the schools, from which the political leaders of the country were continually being produced. These schools were run largely by religious orders on very meager funds. There was a lively Catholic press. As radio and television grew, clerical influence played its part and a day did not go by without one or several appearing on the screen in some sort of specialist guise.

This permeation of civil society by the Roman Catholic ethos was most natural. The clergy had sustained the Catholic Nationalist populace over the centuries of oppression. Furthermore, its ranks were drawn from the common people themselves, and the links between clergy and their families were highly regarded. A final and most important element was the considerable filial loyalty Catholic Nationalists showed for their clergy, bishops and popes. This respect for authority—for the guidance of the church—has appeared throughout the examples of church-state interaction given above. But it has also appeared in survey investigations into personal religiosity in the form of high levels of authoritarianism (cf. Nic Ghiolla Phadraig 1980).

But surely, one might say, this is all in the past. Authoritarianism in the South is on the wane. From the 1950s onward, possibly under the effects of an improved standard of living as Ireland opened up to foreign investment, its people became more broadminded. Later, under the effects of the Second Vatican Council 1962-1965, a liberal theological climate took shape, spearheaded by religious orders such as the Dominicans and the Jesuits. Criticism of the Irish constitution itself began to come from both clerical and lay quarters as a new intelligentsia emerged. Even the famous paragraphs of article 42 intending to give pride of place to the Roman Catholic Church in the state were removed by referendum in 1972. Indeed, many would argue, the danger is now that public morality will decline—and has already begun to—under the influence of international youth culture which flies in the face of traditional morality and which is anti-authoritarian in spirit. In any event, surely this change has led to a greater sense of tolerance in the South and to a more open approach to the Northern question.

It is time for Hamlet to make an appearance: for that is indeed the question and the tragedy of the situation. For, despite all the supposed changes taking place, the church leadership at least seems most reluctant to countenance any constitutional changes which will lessen the impact of Roman Catholic moral teaching on the public sphere. Indeed, only a week before penning this script, the writer heard a leading member of the Irish hierarchy repeat the old adage that the Irish constitution is secular, implying that there really was not much to be done to it for the moment. There still appears to be a widespread feeling among the bishops—despite the increasing number of young enterprising clerics among their numbers—that there is no real problem on this score.

There continues to be hierarchical opposition to increasing the availability of contraception (a Supreme Court decision declared their ban to be against the dispositions of the constitution—contraceptives are now available but only on medical prescription). They also oppose the introduction of divorce and show a marked lack of enthusiasm to experiment with shared Protestant-Catholic schools (a lack which the Anglican Church of Ireland also shares—both churches own their schools and their clergy have open access). Recently the bishops supported a referendum to have "the right of the life of the unborn" inscribed in the constitution. Article 40, paragraph 3, section 3 now reads:

> The State acknowledges the right to life of the unborn and, with due regard to the equal right to life of the mother, guarantees in its laws to respect, and, as far as practicable, by its laws defend and vindicate that right (Ninth Amendment of the Constitution Act, 1984).

Antiabortionism is the view of the vast majority of the population of Ireland North or South and of the various churches. It was already forbidden by law to procure an abortion. Its constitutionalization is a direct result, not of this already widespread opinion, but of Roman Catholic pressure, particularly from the right. It is proof of a continuing mode of enforcing Roman Catholic morality on the Irish state as such. Additional proof comes from the Hierarchy's recent statement to the New Ireland Forum (1984) both in the Forum Report (vol. 12) and in their written submission (Irish Episcopal Conference 1984). They not only repeat their oft-stated attitude to Catholic schools, defending them from any contribution to sectarianism in Ireland, but oppose the introduction of divorce and any weakening of legislation protecting the family. They further express reservations about the concept of pluralism and do not see why minority rights should be any more sacred than majority ones. Finally, they excuse Christian divisions from having contributed to the present Irish conflict (cf. also *The Tablet* 1983 and 1983/4).

In this writer's judgment, the church as an organization continues to be aligned to the forces of conservatism in the Catholic Nationalist bloc, particularly to that wing which refuses to consider a new Irish constitution *before* a settlement with the Protestant Loyalists is reached.

The Protestant-Loyalist State

Lest anyone should see the entire problem of the religious determination of the state to be located solely in the Irish Republic, one must look, however briefly at the statelet of Northern Ireland. It was deliberately constructed around the Protestant Loyalists of the North to the detriment of the large minority of Catholic Nationalists who ended up within its boundaries. The Protestant Loyalists had shown, both during World War I and in the decade preceding it, that they would not stomach a united Ireland without a fight. In 1912, the Westminster parliament under the liberal Asquith prepared to give Ireland "home rule" in the face of conservative party opposition. The Ulster Unionists, as they were known, under the leadership of James Craig and Sir Edward Carson, began to arm and train a Protestant Loyalist force, formed a provisional government which would come into action should Britain abandon them, and establish "a solemn league and covenant," to which the vast majority of the Protestant-Loyalist population committed itself. There was also an evangelical revival which was markedly anti-Catholic. In 1914, senior (Protestant) officers in the army stationed at the Curragh near Dublin declared that they were prepared to resign their commissions rather than take up arms to quell a Protestant Loyalist rebellion. Leading members of the British Conservative party were also committed to this peculiar rebellion to remain British so that, when Irish independence finally came in 1921, Protestant Loyalists were sufficiently strong, both militarily and in terms of British support, to obtain their aim: the setting up of statelet in Northern Ireland which would still be an integral part of the United Kingdom. What eventually emerged over the next few years was a state which had been meticulously constructed in its geographical contours so as to be large enough as to constitute a viable politicoeconomic unit and small enough to guarantee a Protestant-Loyalist majority for the foreseeable future.

The new statelet of Northern Ireland was to be subject to Britain in terms of taxation and foreign policy, but in all other matters was to have its own parliament at Stormont Castle outside Belfast. It was the intention of the British government that parliament be elected on a proportional system. But having begun to use it, Stormont abolished the system in favor of "first past the post," for the simple reason that this traditional method guaranteed Protestant Loyalist ascendancy. The previous gerrymandering of the electoral boundaries ensured that, in local government elections to town councils, Protestant Loyalists would hold the reins of government even if they were numerically a minority in the locality. Thus began a period of continuous discrimination against Catholic Nationalists in the allocation of public monies for housing and welfare.

It could be pointed out that the only issue on which specifically Protestant legislation occurred was in the establishment of local by-laws bringing in Sunday observance—in the closure of bars, public houses and dance halls as well as municipal sporting facilities for the duration of the sabbath. But that does not mean that religious matters did not pertain to the existence of the Northern state. The Northern state was no less Protestant than the Southern state was Catholic. It is certainly *easier* to identify the Catholic elements in the South, particularly because it had a written constitution. In the North one has to look elsewhere: to the fact that the entire apparatus of state in the North was dominated by Protestant Loyalists— electoral boundaries, civil service, police force—particularly the reserve force known as the "B specials" which was recruited exclusively from Protestant Loyalists. The various organizations within civil society, from the less powerful golf clubs to the directly influential politicoreligious organizations and secret societies (the Orange Order, the Black Preceptory, the Apprentice Boys), all spelled out one message: a Protestant state for a Protestant people, as James Craig, the first prime minister of the new statelet, called it. In 1931, even a Protestant league of employers was founded to prevent Catholic Nationalists getting jobs from Protestant employers or even working with Protestants. The Protestant Loyalists leadership were totally open in their sectarianism. "Home rule" did indeed for them signify "Rome rule" and for their own state, they intended the converse to be the case.

For anyone who doubts the theory that the modern state can be the vehicle of dominant groups or alliances in society, or that religious interests can be substantially represented in such alliances, the examples of the states of Ireland are surely sufficient evidence.

Conclusions

Earlier, mention was made of the New Ireland Forum. This was an initiative sponsored by the major nationalist party in Northern Ireland to bring together politicians from both sides of the divide to discuss the future of the island as a whole. In reality only the four major nationalist parties participated. Loyalist parties refused to participate, and the Provisional Sinn Fein, the political wing of the Provisional Irish Republican Army, was excluded by the fact that the ground rules for the Forum only allowed parties accepting constitutional politics to participate. The Forum completed its consultations and reported in the summer of 1984. There was one vital breakthrough for the nationalist consciousness. All four parties committed themselves to the recognition of the Protestant Loyalist groups as having legitimate aspirations and affirmed the need for the recognition of *two sets of legitimate rights* coexisting in the island as a whole.

> Constitutional nationalists are determined to secure justice for all traditions. . . . The new Ireland must be a society within which, subject only to public order, all cultural, political and religious beliefs can be freely expressed and practiced.

This was made explicit in terms of the sense of British identity which Protestant Loyalists experienced:

> This implies in particular, in respect of Northern Protestants, that the civil and religious liberties that they uphold and enjoy will be fully protected and their sense of Britishness accommodated (New Ireland Forum 1984, vol. 1:22-23).

For the very first time, the leadership of all the major constitutional nationalist parties in Ireland—and they represent 90 percent of the nationalist population—had abandoned the concept of the tyranny of the majority will, and "the people of Ireland" were no longer seen as the Catholic-Nationalist population. There were still traces of ethnocentrism in their nationalist viewpoint elsewhere in the report: for instance, they still referred to *the historic integrity of Ireland* (page 28), which tends to imply some naturalistic concept of national unity, when Ireland as a political unit only ever existed as a British administered territory. But such traces hardly invalidate the enormous step forward.

Unfortunately, it is a step not yet taken by the other interested parties, namely the Protestant Loyalists, the British government and the Irish Roman Catholic Episcopal conference.[1] All three still operate on the basis of majority dominance in the state. The British Conservative party, led by Margaret Thatcher, insists that there will be no change in the constitutional dispositions of Northern Ireland without the consent of "the majority in Northern Ireland." The phrase which Protestant Loyalists use to identify the same group is *the people of Northern Ireland*, which excludes the Catholic Nationalists of the North in the same way as de Valera's "Irish Nation" excluded the Protestants. All such concepts have long centered on the merging of two ideas: Rousseau's notion of *the popular will*—of individuals coming together to make the social contract; and the conception of a people who (in the stronger form) have a natural right to become a nation or (in the weaker form) to belong to the nation of their choice. The implication is that the majority has every right to decide what rights minorities are to have in the state.

It is interesting to note that the Irish Catholic Bishops share a similar practical attitude both to the British and to the Protestant Loyalists, even though their position stems from a different theoretical position. Conservative and authoritarian religious tendencies have a marked inclination to embody themselves in society in a sectarian form. The medieval church, which tolerated no other religious groupings inside Christendom apart from the Jews (whom it subordinated to the role of a semipersecuted necessity) is a prime example. The case of Irish Catholic nationalism represents a particular conjuncture of an imported religious form (a papal, mediterranean-centered notion of church-state relationships) and an indigenous national liberation movement. It forged a sectarian state structure in Ireland. In other words, there is an elective affinity between what David Martin (1978) has termed monopoly catholicism and sectarian politics (Fulton 1984). The self-assertion of the Catholic Nationalist bloc in Ireland came to be as totalizing as that of the Protestant ascendancy which preceded it under the British domination of the island. It was partly (though far from solely) as a response to this that the Protestant Loyalist bloc developed its solidarity and installed itself in its Ulster fortress.

At the time of Irish independence, the Protestant Loyalists could not bear the loss of the dominance in which they had shared under British rule over the whole island. It is difficult to gauge today how strong that feeling still is and to what extent it is overruled by fear of absorption into a Catholic Nationalist state. What remains clear is that, both in the formation of the present crisis, as well as in the perceptions of its current protagonists, religious factors played and continue to play a significant role.

Note

1. Editors' note: This paper was completed before the 1985 agreement between the British government and the government of the Republic of Ireland to grant the latter an advisory role in certain matters affecting Northern Ireland and to work toward a democratic solution to the major problems in Northern Ireland. Both the IRA and the Protestant Loyalists have rejected this move.

Bibliography

Bender, L. 1960. *Ius Publicum Ecclesiasticum*. Hilversum: P. Brand.
Canon Law. 1917. *Codex Iuris Canonici*. Rome: Vatican. Translations from S. Woywood, *A Practical Commentary on the Code of Canon Law*. New York: Wagner Inc. (1957).

Constitution of Ireland 1937. Dublin: Government Publications.

Freemantle, A., ed. 1956. *The Papal Encyclicals.* New York: New American Library of World Literature, Inc.

Fulton, J. "Religion, Nationalism and the State in the Irish Conflict." Forthcoming.

Irish Episcopal Conference. 1984. *Submission to the New Ireland Forum.* Dublin: Veritas.

Leo XIII. 1903. *The Great Encyclical Letters of Pope Leo XIII.* New York: Benzinger.

Longford, the Earl of and T.P. O'Neill. 1970. *Eamon de Valera.* Dublin: Gill and Macmillan.

Martin, D. 1978. *A General Theory of Secularization.* Oxford: Blackwells.

Miller, D.W. 1973. *Church, State and Nation in Ireland 1898-1921.* Dublin: Gill and Macmillan.

Montesquieu, Baron de. 1848/1878. *The Spirit of the Laws.* Trans. T. Nugent. London: G. Bell and Sons.

New Ireland Forum. 1984. *Report,* vol. 1 and *Public Sessions,* vol. 2-13. Dublin: Government Publications.

Nic Ghiolla Phadraig, M. "The Legitimation of Social and Religious Norms." Ph.D. Thesis, University College Dublin, 1980.

Pius XI. 1929. *Christian Education of Youth.* London: Catholic Truth Society.

_____. 1930. *On Christian Marriage.* London: Catholic Truth Society.

_____. 1931. *On Reconstructing the Social Order.* London: Catholic Truth Society.

The Tablet. 1983. Articles on the Irish antiabortion amendment to the Irish Constitution: Pp. 346-47, 816-18, 832, 887, 904.

The Tablet. 1983/4. Articles on the New Ireland Forum: volume 1983: Pp. 264-65; volume 1984: Pp. 52-53, 60-61.

Van Noort, G. 1960. *Tractatus De Ecclesia Christi.* 5th ed. Hilversum, Holland: P. Brand.

Whyte, J.H. 1980. *Church and State in Modern Ireland 1923-79.* Dublin: Gill and Macmillan; Totowa, New Jersey: Barnes and Noble.

19

The British Right to Discriminate

Eileen Barker

Despite the enormous constitutional differences between the two countries, Great Britain and the United States of America share a remarkably similar range of beliefs about the place of religion in society. The styles are different, of course, but the leaders of both nations make—and are expected to make—frequent and fervent references to a God who is assumed to be on their side and whose natural law lies at the foundation of their respective constitutional arrangements. The citizens of both nations insist that theirs is a country of religious freedom and toleration. Both countries play host to and tolerate a wide variety of religious, political, and other kinds of beliefs and nonbeliefs. Successive waves of immigration and the enormous increase in international communication, facilitated by travel and the media, have resulted in both countries acquiring pluralistic natures.

What similarities there are have been derived from diametrical directions. The United States of America is a republic, Britain is a monarchy. The United States has a written Constitution of which the First Amendment reads:

> Congress shall make no law respecting an establishment of religion, or prohibiting the free exercise thereof; or abridging the freedom of speech, or of the press; or the right of the people peaceably to assemble, and to petition the Government for a redress of grievances.

Britain has no First Amendment; she has no written constitution with provisions concerning fundamental rights and freedoms. Although there are certain laws which are termed *constitutional* (such as the 1707 Act of Union with Scotland), all laws passed by Parliament are of equal standing. There is no supreme law which takes precedence over ordinary laws; there are no fundamental rights (such as those enshrined in the United States Bill of Rights) by which standard all other laws must be tested. No law can be challenged directly on the ground that its enactment could violate a more basic constitutional right. Even the concept of rights is a thin one with respect to justice in England, where it is more usual to talk of civil liberties. A right exists when there is a positive law on the subject, while a liberty exists when there is no law against it. Those human rights which do exist in Britain are protected by public opinion rather than by law.

There are some laws giving rights and protections to British citizens. Certain rights are provided by the 1944 Education Act; the 1970 Equal Pay Act obliges firms to pay men and women doing the same job the same wage; the 1976 Race Relations Act forbids discrimination on the grounds of race. There are no laws protecting the rights of religious minorities in Britain. It is one of the ironies of history that Northern Ireland is the only place within the United Kingdom in which discrimination on the basis of religion is unlawful.

Along with other nations, Britain accepts the legal significance of the Universal Declaration of Human Rights which includes:

Article 2
Everyone is entitled to all the rights and freedoms set forth in this Declaration, without distinction of any kind, such as race, colour, sex, language, religion, political or other opinion, national or social origin, property, birth or other status.

Article 18
Everyone has the right to freedom of thought, conscience and religion; this right includes freedom to change his religion or belief, and freedom, either alone or in community with others and in public or private, to manifest his religion or belief in teaching, practice, worship and observance.

Following the Universal Declaration of Human Rights, the European Convention on Human Rights and Fundamental Freedoms came into force in 1953. This included Article 18 of the Universal Declaration of Human Rights, with the additional rider:

Freedom to manifest one's religion or beliefs shall be subject only to such limitations as are prescribed by law and are necessary in a democratic society in the interests of public safety, for the protection of public order, health or morals, or for the protection of the rights and freedoms of others.

But although the United Kingdom is a party to the European Convention, its laws are sometimes not in conformity with some of the Convention's provisions, and there is a strong difference of opinion about the desirability of incorporating the European Convention into domestic law in Britain.

Although cases may not be brought into British courts under the convention's provisions, the United Kingdom does permit individual petitioners to take cases to the European Commission at Strasbourg where they are tested by reference to Britain's international obligations under the Convention. Not only are there more cases brought against the United Kingdom than against any other member nation, but the number of cases decided against her is more than twice as great as that of her closest rival in such matters, Austria. Those who advocate the incorporation of the European Convention into British law interpret the large number of such judgments as a clear indication of how, by not accepting the principle of the Convention being part of domestic law, Britain is unnecessarily exposed at the international level regarding matters that are remedied within the national system in other Convention countries.

Britain not only has no constitution protecting all religious groups, it has an established church. Although the split from Rome resulted from Henry VIII's desire to marry Anne Boleyn, it was during the reign of Elizabeth I, with the Second Act of Supremacy in 1559, that the Church of England was "by law established": the Church and the realm thereby being deemed to be not complementary but identical. Attendance at church became compulsory by statute; nonattendance was punishable by fine and imprisonment. After the Restoration, the Declarations of Indulgence (1662-1688) suspended the use of the penal laws against dissenters from the Church of England. Today the Church of England is the established Church in England, but not in the rest of Britain. The Presbyterian Church of Scotland has been the established church in Scotland since the Act of Union in 1707; the Church in Wales was disestablished in Wales in 1920. The sovereign, who must be a member of the Church of England, is known as the "defender of the faith." The Church is also linked with the legislature through the House of Lords in which the two archbishops (of Canterbury and York) and twenty-four senior diocesan bishops have seats. Clergy of the Churches of England, Scotland and Ireland and the Roman Catholic Church are legally disqualified from sitting in the House of Commons.

As the Pilgrim fathers bore witness, establishment has, historically, been a source of considerable discrimination. There was a period when to be a Roman Catholic was considered not a religious problem, but was defined as treason. During the reign of Elizabeth 1, Catholic priests were not burned, but drawn and quartered, since they had committed the secular offense of acknowledging papal rather than royal supremacy. After the Restoration, it became accepted that Catholics and Nonconformists could not be totally eradicated, but their opportunities were severely curtailed, and their existence was made extremely unpleasant and difficult. Toward the end of the seventeenth century, heresy had ceased to be a civil offense (the Ecclesiastical Jurisdiction Act, 1677). Freedom of worship was granted to Protestant dissenters, but not to Catholics or Unitarians (the Toleration Act, 1689). During the 1820s, Nonconformists (Repeal of the Test and Corporation Acts, 1828) and Roman Catholics (the Roman Catholic Relief Act, 1829) were granted political emancipation. In 1858, Jews were able to become members of Parliament (the Jewish Relief Act), but it was not until 1871 (eighty years after the enactment of the First Amendment in the United States) that religious tests for admission to universities were finally abolished.

Today it is not in the universities, but in the lower schools that the difference between Britain and the United States is great. In the United States, the First Amendment has been interpreted as implying that no religion may be taught in the public schools. In Britain, the 1944 Education Act decreed that the one subject that must be taught in schools is religious instruction. There are some curiously paradoxical manifestations of this difference. For example, Dolbeare and Hammond and others have shown that religion is still taught in certain areas of the United States, while complaints have been made that religion taught in British schools is frequently nothing more than a superficial overview of comparative ethics. The growth of the "creation science" movement in America has led to strong, and in several instances successful, lobbying for equal time to be given both to Genesis and to evolutionary accounts of creation. Such a thing is inconceivable in England. In 1977, when the local authority in Dallas was insisting that the historical story of Adam and Eve be taught to students, an English local authority was holding the dismissal of a religious education teacher for doing that. Judge Overton's recent ruling in Arkansas that creationism is religion, not science, and that it is, therefore, unconstitutional for it to be taught in the schools, may have revoked Act 590, but, according to several surveys, there are still many Americans who believe that the Genesis account should be taught in the schools. I have been told that Oklahoma is one of the states that has not sought an "equal time" bill because if it were enacted their schools would have to introduce the teaching of evolution.

The special status of the Church of England is well illustrated by the treatment of blasphemy. Still cited in the courts is a case from 1838 in which the Reverend Michael Gathercole was charged with libeling the Roman Catholic Church and the jury was directed that:

> A person may, without being liable for prosecution for it, attack Judaism, or Mahomedanism, or even any sect of the Christian Religion (save the established religion of the country); and the only reason why the latter is in a different situation from the others is, because it is the form established by law, and is therefore a part of the constitution of the country. In like manner, and

for the same reason, any general attack on Christianity is the subject of criminal prosecution, because Christianity is the established religion of the country. The defendant here has a right to entertain his opinions, to express them, and to discuss the subject of the Roman Catholic religion and its institutions. . . . If it was merely an attack upon the Roman Catholic Church . . . then he is entitled to an acquittal. . . .

Recently, Mary Whitehouse, a well-known British watchdog of public morality, successfully initiated a private prosecution of *Gay News* when it published a poem in which a Roman soldier expressed a homosexual love for Jesus. This ruling resulted in a governmental paper which proposed that the common law offenses of blasphemy and blasphemous libel should be abolished, partly on the grounds that the present blasphemy law does not extend beyond the Christian religion. Christian denominations are protected only to the extent that their fundamental beliefs are consistent with those of the established church. It is interesting that, in the *Gay News* case, Lord Scarman had, for the same reason, come to the opposite conclusion:

There is a case of legislation extending it [blasphemous libel] to protect the religious beliefs and feelings of non-Christians. . . . My criticism of the common law offence of blasphemy is not that it exists but that it is not sufficiently comprehensive. . . . It is shackled by the claims of history.

Advocates for both the abolition and the extension of the blasphemy laws have pointed to the unfairness in a plural society of making a special case for the Church of England "by law established." One is unlikely to hear public statements nowadays that explicitly advocate a discriminatory approach to religion. The religious affairs correspondent of the London *Times* wrote:

Neither the courts nor parliament are needed to enforce the religious tolerance which is such a strong feature of the British way of life. Racial prejudice, and discrimination purely on grounds of faith, are not significant social evils in 1982 (5 August 1982).

Nonetheless, a deep-seated attitude assumes that there is one true faith and that although other faiths should be tolerated, adherents of such faiths must expect to be less equal than those who adhere to the majority religion. This may even be justified on the practical grounds of preventing discrimination. There was, for example, the case of a Muslim teacher who was told that he would be considered a part-time teacher, paid for only four days a week, because he had to miss about three-quarters of an hour of his teaching duty every Friday when his religious duty demanded that he attend prayers at a mosque. The 1944 Education Act states that "No teacher in [a county or voluntary] school shall . . . receive any less emolument . . . by reason of . . . his attending or omitting to attend religious worship," but the Muslim lost the case. He appealed. Lord Scarman invoked the European Convention as an interpretive aid to uphold the appeal, but the two other lords dismissed it. Lord Denning ruled that "The Convention is not part of our English law," and that although we would always have regard for it, "it is drawn in such vague terms that it can be used for all sorts of unreasonable claims." Lord Denning argued that if a minority group were allowed not to fit in with the practices of the majority, this would lead to resentment and "so the cause of racial integration would suffer."

Lord Denning may well be correct in his assessment of possible reactions to the outcome of such cases, but one might ask whether an outbreak of anti-Semitism was averted when, in 1961, Jewish shopkeepers were not exempted from Pennsylvania's Sunday closing law (*Braunfield* v. *Brown*); or whether, in 1963, there was an outbreak of resentment against Seventh-Day Adventists when it was ruled unconstitutional that South Carolina denied a member of that faith unemployment compensation after she had been discharged by her employer for not working on Saturday (*Sherbert* v. *Verner*).

Religious discrimination does occur in England. What is less obvious is the way in which the courts discriminate not just in favor of the established religion, but in favor of more traditional, socially accepted religions as opposed to the new religious movements. People whose religious beliefs and/or observances clash with a secular timetable that is, nonetheless, in accordance with the established religion are expected to either abandon those beliefs/observances or accept whatever consequences follow. This is more of a "we-were-here-first-and-if-you-don't-like-it-you-can-lump-it" attitude, than one of positive discrimination. People can worship on Saturday or Friday, but the (Anglican) British cannot be expected to be inconvenienced as a result.

There are exceptions, and it is interesting to note the pattern these exceptions take. Since 1950, it has, for example, been possible for Jewish shopkeepers to close on Saturdays and to open on Sunday mornings in England and Wales. But there are limits to the extent that the British can "reasonably" be expected to accommodate Jewish citizens. A Mr. and Mrs. Ostreicher lodged an objection when the secretary of state for the environment decided to hold a public inquiry on a matter that concerned them (the compulsory purchase of houses they owned) on the seventh day of Passover. Lord Denning ruled that "the men at the department acted perfectly reasonably" when they arranged the date for 21 April—carefully avoiding Good Friday and Easter Monday—which, he said, would "seem to all ordinary people to be a quite suitable date."

Ordinary people have even more influence on the opinions of what is reasonable, or right and proper, regarding the new religious movements. There have, during the past few years, been several cases in Britain (and the rest of Europe) involving cults. Although there are not as many of these cases as in the United States, they are significant. The first such case to attract attention in Britain concerned the Church of Scientology. In 1968 the then minister of health, Kenneth Robinson, stated in the House of Commons that:

> Scientology is a pseudo-philosophical cult. . . . Since the Anderson report on Scientology (published in 1965 in the State of Victoria, Australia), coupled with the evidence already available in this country, sufficiently established the general undesirability and potential dangers of the cult, we took the view that there was little point in holding another enquiry.

> The Government are satisfied, having reviewed all the available evidence, that Scientology is socially harmful. It alienates members of families from each other and attributes squalid and disgraceful motives to all who oppose it; its authoritarian principles and practices are a potential menace to the personality and well-being of those so deluded as to become its followers; above all, its methods can be a danger to the health of those who submit to them. There is evidence that children are now being indoctrinated (25 July 1968).

Although there was no power under existing law to prohibit the practice of Scientology, the government had "concluded that it is so objectionable that it would be right to take all steps within their power to curb its growth." Accordingly, foreign nationals would no longer be eligible for admission as students at the Hubbard College at East Grinstead, or any other Scientology establishment, and work permits would not be granted to foreigners for employment at a Scientology establishment.

Richard Crossman, Kenneth Robinson's successor at the Ministry of Health, makes several references in the third volume of *The Crossman Diaries* to the embarrassment experienced by the government as a result of imposing the ban before a proper inquiry had been concluded. Sir John Foster was asked to look into Scientology. His report (presented in 1971) concluded that, although he was not prepared to say that Scientology establishments could come under the description of "bona fide educational establishments," it seemed wrong not to allow visitors entry because they were proposing to do something that was legal for Britons to do. Scientologists should be granted or refused work permits according to the same criteria as everyone else. That they or their proposed employers are Scientologists should be regarded as irrelevant.

In 1974 a Dutch woman, Yvonne Van Duyn, who had been offered employment as a secretary at Hubbard College, was refused entry to the United Kingdom on the grounds that the secretary of state considered it "undesirable to give anyone leave to enter the United Kingdom on the business of or in the employment of that organization." The case was taken to the European Court of Justice which pronounced that the United Kingdom was entitled, for reasons of public policy, to refuse the right of entry to a national of another member state. The ban on foreign Scientologists was in force for twelve years before it was officially lifted. Three main reasons were given: (1) the ban was unenforceable as Scientologists did not need to disclose themselves as such at ports of entry; (2) the ban might be difficult to defend before the European Court of Human Rights at Strasbourg; and (3) it was unfair, since Scientology was the only movement for which Britain's general religious tolerance was thus suspended.

Legal concern over the new religions in Britain first focused on Scientology, and although other movements have had problems in the courts, the Unification Church is the one that has been publicized most frequently and most spectacularly during the past ten years. There have been several minor cases (concerning peddlers' licenses, or charges of obstruction), but the one that was to make history as the longest civil action in Britain, was that against Associated Newspapers. A popular tabloid, the *Daily Mail*, had published an article accusing the Unification Church of brainwashing its members and of breaking up families. The Moonies lost their libel suit and the subsequent appeal, and were refused permission to take the matter further to the House of Lords. During the litigation, each side was allowed two expert witnesses, and each produced one on brainwashing and one on theology. For the *Daily Mail*, the Reverend Dr. Iain Torrance, a minister of the Church of Scotland, testified that "true Christianity" could be distinguished from what was not. It was, he said, a matter of degree: at a first level, Luther had protested against certain indulgences and transubstantiation, but "now Christianity has absorbed his protests"; at a second level, there were certain fundamental heresies in Christology, but "for fifteen hundred years Christianity has turned its face from those." At the third level, Dr. Torrance testified, the Unification Church went even further: "There is an old-fashioned word for what they do and that is, I think, blasphemy." When asked by the Moonies' counsel whether it might not be a lesson of history that it is unwise to make an assertion about what is true doctrine, and to disqualify people who do not subscribe to it as unchristian, Dr. Torrance replied that "at times it is our responsibility to do so."

It was clear that Dr. Torrance was not the only person in the court who believed it his duty to point out that Unification beliefs are not true. It was constantly suggested that the theology is unbelievable and that the Unification Church is, therefore, a bogus religion. The following is from the judge's summing up for the jury:

> Members of the jury, about those beliefs, [the appellant, Mr. Orme] has uncompromisingly stated that he believes Mr. Moon to be the Messiah. One is perfectly entitled to believe that anyone is the Messiah, the Lord of the Second Advent, and, as I have said many times, we must respect people's religious views. *But* Mr. Orme is a *highly intelligent* man. You have heard the structure of Mr. Moon's lifestyle and foundation. You ask yourselves whether a *reasonable* man could believe that Mr. Moon is in fact the Messiah and the Lord of the Second Advent. *Is he a dupe?* Was he a dupe originally and then became converted? *Or is he a fraud?* [emphasis added]

The court of appeal allowed that the jury was improperly invited to test the quality of the plaintiff's beliefs by their reasonableness, but this was, in the opinion of the appeal judges, a "minor deviation from relevancy [which] was not likely to have confused the jury." Throughout both the trial and the appeal it was clear that Britain has no First Amendment, and reference was continually made to the strangeness, bizarreness, unorthodoxy, and incomprehensibility of Unification beliefs.

The present state of British law on discrimination permits a curiously effective way of insuring that discrimination can exert its greatest effect on new religious movements, and yet assume some protection for older, more traditional religions. Such a state is the unintended consequence of the present law which makes racial, but not religious, discrimination illegal.

A series of cases which tested the laws concerning discrimination in Britain concerned the wearing of turbans in the Sikh community. There was the case of the turbaned bus conductor who, it was ruled, did not have to wear a uniform hat. The passing of the Motor-Cycle Crash Helmets (religious exemption) Act in 1976 allowed motorcycling Sikhs not to wear crash helmets; and then followed a five-year legal battle concerning a Sikh schoolboy who had been told by the headmaster of the school he wished to attend that he had to remove his turban and cut his hair before he could be admitted. The initial judgment at the county court dismissed the Sikh's claim that the headmaster had committed an unlawful act of discrimination, and the court of appeal upheld this decision on the ground that Sikhs did not constitute a racial group within the meaning of the Race Relations Act of 1976. Lord Denning declared that

> [The Act] did not include religion or politics or culture. One could discriminate as much as one liked against Roman Catholics or communists or "hippies" without being in breach of the law. . . .

However, he continued, the one distinguishing characteristic of Jews was a racial characteristic. Consequently:

> There must be no discrimination against the Jews in England. Anti-semitism, which had produced great evils elsewhere must not be allowed here. . . .

> "Sikh" came from the Sanskrit word for "disciple." Sikhs were the disciples or followers of Guru Nanak who was born in 1469. . . .

> There was no difference in language or blood which distinguished the Sikhs from the other people in India who were largely the product of successive invasions which had swept into the country. . . .

> Professor Bowles of Syracuse University, New York, had said that the difference between Muslims, Sikhs and Hindus was mainly cultural, not biological.

> No doubt (Sikhs) were a distinct community, just as other religious and cultural communities. But that was not enough.

> The Sikhs were a fine community upholding the highest standards but they were not a "racial group." It was not unlawful to discriminate against them.

> The headmaster had not discriminated against the Sikhs at all.

It is clear that the Jews, largely integrated and respected members of the British community, are protected by the law from discrimination. But the Sikhs, too, have now become generally respected members of the British community. There followed an uproar. The British Council of Churches added its voice to the protests, its community and race relations unit writing to the home secretary to ask for the law to be changed to clarify that discrimination against Sikhs was in the same category as discrimination against Jews. It was pointed out that during its committee stage in the House of Commons, an amendment had been proposed that the Race Relations Act include discrimination on the grounds of religion. The amendment was withdrawn when a minister of state at the Home Office pointed out that the Bill, by introducing the concept of indirect discrimination, did "a great deal to protect those who are discriminated against by reason of their religious observance." The minister had even given a hypothetical example that it would be indirect discrimination for an employer to insist that a Sikh working as a chauffeur wear a peaked cap.

Nine months after the court of appeal said that Sikhs were a religious group, not a race, the House of Lords allowed an appeal against the decision on the grounds that the Sikhs *could* be defined as an ethnic group. It was, they ruled

> possible for a person to fall into a particular racial group either by birth or by adherence, and it made no difference, so far as the 1976 Act was concerned, by which route he found his way into the group.

It is possible for those who would by any accepted criteria be classified as members of a religion, to be redefined as an ethnic minority so long as they have adhered together over a sufficiently long test period. That the Hebrew faith is passed through the mother only, and gentiles can convert to Judaism, or that "the difference between Muslims, Sikhs and Hindus is mainly cultural, not biological" can, by what might seem to be a taxonomic sleight of hand, be seen as irrelevant in making the distinction between race and religion. So long as *ethnicity* can be defined with reference to adherence over time, the longer a religious movement has been around, the greater the chance it has of being protected by the law (other things being equal). The Sikhs have just managed to pass through this fine filter of British justice. It is unlikely that such a filter could operate so overtly in the United States of America.

I do not wish to suggest that religious minorities in Britain are the victims of far more intolerance or discrimination than they are in the United States or in any of the European countries in which there is no established church and religious discrimination is forbidden by law. Were I to be a member of some strange new cult, I would be unlikely to flee the shores of my native land in a modern-day Mayflower, for I could by no means be certain of landing in a country in which my rights would not be at least as well protected as they are *de facto,* if not *de jure,* in Britain.

Why is there so little difference between the American and British treatment of religions when their legal status in the two countries is so vastly different? Establishment means that other faiths have no hope of being viewed equally in the sight of the law. The absence of constitutional protection (or, indeed, legal protection of any kind) against religious discrimination means that members of minority faiths have little hope of redress should they suffer on account of their faith—unless they are able to take their case to the European Court at Strasbourg. Pronouncements made in the British courts reveal, on occasion, what must seem to those conversant with the niceties of First Amendment implications, an extraordinarily blatant parochialism. There is ignorance, one might almost say innocence, of such concepts as epistemological or social relativism. It is not argued that the British brand of Protestantism is the real truth. It is merely taken for granted that it is the truest, and that it is the sort of religion that any right-thinking citizen would want to guide his spiritual and, if necessary, his secular life. But this is not a forcefully held belief, high in the consciousness of any but a tiny minority of Britons. It is, rather, an absent-mindedly taken-for-granted acceptance of what is right and proper.

Religion is rarely questioned—either positively or negatively—it is just there as part of the background to British life. Were it to become too obviously intrusive, this would be as disturbing as its disappearance. The established church is neither fundamentalist nor totalitarian, nor is it particularly evangelical. Most of its members (including its officials) are perfectly happy to let others believe whatever they wish to believe, but they will start to raise an eyebrow and, if necessary, react in some measure if their established way of life is threatened. Outsiders may be tolerated, but it is felt that they can hardly expect to claim the privileges of establishment. This is not to say that the secular establishment is coterminous with the religious establishment. The former has opened its doors to those outside the Episcopalian fold; not a few judges, including those holding high office, are Catholics. One has even been able to find the odd Buddhist (convert, of course) sitting on the bench.

It is possible that the very existence of establishment means that those who are accepted as part of the secular establishment do not feel as threatened as those in the (relatively speaking) nonestablished establishment of the United States. Such a suggestion pays no attention to the rapidly changing situation in both societies, and it can give us no more than a tentative clue as to how the recent boundary testing that the newer religions have instigated within the legislature may be resolved.

About the Contributors

Eileen Barker is dean of undergraduate studies at the London School of Economics. She is the author of *The Making of a Moonie: Brainwashing or Choice?* and editor of *Of Gods and Men: New Religious Movements in the West* and *New Religious Movements: A Perspective for Understanding Society;* and has contributed to more than sixty journals and books. She is also author of *Armageddon and Aquarius: New Religions in Contemporary Christiandom* (forthcoming).

James A. Beckford, senior lecturer in sociology at the University of Durham, England, is the author of *The Trumpet of Prophecy: A Sociological Study of Jehovah's Witnesses* and *Religious Organizations.* His recent research on public responses to new religious movements is presented in *Cult Controversies.* He is editor of *Current Sociology,* official journal of the International Sociological Association, and President of the Association's Research Committee for the Sociology of Religion. He is currently writing a book on the problem of religion in advanced urban societies.

Hamid Dabashi is a lecturer of sociology at the University of Pennsylvania. His publications include "Shariti's Islam: Revolutionary Uses of Faith in a Post-Traditional Society" (*Islamic Quarterly*); "Revolutions of Our Time: Religious Politics in Modernity" (*Contemporary Sociology*); and "A View of Mulla Sadra's Social Thought: Social Order in a Sacred Order" (*Iran Nameh*). His forthcoming volume on Muhammad's charismatic authority examines the emergence of various cultural paradigms in the post-Muhammadan period.

N. J. Demerath III is currently professor and chair of sociology at the University of Massachusetts, Amherst. A long time student of the sociology of culture, he has written extensively on religion specifically. He is presently engaged in an empirical assessment of church-state relationships in a mid-sized northeast U.S. city.

John Fulton, a sociologist, teaches at St. Mary's College in Twickenham, England. He is the author of a number of articles and papers dealing with the interplay of religious, class and nationalist factors in the conflict in Northern Ireland, as well as a recent theoretical article, "Experience, Alienation and the Anthropological Condition of Religion," which appeared in *The Annual Review of the Social Sciences of Religion*, 1981.

Phillip E. Hammond is professor of religious studies and sociology, University of California, Santa Barbara, and chair of Religious Studies. The author of many books, he has specialized on the topic of religion and political culture. He recently edited *The Sacred in a Secular Age* and is coeditor, with David Bromley, of *The Future of New Religious Movements*.

Dean M. Kelley has been the Executive for religious and civil liberty of the National Council of Churches since 1960. He is the author of *Why Conservative Churches Are Growing* and *Why Churches Should Not Pay Taxes;* the special editor of the November 1979 issue of *Annals of the American Academy of Political and Social Science* on "The Uneasy Boundary: Church and State"; and editor of *Government Intervention in Religious Affairs*.

John Markoff is associate professor of sociology and history at the University of Pittsburgh and author of a number of articles of historical-sociological concern. He is currently preparing a book on the rights of the rural lords at the beginning of the French Revolution.

Robert S. Michaelson is professor of religious studies, University of California, Santa Barbara. He is the author of *Piety in the Public School* and *The American Search for Soul*. American Indian religious freedom and public policy issues in a historical and comparative context are among his recent research interests.

Ewa Morawska is assistant professor of sociology at the University of Pennsylvania. She is the author of several books and articles, including *Polish-American Community*, coauthored with Irwin Sanders; *The Poles of Toronto*, with Rudolph Kogler and Benedykt Heydenkorn; *The Maintenance of Ethnicity: Polish American Community in Boston;* and *For Bread With Butter: Life-Worlds of East Central Europeans in Johnstown, Pennsylvania, 1890-1940*.

Leo Pfeffer is Professor of Constitutional Law, Long Island University. He is also special Counsel, American Jewish Congress. He has authored *Religion, State and the Burger Court*. He has contributed an article and an autobiography to *Religion and the State: Essays in Honor of Leo Pfeffer*.

Daniel Regan, associate professor of sociology at the University of Pittsburgh, is completing a monograph on freedom of speech and expression in Malaysia. He is also conducting an empirical study of the political consequences of corruption and anticorruption in Indonesia and Malaysia. Past work includes articles and chapters on Southeast Asian intellectuals (including their religious orientations), civil religion, and medical professionals in the Third World, included in *Sociological Analysis, Journal of Asian and African Studies,* and *Journal of Southeast Asian Studies,* among others.

Thomas Robbins, a sociologist of religion, has held research or teaching appointments at various universities including Yale, Queens College, The Graduate Theological Union and Central Michigan University. He is co-editor of *In Gods We Trust* and *Cults, Culture and the Law.* He has published numerous articles on religious movements, which have appeared in *Daedalus, Society, Social Problems, Concilium* and various sociology and religious studies journals.

Roland Robertson is professor of sociology and religious studies, University of Pittsburgh. He is author of many articles and books on religion, international relations, and sociological theory; including *Meaning and Change, Identity and Authority, International Systems and the Modernization of Societies,* and *The Sociological Interpretation of Religion.*

Leland W. Robinson is associate professor of sociology at the University of Tennessee at Chattanooga. He is the author of several articles on revolutionary movements and on the role of religion in social change. His most recent paper, "The Elitist Thesis and the Rhodesian Revolution: Implications for South Africa," appears in an edited volume titled *Inequality and Contemporary Revolutions.*

Bryan S. Turner is Professor of Sociology, Flinders University, South Australia. He is the author of a number of books, including *Religion and Social Theory, Weber and Islam, Marx and the End of Orientalism, Capitalism and Class in the Middle East,* and *For Weber.*

Rhys H. Williams is a graduate student in sociology at the University of Massachusetts, Amherst. His scholarly interests include religion, politics, and culture; he is currently at work on a research project studying religion and political power in a local community context.

Index